Routledge•Cavendish Questions & Answers Series

European Union Law
2009–2010

Q&A

Routledge•Cavendish Questions & Answers Series

European Union Law

2009–2010

MIKE CUTHBERT

BSc (Econ), LLB, LLM, BA (Law)
Principal Lecturer, University of Northampton

Routledge·Cavendish
Taylor & Francis Group
LONDON AND NEW YORK

Seventh edition published 2009
by Routledge-Cavendish
2 Park Square, Milton Park, Abingdon, Oxon, OX14 4RN

Simultaneously published in the USA and Canada
by Routledge-Cavendish
270 Madison Avenue, New York, NY 10016

*Routledge-Cavendish is an imprint of the Taylor & Francis Group,
an informa business*

© 1993, 2007, 2009 Mike Cuthbert

Previous editions published by Cavendish Publishing Limited
First edition   1993
Second edition   1997
Third edition   1997
Fourth edition   2001
Fifth edition   2003

Previous editions published by Routledge-Cavendish
Sixth edition   2007

Reprinted 2010

Typeset in Garamond by
RefineCatch Limited, Bungay, Suffolk
Printed and bound in Great Britain by
TJ International Ltd, Padstow, Cornwall

British Library Cataloguing in Publication Data
A catalogue record for this book is available from the British Library

Library of Congress Cataloging-in-Publication Data
Cuthbert, Mike.
European Union law : 2009–2010 / Mike Cuthbert.—7th ed.
p. cm.—(Routledge-Cavendish questions and answers series)
Rev. ed. of: European Union law. 6th ed. 2008.
Includes bibliographical references.
1. Law—European Union countries.   2. Law—European Union countries—
Examinations, questions, etc.   3. European Union.
I. European Union law.   II. Title.
KJE949.E955 2009
341.242'2076—dc22
2008044852

ISBN 10: 0–415–48271–2
ISBN 13: 978–0–415–48271–4

CONTENTS

Table of Cases   *vii*
Table of Legislation   *xvii*
Table of Equivalences   *xxv*
Introduction   *xxix*

1   Community Institutions   1

2   Sources of Law   21

3   EC Law and National Law   33

4   Judicial Remedies and Review (1): Direct Actions   51

5   Judicial Remedies and Review (2): Indirect
    Action – Preliminary References   71

6   The Free Movement of Goods   91

7   Competition Policy   109

8   The Free Movement of Workers   133

9   The Freedom of Establishment and the Freedom to
    Provide Services   149

10 Freedom from Discrimination   165

11 External Relations   181

12 The Internal Market and Beyond   193

Index   *205*

TABLE OF CASES

Note: Where recent cases have not been widely reported, it is possible to read the judgment on the ECJ website. Go to www.curia.eu.int, select 'Proceedings' and 'case law'. Use the case number to search for the case you want to read.

Adams v Commission (Case 145/83) [1986] 1 CMLR 506 118

AGS Assedic Pas-de-Calais v Dumon & Froment (1995) (Case 235/1995)
[1998] ECR 1–4531 81

Ahlström and Others v Commission (Woodpulp case) [1988] ECR 5193;
[1988] 4 CMLR 901; [1993] ECR 1–1307; [1903] 4 CMLR 407 131

Airtours plc v Commission (Case T-342/99) [2002] 5 CMLR 7 131

AKZO Chemie BV (Case 53/85) [1986] ECR 1965 .... 111, 121, 124

Alphons Lutticke (Case 57/65) [1966] ECR 205 38

Amsterdam Bulb RV v Produckschap voor Siergewassen (Case 50/76)
[1977] ECR 137 28

Arcaro (Criminal proceedings) (Case C-168/95) [1997] All ER (EC) 82 40

Arsenal Football Club plc v Reed (Case 206/01) (2002) 100

Auer (No 1) (Case 136/78) (1979) 154

Bacardi-Martini v Newcastle United FC (Case 318/00) (2003) ECR 1–905 81

Barber v Guardian Royal Exchange (Case C-262/88)
[1990] IRLR 400 .... 171, 172, 176, 178, 179

Baumbast v Secretary of State for the Home Department [2002] ECR 1–8417 ...... 138, 140

Bayerische HNL Vermehrungsbetriebe GmbH v Council and Commission
(Cases 83/76, 94/76, 4/77.15/77 AND 40/77 [1978] ECR 1209 69

Becker V Finanzamt Munster-Innenstadt (Case 8/81) [1982] ECR 53 43

Bela-Muble Josef Bergman v Grows Farm (Skimmed Milk case) (Case 114/76)
[1977] ECR 1211 .... 24, 84

Belgian Bakery Case see Oebel

Berlin Butter case see Ran v BALM

Bilka-Kaufhaus v Weber von Harz (case 170/84)

[1986] ECR 1607 .... 167, 170, 171, 173, 175, 179

Blaizot v University of Liège (1987) (Case 24/86) [1989] 1 CMLR 57 151

Bonsignore v Oberstadtdirektor of the City of Cologne (Case 67/74)

[1975] ECR 297 .... 143, 146

Bosman *see* URBSA V Bosman

Bourgoin SA v Minister of Agriculture, Fisheries and Food [1986] 1 CMLR 267 64

Brasserie du Pêcheur (Case C-46/93)[1996] 1 CMLR 889 .... 44, 46, 48, 64

Bresciani (Case 87/75) [1976] ECR 129 .... 40, 182, 184

Bristol Myers Squibb v Parnova (427/93) 103

British-American Co and Reynolds Industries Inc v Commission

(Philip Morris Inc Intervening) (Cases 142/84 and 156/84)

[1987] ECR 4487; (1987) The Times, 30 November 132

BRT v SABAM [1974] ECR 51; [1974] CMLR 238 6 (Case 127/73) 116

Bulmer v Bollinger [1974] 2 All ER 1226 .... 29, 77, 84

Burton v British Railways Board (Case 19/81) [1982] ECR 555 179

Calpak SpA v Commission (Cases 789/79 and 790/79) [1980] ECR 1949 .... 57, 83

CAM SA v Commission (Case 100/74) [1975] ECR 1393 57

Camera Care Ltd v Commission (Case 792/79R) [1980] 1 CMLR 334 120

Carpenter v Secretary of State for the Home Department (Case 60/00)

[2003] ECR 1–6279 140

Cassis de Dijon (Case 120/78)

[1978] ECR 64 .... 91, 92, 93, 94, 95, 96, 97, 98, 99, 100, 103, 104

Centrafarm v American Home Products (Case 3/78) [1978] ECR 1823 102

Centrafarm v Sterling Drug (Case 15/74) [1974] ECR 1147 .... 103, 106

Centrafarm BV v Winthrop BV (Case 16/74) [1974] ECR 1183 101

Centros Ltd (Case 212/97) (1999) ECR 1–1459 .... 139, 157

Chen v Secretary of State for the Home Department (Case 200/202)

[2004] 3 CMLR 48 140

CILFIT SA v Ministry of Health (Case 283/81)

[1982] ECR 3415 .... 71, 74, 76, 78, 80, 87, 88, 89

CNPAAP v Council (Case 87/95P)[1996] ECR 1–2003 61

Cohn-Bendit (1979) Conseil d'Etat, 22 December 1978 .... 43, 89

Colditz (Case 9/67) [1967] ECR 229 29

Colim NV v Bigg's Continent Noord NV (Case C-33/97) [1999] ECR 1 3975 98

Commercial Solvents (Cases 6 and 7/73) [1974] ECR 223 .... 112, 113, 122

Commission v Belgium (1981) (Case 149/79) [1980] ECR 3881;
    [1981] 2 CMLR 413 142
Commission v Council (Case 81/72) [1973] ECR 575 25
Commission v Denmark [1986] (Case 302/86) [1989] ECR 4607 94
Commission v France (Case 7/71) (EURATOM case) [1971] ECR 1003 53
Commission v Germany Re German Sausage (Case 274/87) [1989] 2 CMLR 733 ...... 94, 99
Commission v Ireland (Case 249/81) [1982] ECR 4005 .... 92, 105
Commission v UK (Turkey case) (Case 40/82) [1982] ECR 2793 54
Commission v UK (Case C-146/89) [1989] 3 CMLR 601 65
Commission v UK (Case 466/98) (2002) 184, 187
Commissioners of Customs and Excise v Samex ApS [1983] 3 CMLR 194 78
Confederazione Italiana Dirigenta de Azienda v EC Council (Case 297/86)
    [1988] ECR 3531 13
Consten and Grundig v Commission (Cases 56 and 58/64) [1964] CMLR 489 ...... 124, 125
Continental Can (Case 6/72) [1972] CMLR D 11 .... 29, 111, 121, 122, 124, 128, 131
Cornelis Kramer (Cases 3, 4 and 6/76) [1976] ECR 1279 .... 185, 186, 187, 189
Costa v ENEL (Case 6/64) [1964] ECE 585 .... 30, 35, 63, 73, 74
Courage Ltd v Crehan (Case 453/99) [2002] ICR 457 .... 113, 116

D v Council (Case 122/99) [2001] ECR 1–4319 168
Da Costa en Schaake (Cases 28–30/62) [1963] ECR 31 87
Danfoss (Case 109/88) [1989] ECR 3199 175
Defrenne v Sabena (No 2) (Case 43/75)
    [1976] ECR 455 .... 30, 38, 39, 46, 166, 167, 169, 170, 173, 176, 179
Defrenne and Newstead v Dept of Transport (Case 192/85) [1988] 1 WLR 612 167
Deuka v EVGF (Case 78/74) [1975] ECR 421 25
Deutsche Apothekerverband (Case 322/01) (2003) ECR 1–14877 98
Deutsche Grammophon (78/79) [1981] ECR 487 101
Dias (Case 343/90) [1992] ECR 1 81
Dillenkofer and Others v Germany (Cases T-178, 179, 180–90/94)
    [1996] ECR 1–4845 .... 44, 65
Duke v GEC Reliance [1988] AC 618 .... 43, 47
Dyestuff case see ICI v Commission (Dyestuff case) (48/69)

EC Commission v Italy [1972] Case 39/72 [1973] ECR 101 28
EC Council v European Parliament (Case 34/86) [1986] 1 CMLR 138 6
Emmott v Minister for Social Welfare (Case C-208/90) [1991] 3 CMLR 894 43
Enderby v Frenchay HA (Case 127/92) [1994] 1 CMLR 8 .... 170, 173, 174

ERT case (1989) (Case C-260/89) [1991] ECR 1 25

ERTA (Case 22/70) [1971] ECR 263 .... 73, 185, 187, 188, 191

Extramet Industrie v Council [1991] ECR 1–2051 61

Factortame cases *see* R v Secretary of State for Transport ex p Factortame Ltd

Firma Foto-Frost v Hauptzollamt Lübeck-Ost (Case 314/85) [1988] 3 CMLR 57 ...... 75, 85

Foglia v Novello (No 1) (Case 104/79) [1980] ECR 745 .... 79, 80

Foglia v Novello (No 2) [1982] (Case 244/80) [1982] 1 CMLR 585 .... 80, 81

Foster v British Gas plc (Case C-188/90) [1990] ECR-1 43

Fragd Case (Case 33/84) [1985] ECR 1605 [1990] 36

France v UK (Re Fishing Net Sizes) [1978] (Case 141/78) [1979] ECR 2923 52

Francovitch v Italian State (Cases C-6/90) [1992] IRLR 84 .... 44, 48, 55, 62, 63, 64, 74

Frontini (Case 183/73) [1974] 2 CMLR 372 35

Fruit and Vegetable (Cases 16 and 17/62) [1962] ECR 471 57

Garden Cottage Foods Ltd v Milk Marketing Board [1984] AC 130 116

Garland v BREL (Case 12/81) [1982] ECR 359; [1983] 2 AC 751 .... 47, 89, 167, 171, 179

Gencor Ltd v Commission (Case T-102/96) [1999] ECR 1–1753 131

Givane v Secretary of State for the Home Department (Case 257/00)
[2003] ECR 1–345 138

Grad v Finanzamt Traunstein (Case 9/70) [1970] ECR 825 .... 39, 40, 42

Grant v South-West Trains [1998] All ER (EC) 193 .... 168, 173, 175

Gravier v City of Liège (1984) (Case 293/83) [1985] ECR 593 .... 150, 151

Greenham and Abel (Case 95/01) [2004] 3 CMLR 33 98

Haegeman v Belgian State (Case 181/73) [1974] ECR 449 .... 73, 182, 183, 184

Henn and Darby v DPP [1981] AC 580 .... 78, 88, 89

Hoechst (Case T-10/89) [1989] ECR 2859 119

Hoffman-La Roche v Centrafarm (Case 102/77) [1978] ECR 1139 .... 102, 103, 123

Hugin v Commission (Cash Register case) (Case 22/78) [1979] ECR 1869 112

ICI v Colmer (1996) (Case 264/96) [1998] ECR 1–4695 82

ICI v Commission (Dyestuff case) (Cases 48, 49 and 51–57/69)
[1972] CMLR 557 .... 114, 124, 126

International Chemical Corp SpA v Amministrazione delle Finanze dello Stato
(Case 66/80) [1981] ECR 1191 .... 75, 85

International Fruit Co (Cases 21–24/72) [1972] ECR 1219 .... 40, 182, 184

Internationale Handelsgesellschaft mbH (Case 11/70) [1970] ECR 1125 ...... 24, 25, 33, 35

Irish Creamery Milk Suppliers Association v Ireland (Cases 36, 71/80)
  [1981] ECR 735 76
Isolglucose case *see* Royal Scholten-Honig v Intervention Board for Agriculture

Japanese Ball Bearing cases (Cases 113, 118–21/77) [1977] ECR 1185 58
Jégo-Quéré et de SA v Commission (Case T-177/01) [2002] 2 CMLR 44 61
Jenkins v Kingsgate (Clothing Productions) Ltd (Case 96/80) [1981] ECR 911 167
Johnston v Chief Constable of the Royal Ulster Constabulary (Case 22/84)
  [1986] ECR 1651 .... 26, 168

Kalanka v Bremen (Case 450/93) [1995] ECR 1–3051 168
Kampelmann (Case 253/96) (1997) ECR 1–6907 47
KB v NHS Pensions Agency (Case 117/01) [2004] 1 CMLR 28 .... 168, 173, 175
Keck and Mithouard (Cases 267–68/91) [1993] ECR 1–6097 .... 96, 98
Kempf v Staatssecretaris van Justitie (Case 139/85) [1986] ECR 1741;
  [1987] 1 CMLR 764 .... 136, 142
Kirklees MBC v Wickes Building Supplies Ltd [1992] 3 All ER 717 64
Kolpinghuis Nijmegen (Case 80/86) [1989] 2 CMLR 18 40

Laurie-Blum (Case 66/85) [1987] 3 CMLR 389 .... 134, 138, 141, 142, 143, 144, 150
Les Verts v Parliament (Case 249/85) [1987] 2 CMLR 343 68
Levez v Jennings (1999) All ER (EC) 181 .... 49, 175
Levin v Staatssecretaris van Justitie (Case 53/81) [1982] ECR 1035 .... 135, 136, 138,
                                                                                                    141, 142
Lister v Forth Dry Dock and Engineering Co Ltd [1990] 1 AC 546 .... 40, 46, 48
Luisi v Ministero del Tesoro (1983) (Cases 286/82 and 26/83) [1984] ECR 377 .... 150, 151

M6 and Others v Commission (Case 112/99) [2001] ECR II-2459 116
Macarthys v Smith (Case 129/79) [1980] 2 CMLR 205 ECR 1275 .... 47, 169
Maize and Starch case *see* Maizena v Council
Maizena v Council (Case 139/79) [1980] ECR 3393 .... 4, 85
Markus v Hauptzollamt Hamburg-Jonas (Case 14/69) [1969] ECR 349 31
Marleasing SA v La Commercial Internacional de Alimentacion SA
  (Case C-106/89) [1992] CMLR 305; [1990] ECR 1 .... 40, 45, 48
Marschall v Land Nordrhein-Westfalen (Case 409/95 [1997] ECR 1–6363 168
Marshall v Southampton and South West Hampshire AHA (Case 152/84)
  [1986] ECR 723 .... 40, 43, 46, 47, 168, 176, 178
Meijer v Department of Trade (Case 118/78) [1979] ECR 1387 55

Meiliche (Case 83/91) [1992] ECR 1 81
Morganbesser [2004] 1 CMLR 24 139

National Panasonic (UK) v commission (Case 136/79) [1980] ECR 2033 119
Netherlands State v Reed (Case 59/85) [1986] ECR1283; [1987] 2 CMLR 448 153
Nimz v Freie und Hansestadt Hamburg (Case 184/89) [1992] 3 CMLR 699 174
Ninni-Orasche (Case 412/01) [2004] 1 CMLR 19 .... 136, 173

Oebel (Belgian Bakery Case) (Case 155/80) [1981] ECR 1993 93
Oliveri (Case 493/01) [2005] 1 CMLR 18 147
Omega (Case 36/02) [2005] 1 CMLR 5 140
Ordre des Avocats v Klopp (Case 107/83) [1984] ECR 2971 156
Orfanopulos (Case 482/01) 1CMLR 18 147

P v S and Cornwall County Council [1996] 2 CMLR 247 .... 168, 175
Patented Feedingstuffs, Re [1989] 2 CMLR 902 89
Patrick v Ministre des Affaires Culturelles (1978) (Case 11/77) [1977] ECR 1199 162
Perfume cases (Case 99/79) SA Lancome v Etos BV [1980] ECR 2511 116
Pfizer Inc v Eurim-Pharm GmbH (Case 1/81) [1981] ECR 2913 102
Pharmacia & Upjohn SA v Paranova SA (379/97) 101
Philip Morris case [1987] see British-American Co and Reynolds Industries Inc v
   Commission (Philip Morris Inc Intervening)
Pickstone v Freemans plc [1989] 1 AC 66 .... 45, 47, 48
Pioneer Hi-Fi case [1980] 1 CMLR 457 119
Plaumann v Commission (1962) Case 65/72 [1963] ECR 95 .... 58, 60, 61, 66, 84
Politi v Italian Ministry of Finance (Case 43/71) [1971] 2 ECR 1039 28
Polypropylene case (1986) OJL 230/1 113
Prais v Council (1975) (Case 130/75) [1976] ECR 1589 .... 24, 169
Procureur du Roi v Dassonville (Case 8/74) [1974] ECR 837 ...... 91, 92, 93, 94, 96, 97, 98
Procureur du Roi v Royer (case 48/75) [1976] ECR 497 .... 134, 135, 151

R v British Coal Corp ex p Vardy [1993] 1 CMLR 721 48
R v Henn and Darby (cASE 34/79) [1981] AC 850 78
R v HM Treasury ex p BT (Case 392/93) [1996] IRLR 300 49
R v HM Treasury ex p Daily Mail and General Trust plc (1987) (Case 81/87)
   [1989] 1 All ER 328 77
R v Immigration Appeal Tribunal ex p Antonissen (Case 292/89)
   [1991] 2 CMLR 135, 138

R v Intervention Board for Agricultural Produce ex p ED and F Man (Sugar) Ltd
(Case 181/84) [1985] 3 CMLR 759 .... 84, 85, 123
R v Pieck (Case 157/79) [1980] ECR 2171 78
R v Plymouth JJ ex p Rogers [1982] 3 CMLR 221 78
R v Secretary of State for Employment ex p EOC [1994] 1 All ER 910 37
R v Secretary of State for the Home Department ex p Dannenburg
[1984] 2 All ER 481 152
R v Secretary of State for Transport ex p Factortame Ltd (No 2) (Case C-213/89)
[1991] 3 CMLR 769 .... 63, 74
R v Secretary of State for Transport ex p Factortame Ltd (No 3) (Case C221/89)
[1991] 3 WLR 288; [1996] ECR 1 .... 46, 48, 64, 86
R v Secretary of State for Transport ex p Factortame Ltd (No 4) (Case C-48/93)
[1999] 4 All ER 906 .... 49, 65
R v Tymen (Case 269/80) [1981] 2 CMLR 544 78
R (on the application of British American Tobacco) v Secretary of State for Health
[2003] All ER (EC) 604 86
Ran v BALM (Berlin Butter case) (Cases 133–36/85) [1987] ECR 2289 84
Ratti (Case 148/78) [1979] ECR 1629 .... 39, 43, 46
Raulin (1989) (Case 357/89) [1992] ECR 1–1027 136
Rewe-Zentrale v Hauptzollamt Emmerich (Case 37/70) [1971] ECR 23 81
Rewe-Zentralfinanz v Hauptzollamt Landau/Pfalz (Case 45/75) [1976] ECR 181 116
Reyners (Case 2/74) [1974] ECR 631 .... 160, 162
Rheinmublen (Cases 146 and 166/73) [1974] ECR 139 .... 76, 77, 78
Rinner-Kuhn v FWW Spezial Gebäudereinigung GmbH (Case 171/88)
[1989] ECR 2743 .... 167, 170, 172
Riseria Luigi Geddo v Ente Nazionale Rise (Case 2/73) [1974] ECR 865 .... 92, 96
Roberts v Birds Eye Walls Ltd (Case 132/92) [1994] ICR 338 172
Roquette Frères v Council (Case 173/79) [1980] ECR 3333 .... 4, 65, 67
Royal Scholten-Honig v Intervention Board for Agriculture (Isoglucose
case) (Case 103/77 amd 145/77) [1978] ECR 2037 .... 57, 67
Rutili v Ministre de l'Interieure (Case 36/75) [1975] ECR 1219;
[1976] 1 CMLR 140 .... 43, 143, 145, 151

Sabbatini v European Parliament (Case 20/71) [1972] ECR 345 .... 24, 169
Schneider Electric SA v Commission (Cases T-310/01, T-77/02)
[2002] ECR II-4071 131
Schoenenburg (Case 88/77) [1978] ECR 473 55

Schoppenstedt (Case 5/71) [1971] ECR 975 .... 59, 69

Sebago Inc v GB Unie SA (173/98) 103

Secretary of State for the Home Department v Akrich (Case 109/01)
    [2003] 3 CMLR 26 138

Segers (Case 79/85) [1986] ECR 2375 .... 139, 158

Sgarlata v Commission (Case 79/85) [1965] ECR 215 83

Shell-Berre, Re [1964] CMLR 462 86

Silhouette International v Hartlauer Handelsgesellschaft (Case 335/96)
    [1998] 2 CMLR953 102

Simmenthal SpA (No 2) (Case 106/77) [1978] ECR 278 .... 33, 36, 46, 63

Skimmed Milk Powder case see Bela-Muble Josef Bergman v Grows Farm
    (Skimmed Milk case)

Sotgui v Deutsche Bundespost (Case 152/73) [1974] ECR 153 .... 142, 145

Stauder v City of Ulm (Case 29/69) [1969] ECR 419 .... 25, 30

Stock Exchange Case (1993) 2 CMLR 677 78

Sutton v Secretary of State for Social Security (Case 66/95) [1997] 2 CMLR 382 .... 49, 65

Telemarsicabruzzo SpA v Circostel (Case 320–322/90) [1993] ECR 1–393 81

Tetra Laval v Commission (Cases T-5/02, T-80/02)
    (2002) ECR II-4381 & ECR II-4519 132

Thieffry (Case 71/76) [1977] ECR 765 162

Toepfer v Commission (Case 106 and 107/63) [1965] ECR 10919 83

Transocean Marine Paint Association v Commission (Case 17/74) [1974] ECR 1063 26

Turkey case see Commission v UK 54

TWD Textilwerke Deggendorf GmbH v Germany (Case C-188/92) [1994] ECR 1 59

Union de Pequeños Agricultores (cASE 50/00p) (2002) 58, 60, 61

United Brands Co v Commission (27/76) [1976] ECR 207 .... 111, 112, 122, 123, 127

URBSA V Bosman [1996] 1 CMLR 645 164

Van Binsbergen (Case 33/74) [1974] ECR 229 .... 160, 162

Van Duyn v Home Office (Case 41/75)[1975] 1 CMLR 1;
    [1974] ECR 1337 .... 42, 46, 151, 152, 177

Van Gend en Loos (Case 26/62)
    [1963] ECR 1 .... 33, 35, 38, 39, 41, 42, 45, 55, 73, 87, 177, 199

Verbond van Nederlands Ondernemingen (VNO) (Case 51/76) [1977] ECR 113 39

von Colson (Case 14/83) [1984] ECR 1891 .... 40, 44, 45, 47

Walgrave and Koch v Ass Union Cycliste (Case 36/74) [1974] ECR 1405 .... 160, 163

Watson v Belman (Case 118/75) [1976] ECR 1185 151

Webb v EMO Air Cargo (UK) Ltd [1992] IRLR 116; [1994] IRLR 116 .... 48, 168

Williams v Dutch Secretary of State [1977] 1 CMLR 669 138

Woodpulp case *see* Ahlström and Others v Commission

Worrington v Lloyds Bank Ltd [1982] 3 All ER 373 179

Zino Davidoff SA v A&G Imports Ltd (No 1) [1999] 3 WLR 849 .... 102, 103

Zuckerfabrik Watenstedt (Case 6/68) [1968] ECR 409 .... 27, 58

TABLE OF LEGISLATION

▌DIRECTIVES

Directive 64/221 (Movement and residence of foreign nationals) 43, 133, 149, 150

    Art 3 .... 146, 147

    Art 3(1) 146, 147, 152

    Art 3(2) 146, 147

    Art 6 152

    Art 8 152

Directive 68/360 (Rights of entry into EU

    for workers and their families) 133, 134, 135, 138

Directive 70/50 (Free trade between Member States) 92, 96

    Art 3 97

Directive 73/148 (Rights of entry and residence) 149

Directive 75/34 (Rights to remain after employment for the self-employed

    and their families) 149

Directive 75/117 (Equal pay) 165, 166, 167

    Art 1 170

Directive 76/207

    (Equal Treatment Directive) 26, 40, 47, 48, 165, 166, 169, 173, 175, 178

    Art 1(2) 178

    Art 2 168

    Art 2(1) 173

    Art 2(4) 168

    Art 5(1) 178

Directive 77/249 (Free movement of lawyers) 153, 154

Directive 77/338 (Sixth (VAT) Directive) 43

Directive 79/7 (Equal treatment in matters of social security) 165, 179

Directive 80/987 (Protection of employees in cases of insolvency of employers) 62, 63

Directive 86/378 (Equal treatment for occupational pension schemes) 165

Directive 86/613 (Equal treatment for self-employed) 165
Directive 89/48 (Mutual Recognition of Professional Qualification) 139, 149, 153, 155
   Art 1(a) 155
   Art 3 155
Directive 89/104/EEC (Trade Marks) 100
Directive 90/366 (Rights to students undertaking a vocational course at a
   university in another member state) 152, 153
Directive 91/533 (Employees) 47
Directive 93/96 (Students) 150, 152
Directive 98/5 (Lawyers Directive) 155
Directive 2000/43 (Equal treatment between persons irrespective of race or
   ethnic origin) 166, 169
Directive 2000/78 (Framework Directive for equal treatment in employment
   and occupation) 166, 169, 175
Directive 2002/73 (Equal Treatment Directive) 166, 169, 173, 175
Directive 2004/38 (Citizens' Free Movement Rights) 153

REGULATIONS

Regulation 1/2003 .... 19, 115, 116, 117, 118, 119
Regulation 17/62 (Implementing EC Treaty) 125
Regulation 139/2004 .... 19, 124, 129, 132
Regulation 769/68 (National sugar prices) 68
Regulation 1111/77 (Laying down common provisions for Isoglucose) 67
Regulation 1251/70 (Right to remain in EU State after employment) 133
Regulation 1310/97 (Merger) 129
   Art 1(3) 129
Regulation 1408/71 (EC legislation on social security) 135
Regulation 1612/68 (Freedom of movement of workers within
   the Community) 133, 134, 141, 144
   Art 1 141
   Art 10(1) 135, 138
Regulation 2173/85 (Establishing Economic Interest Groupings) 159
Regulations 4064/89 (Merger) 19, 124, 129, 132
   Art 4(1) 130
   Art 8 130

TREATIES AND CONVENTIONS

Act of Accession 1972
  Art 102 190

Charter of Fundamental Rights 25, 198
  Art 47 60
Constitutional Treaty 19, 26, 194, 198, 201
  Arts 1–19 199

EC Treaty 1, 3, 35, 37, 125, 154, 187
  Annex II 87
  Art 2 .... 106, 117, 144, 163, 168
  Art 2(1) 93
  Art 3 .... 93, 106, 166
  Art 3(c) 163
  Art 3(g) 117, 120
  Art 5 .... 45, 63, 203
  Art 6 26
  Art 6(1) 130
  Art 6(a) 169
  Art 7 .... 24, 203
  Art 10 .... 36, 45, 46, 63
  Art 11(2) 16
  Art 12 .... 35, 38, 42
  Art 13 .... 166, 169, 175
  Art 14 96
  Art 14(1)(a) 130
  Art 14(2) 130
  Art 18 140
  Art 23 91
  Art 25 .... 35, 38, 42, 87, 91
  Art 25(3) 66
  Art 28 .... 64, 88, 89, 91, 92, 93, 94, 95, 96, 97, 98, 99, 100, 104, 105, 106, 107
  Art 29 .... 91, 92, 100
  Art 30 .... 54, 64, 88, 89, 91, 93, 94, 95, 97, 99, 100, 101, 102, 104, 105, 106, 107
  Art 31 87
  Art 36 .... 102, 104, 107

Art 37(3) 69

Art 39 .... 133, 134, 135, 137, 138, 140, 141, 142, 143, 144,
145, 146, 147, 149, 150, 151, 163, 177

Arts 39–42 30

Art 39(4) 138

Art 40 28

Art 43 .... 134, 137, 139, 140, 142, 149, 150, 157, 161, 162

Arts 43–48 153

Art 44 .... 157, 158

Art 45 161

Art 46 .... 140, 149

Art 47 154

Art 48 .... 139, 143, 144, 145, 157, 158, 163, 177

Art 48(4) 142, 143

Art 49 .... 134, 137, 140, 142, 149, 150, 151, 157, 158, 162, 163

Arts 49–55 140

Art 50 .... 149, 151, 157, 162, 163

Art 52 161

Art 55 161

Art 59 .... 162, 163

Art 60 .... 162, 163

Art 71 188

Art 75 188

Art 81 .... 19, 109, 110, 113, 114, 115, 116, 117, 118, 119, 120, 125, 126, 127, 129

Art 81(3) 114, 116, 118, 131

Art 82 .... 19, 29, 109, 110, 111, 112, 113, 114, 117, 118,
119, 120, 121, 123, 124, 128, 129, 131

Art 85 .... 119, 125, 127, 129

Art 85(1) 125

Art 85(2) 126

Art 86 .... 19, 29, 112, 119, 124, 128, 129

Art 87 .... 105, 109, 117, 120

Art 88 .... 109, 117, 120

Art 90 .... 81, 91

Art 92 105

Art 95 .... 81, 167

Art 113 .... 186, 191

Art 114 .... 186, 191
Art 119 .... 38, 166, 170, 171, 172, 173, 174, 176, 177, 179
Arts 131–134 .... 181, 182, 185
Art 132 190
Art 133 .... 182, 183, 185, 186, 190, 191
Art 136 30
Art 141 .... 24, 30, 38, 39, 165, 166, 167, 169, 170, 171, 172, 173, 174, 175, 176, 177, 179, 180
Art 141(4) 168
Art 149 16
Art 169 .... 48, 53, 55, 64, 106, 177
Art 171 .... 54, 64
Art 173 .... 68, 69, 73, 120, 125, 127, 128, 186, 188
Art 173(1) 68
Art 173(2) 66, 68
Art 174 68
Art 177 .... 35, 36, 42, 43, 64, 72, 93, 106, 144, 145, 146, 147, 161, 162, 163, 170, 171, 177, 178, 179, 184, 186, 189
Art 177(1)(b) 73
Art 177(2) 86
Art 189 .... 3, 30, 42, 46
Arts 189–199 2
Art 199 89
Art 201 3
Arts 202–207 2
Arts 203–210 14
Art 205 15
Art 208 .... 18, 189
Art 210 186
Art 211 .... 17, 18, 52, 53, 195
Arts 211–214 2
Art 213 20
Art 215(2) 68
Art 216 20
Art 220 .... 7, 23, 80
Arts 220–245 2

Art 222 .... 8, 101, 126
Art 223 8
Art 225 11
Art 226 .... 9, 18, 20, 46, 51, 52, 53, 54, 55, 64, 105, 106, 177
Art 227 .... 9, 38, 46, 51, 52, 54, 55
Art 228 .... 9, 18, 46, 51, 52, 54, 64, 186, 190
Art 229 120
Art 230 .... 9, 12, 23, 27, 30, 51, 56, 57, 58, 59, 60, 66, 68, 69, 73, 82, 83,
                        84, 85, 116, 117, 118, 119, 120, 125, 127, 128, 186, 188, 204
Art 230(4) 59, 60, 61, 62
Art 230(5) 61
Art 231 .... 59, 68, 83, 85
Art 232 51
Art 234 .... 9, 29, 35, 36, 39, 42, 43, 51, 55, 59, 60, 63, 64, 68, 71,
                        72, 73, 74, 75, 76, 77, 78, 79, 80, 81, 82, 83, 84, 85, 86,
                        87, 88, 93, 97, 98, 106, 144, 145, 146, 147, 161, 162,
                        163, 170, 171, 177, 178, 179, 184, 186, 189
Art 234(2) 74, 76, 86, 87
Art 234(3) 74, 76, 80, 86, 87, 88, 89
Art 235 .... 56, 60, 68
Art 241 .... 9, 51
Art 243 .... 9, 55
Art 249 .... 18, 19, 21, 22, 27, 28, 30, 36, 38, 39, 40, 41, 42, 46, 57, 73, 83, 118
Art 253 .... 27, 31
Art 254 27
Art 257 .... 12, 13
Art 263 12
Art 264 203
Art 265 203
Art 266 89
Art 271 13
Art 272 6
Art 281 .... 181, 185, 186, 189
Art 288 .... 23, 26, 56, 60, 62, 68, 69, 117, 118
Art 293 .... 157, 158
Art 295 .... 101, 126

Art 300 .... 181, 182, 186, 190

Art 301 19

Arts 302–304 .... 181, 182

Art 308 18

Art 310 .... 181, 182, 183

Part 1 .... 186, 189

Preamble 203

European Coal and Steel Community in 1952 .... 1, 12

European Convention on Human Rights 1951

Art 6 60

Art 13 60

General Agreement on Tariffs and Trade (GATT) 18, 185

Art XI 184

Laeken Declaration 2001 .... 194, 196, 197, 199, 200

Lisbon Treaty 19, 194, 197, 201

Luxembourg Accords 1966 16

Merger Treaty 1965 10

Mutual Recognition of Companies and Bodies Corporate 1968 158

North East Atlantic Fisheries Convention 189

Schengen Agreement 137

Single European Act 1986 .... 1, 3, 11, 15, 16, 68

Art 6 4

Art 7 .... 4, 16

Art 18 193

Art 95 193

Preamble 25

Treaty of Amsterdam 1997 .... 1, 7, 20, 62, 169, 193, 194, 204

Art 141(4) 168

Art 251 .... 5, 201

Treaty on European Union 1992 (Maastricht Treaty) 3, 4, 16, 46, 193, 201, 202–4

Arts 17–21 204

Art 48 200

Art 49 203

Art 251 203

Protocol 2 180
Protocol on Social Policy 202
Treaty of Nice 2000 .... 7, 13, 16, 17, 194, 195, 196, 197, 198, 204
s 225(3) 79
Treaty of Rome *see* EC Treaty

Yaounde Convention 40

UK LEGISLATION

European Communities Act 1972 .... 45, 47
ss 2 and 3 35

Obscene Publications Act 1959 75

Sex Discrimination Act 178
s 6(4) 47, 48
Shops Act 1950
s 47 64

Trade Union and Labour Relations Act 1992 48

TABLE OF EQUIVALENCES

TREATY ESTABLISHING THE EUROPEAN COMMUNITY (EC TREATY)

Previous numbering	New numbering
	Art 1(3)
Art 2	Art 2
Art 3	Art 3
Art 3(C)	Art 3(C)
	Art 3(g)
	Art 6
Art 4	Art 7
Art 5	Art 10
	Art 11(2)
Art 6(a)	Art 13
Art 8 (a)	Art 18
Art 9	Art 23
Art 12	Art 25
Art 12(3)	Art 25(3)
Art 30	Art 28
Art 34	Art 29
Art 36	Art 30
Art 37	Art 31
Art 43(3)	Art 37(3)
Art 48	Art 39
Art 48(4)	Art 39(4)
Art 49	Art 40
Art 50	Art 41
Art 51	Art 42
Art 52	Art 43

Art 54 .... Art 44
Art 55 .... Art 45
Art 56 .... Art 46
Art 57 .... Art 47
Art 58 .... Art 48
Arts 59 .... Arts 49
Arts 60 .... Arts 50
Art 61 .... Art 51
Art 63 .... Art 52
Art 64 .... Art 53
Art 65 .... Art 54
Art 66 .... Art 55
Art 75 .... Art 71
Art 85 .... Art 81
Art 85(1) .... Art 81
Art 85(2) .... Art 81
Art 86 .... Art 82
Art 90 .... Art 86
Art 92 .... Art 87
Art 93 .... Art 88
Art 94 .... Art 89
Art 95 .... Art 90
Art 110 .... Art 131
Art 112 .... Art 132
Art 113 .... Art 133
Art 114 .... Art 133
Art 115 .... Art 134
Art 117 .... Art 136
Art 119 .... Art 141
Art 119(4) .... Art 141(4)
Art 130 .... Art 169
Art 137 .... Art 189
Art 139 .... Art 197
Art 144 .... Art 201
Art 145 .... Art 202
Art 146 .... Art 203

Art 147 .... Art 204

Art 148 .... Art 205

Art 150 .... Art 206

Art 151 .... Art 207

Art 152 .... Art 208

Art 154 .... Art 210

Art 155 .... Art 211

Art 156 .... Art 212

Art 157 .... Art 213

Art 158 .... Art 214

Art 160 .... Art 216

Art 164 .... Art 220

Art 165 .... Art 221

Art 166 .... Art 222

Art 167 .... Art 223

Art 168 .... Art 224

Art 168(a) .... Art 225

Art 169 .... Art 226

Art 170 .... Art 227

Art 171 .... Art 228

Art 171(1)(b) .... Art 234

Art 172 .... Art 229

Art 173 .... Art 230

Art 173(1) .... Art 230

Art 173(2) .... Art 230

Art 173(4) .... Art 230(4)

Art 173(5) .... Art 230(5)

Art 174 .... Art 231

Art 175 .... Art 232

Art 176 .... Art 233

Art 177 .... Art 234

Art 177(2) .... Art 234(2)

Art 177(3) .... Art 234(3)

Art 178 .... Art 235

Art 179 .... Art 236

Art 180 .... Art 237

Art 181 .... Art 238
Art 182 .... Art 239
Art 183 .... Art 240
Art 184 .... Art 241
Art 186 .... Art 243
Art 187 .... Art 244
Art 188 .... Art 245
Art 189 .... Art 249
Art 190 .... Art 253
Art 191 .... Art 254
Art 193 .... Art 257
Art 198(a) .... Art 263
Art 198(d) .... Art 266
Art 199 .... Art 266
Art 203 .... Art 272
Art 210 .... Art 281
Art 215(2) .... Art 288
Art 220 .... Art 293
Art 222 .... Art 295
Art 228 .... Art 300
Art 228(a) .... Art 301
Art 229 .... Art 302
Art 230 .... Art 303
Art 231 .... Art 304
Art 235 .... Art 308
Art 238 .... Art 310

INTRODUCTION

European Union law is unlike any other area of law that you may have encountered in your other legal studies. It does not follow the traditions and principles you have come across previously. It is different, and that fact, perhaps with the added importance given to it by the legal profession and business in general, is why it is increasingly attractive to students. However, although it may have different sources, traditions and terminology, the student is still required to approach examinations with the same preparation as any other examination. One problem you will encounter is that the opportunity was taken in the Treaty of Amsterdam to renumber the EC Treaty. This will mean that textbook or journal article references may be to Articles of the Treaty which are no longer correct. Obviously, the old cases, which are so important to the development of Community or Union law, will refer to the old numbering of the Articles. However, if you are aware of the old and new numbering, this should not prove too much of a problem. I refer to the new numbers in the text, but there is a Table of Equivalences on pp. xxv–xxviii to help you find your way between the old and current numbering.

Wide reading and a detailed review of both the syllabus and past examination papers are important for European Union law, just as for contract, tort, etc. Many topics in European law are interrelated, as you will see from the questions in this book. Some students have difficulties because, European law topics being so different from the common law tradition, they are unsure what is important. They cannot see the wood for the trees, in that they study particular topics but find it hard to see the connections. Then, it suddenly clicks. Hopefully, this happens before they enter the examination hall! It will happen sooner if you read one of the many basic textbooks on European law, making sure that it is the latest edition you can find.

The answers to the questions in this book are not the only possible answers. They have been written at a particular time. If I had to write them again I would probably change some of the contents, perhaps bringing in newer cases, or changing the emphasis. However, the main points would remain the same. I hope that, by reading these answers, you will obtain a clearer view of European Union law and the relationship between different topics.

As you will see, there are some basic cases which are the authority for a number of principles of Union law. They appear in answers to many questions. You should ensure that you are familiar with these, and gradually build up your confidence with the topics. Start with the definitions and basic principles, looking for an authority either through a case or an Article of the Treaty, for example.

This approach will help you when you come to the examination hall and read the questions for the first time. Don't panic! You should have grasped the essentials of the European Union law from your studies. In your preparation, you should consider the following suggestions:

- Read the question paper carefully. Underline or highlight what appear to you to be the key points. This is especially important for problem questions, which may be quite long.

- Write, on the question paper or one of the pages of the answer book, any ideas you have when you first read the question. This might include definitions, cases, Treaty Articles, quotations or other references. This is good practice, because it may help you decide the best questions to tackle, but more importantly, when you return to answer that particular question, these notes will help you to concentrate on the new topic. As you are writing other answers, ideas and cases may suddenly come to mind. Write them down before you forget them! You can always put a line through these notes at the end of the examination, so that the examiner will not regard them as part of your answer.

- When you start to answer a particular question, plan your answer carefully. This will help you to adjust to the topic, but it will also help you recover from those moments when your concentration lapses through some distraction. It may also help you find your next point in your answer when you ask yourself 'what shall I write next?' Remember that you will get little credit for rambling, so planning and following your plan are very important.

- Make sure that you deal with all the parts of the question. This applies to all questions and not just those which have separate (a) and (b) parts. If you do not answer the question fully, you are limiting the range of marks you can obtain for your answer. When you are dealing with problem questions, remember that the examiner is not just looking for an answer which shows knowledge of principles. Your answer should show understanding of the principles and the ability to apply them to the facts in the question.

Lastly, make sure that the examiner can read what you have written. This may seem a very simple point, but examiners like to follow the logical thread of your answer. If it takes a while to decipher what you have written, the examiner might not appreciate your answer fully. In this context, I would like to thank Christine Blundell, who through much practice was able to decipher my handwriting and thus helped in the production of part of this book. You will not be so fortunate, as it is not common practice to have a secretary in the examination hall. However, like you, what I have written remains my own responsibility.

Mike Cuthbert
August 2008

CHAPTER 1

COMMUNITY INSTITUTIONS

INTRODUCTION

It is very important to develop a good understanding of the functions, powers and relationships between the main institutions of the European Union. This requires knowledge of four key institutions, which have their origin in the first Community, the European Coal and Steel Community, established in 1952. Although there have been some changes since then, the basic principles have remained the same.

You should try to get a feel for the need for such institutions. It is sometimes forgotten that the European Community was an innovative idea, in the sense that a supranational body was being created by the transfer of sovereignty from Member States to a Community which was to act on behalf of all its members. Therefore, it was important to ensure that the institutions established would provide a forum for an input by the Member States, a body to implement and police policies decided by the Community, a court to settle disputes and provide authoritative judgments and, finally, a body which would allow an input from a wider base of views from the Member States. Hence, the **Treaty of Rome** established the Council of Ministers, the European Commission, the European Court of Justice (ECJ) and the European Assembly, later to be called the European Parliament in the **Single European Act**.

The starting point for an understanding of the EU institutions is their origin, that is, the Treaty Articles. Although these need not be learned by heart, there are key points which must be grasped as you build up an understanding of their functions and relationships. Do not be confused by the fact that the numbering of the Articles has been affected by the **Treaty of Amsterdam**, where the opportunity was taken to reorder them. As some textbooks and old judgments still refer to the 'traditional' numbering, a Table of Equivalences is included on pp. xxv–xxviii to help you. This details old and new Treaty numbers.

One of the best ways to get an overview of the variety of institutions is to read material which is intended for the non-specialist reader. Some of the publications produced by the European Commission are very good and have the added advantage of being free. There is also a very good website (www.europa.eu). Once you have an overview, you should begin to build up a more detailed picture, which shows the more complex functions and relationships between the institutions. However, you should always be alert to practical examples of the friction or otherwise generated by these institutions and reported in the media. Such examples are invaluable in impressing the examiner but, more importantly, they should convince you that you are not dealing with a theoretical group of institutions, but 'a living community'.

Checklist

You need to have a good understanding of the functions, procedures and membership of the main Community institutions, plus an awareness of the less significant ones. You should also look at Chapter 12, where some of the proposed changes to the institutions are mentioned. In particular, you should concentrate on:

- the European Parliament – **Arts 189–199**;
- the Council of Ministers – **Arts 202–207**;
- the European Commission – **Arts 211–214**;
- the ECJ – **Arts 220–245**; and
- the European Council, the Court of First Instance, the Economic and Social Committee, the Committee of Permanent Representatives, the Committee of the Regions and the Court of Auditors.

Question 1

'Although the European Parliament has limited powers, one cannot claim that the Community legislative process is devoid of democratic participation.'

Discuss.

Answer plan

This type of question has become very popular in recent years. This is largely due to developments which have affected the Parliament. The main points to cover in your answer are:

- powers and composition of the European Parliament;
- procedures of the Parliament; and
- role of the Parliament in the legislative process.

Answer

Since 1979, the Members of the European Parliament have been directly elected by their constituents in the Member States. Before that time, when the members were nominated by their respective governments, they had determined, as early as 1962, to call themselves a Parliament, even though the **Treaty of Rome** referred to them as an Assembly. Under **Art 189**, the European Parliament consists of 'representatives of the peoples of the States brought together in the Community'. It was not until the **Single European Act 1986** that the Member States formally recognised the European Parliament by this name.

The European Parliament has certain characteristics similar to national parliaments, such as the UK Parliament at Westminster. There are a number of standing committees, which mirror the major policy areas of the Community. The committees carry out inquiries; hear evidence from experts and interested parties, including the Commission; and issue reports. In addition, parliamentary questions are an important element of control over the Commission. Under **Art 197**, the Commission must reply orally or in writing to questions put to it by MEPs. In fact, the Council and foreign ministers also take part in this process. It is common practice now for the President of the Council of Ministers to make a report to the Parliament at the end of his or her term as President.

There are two important powers associated with the European Parliament. The **Treaty of Rome** made the European Commission responsible to the European Parliament and this is of increasing importance now. Once appointed by the Member States, the 27 Commissioners can only be removed by the European Parliament passing a censure motion by a two-thirds majority vote and an absolute majority of its Members. Such a motion, successfully passed, would force the resignation of the Commission. However, this power under **Art 201** can only be used against the whole Commission and not against individual Commissioners. This power has never been exercised, although it has been threatened on a number of occasions. However, in order to avoid the motion of censure, the Commission did resign in March 1999 although its members remained in office until replaced by a new Commission in September of that year. With a view to making the institutions more democratic, the **Treaty on European Union (TEU)** gave the European Parliament an important role in the process of appointing the President and Members of the Commission. This was achieved by the need for the Commission to be approved by Parliament in a vote of investiture.

Secondly, and perhaps the most important input that would be recognised as part of democratic participation, is the involvement of the European Parliament in making European laws, principally regulations and directives. There are many policy areas of the Treaty which give the Parliament the right to be consulted on proposed legislation. This is illustrated by the phrase, which is very familiar to any student of the Treaty, 'the Council, acting on a proposal from the Commission and after consulting the European Parliament, shall . . .'. The normal procedure is that the proposal from the Commission is first considered by one of the Parliament's committees mentioned above, which will produce a report and a draft resolution. These then go to the full Parliament for debate before its opinion, including any suggested amendments, is sent to the Council. As a result of this opinion, the Commission may modify its proposal, but there is no obligation on either the Council or the Commission to respond to it. However, whatever weight is given to the European Parliament's view, its right to be consulted must be respected. Failure to follow this procedural requirement may lead to the measure being declared invalid.

This happened in the cases of *Roquette v Council* and *Maizena v Council*, both reported in 1980. An interesting discussion took place in these cases with regard to what extent this requirement gave power to the Parliament to block legislation. Is the requirement that the European Parliament should be asked for its opinion, or must it actually give it? The Council argued that if the latter was true, then the Parliament could delay legislation indefinitely by the simple expedient of not giving an opinion. The ECJ interpreted the requirement under the Treaty to mean that the Parliament has to give its opinion. However, it left open the question of what would happen if the Parliament were to be deliberately obstructive and the Council wished to go ahead with the legislation. Such an impasse has not yet occurred.

It is understandable that in these circumstances, where its opinion carried limited importance to the Council, the European Parliament was often called 'a mere talking shop' by national politicians. With the direct elections of 1979, MEPs saw themselves as the true representatives of their constituents and increasingly called for an active part in the legislative process. This was given by **Arts 6** and 7 of the **Single European Act 1986**, which amended the original Treaty. This required a co-operation procedure to be operative in some instances, but by no means all, where the Treaty required the Parliament to be consulted. The main difference is that in theory, the views of the European Parliament carry more importance, although in practice, this change may not be so significant. When the Council receives a proposal from the Commission, it adopts a 'common position', which is sent to the European Parliament. The Parliament now has three months in which to act. If Parliament rejects the common position, the Council can adopt the proposal only by unanimity. If Parliament wishes to amend the proposal, such amendments are sent back to the Commission for consideration. These amendments may be adopted, but there is no obligation on the Commission to do so. The proposal is then sent back to the Council along with any parliamentary amendments it had not accepted and the reasons for this refusal. The Council can accept the amended proposal by a qualified majority or it can amend it by adopting its own amendments or those proposed by the Parliament. This has to be done by a unanimous vote in the Council.

In practice, the co-operation procedure appears to grant the European Parliament very little extra power. It provides for a possible alliance between a Member State and the Parliament in the sense that the Council of Ministers would not have the unanimity to overrule amendments. But does this give more authority to the Member State or the European Parliament? Also, the requirement on the Commission under the co-operation procedure to consider the Parliament's amendments and to give reasons for not adopting them makes a legal requirement of something which was a matter of practice before. In fact, perhaps the most significant increase in the Parliament's powers brought about by the **Single European Act** is the requirement for its approval in relation to the admission of new members to the Community or the conclusion of association agreements with third countries. Under the Act, the European Parliament thus has a veto in such matters.

However, the big step forward in democratic involvement was the introduction of the co-decision procedure in the **Treaty on European Union**. Under this procedure, Parliament shares the decision making power equally with the Council. If Parliament decides to reject the proposal, it cannot be adopted by the Council. To avoid this deadlock, a conciliation committee is convened with a membership drawn from the European Parliament, the Council and the Commission. If agreement is still not reached, the European Parliament can reject the proposal definitively. The **Treaty of Amsterdam 1998** simplified the procedure in **Art 251** to make it more efficient.

An aspect of democratic participation which has always been considered important in any parliament is the involvement of elected representatives in the setting of expenditure and income levels, that is, a budget. Although it is the President of the European Parliament alone who has the power to adopt the budget, the procedure for the Community budget is rather complex and has been varied on several occasions. The effect of these changes has been to transfer certain powers from the Council to the Parliament.

The European Parliament's right to make changes in the budget depends on the distinction between expenditure which is 'compulsory' and that which is 'non-compulsory'. Compulsory expenditure covers that expenditure which is committed under Treaty provisions or Community legislation. The main example is expenditure on the common agricultural policy. Parliament can only propose modifications to this category of expenditure, thus giving the Council the final say in such matters. However, non-compulsory expenditure, which includes all expenditure which is not the inevitable consequence of Community legislation, can be amended by the majority of MEPs voting in favour of such proposals. This expenditure includes the Community social policy, regional and industrial policies, and accounts for about 42% of the total Community budget. For this type of expenditure, it is the European Parliament which has final control. Therefore, although the Parliament does have some powers of approval as far as the budget is concerned, these are weak with regard to compulsory expenditure, which comprises the majority of the total budget.

However, in 1975, the European Parliament was given increased powers in relation to the Community budget by a conciliation procedure. The aim of these powers is to give the Parliament more effective participation in the budgetary process by seeking agreement between the Parliament and the Council of Ministers. If the Parliament refuses to pass the budget as presented to it by the Council, a number of important consequences follow. First, the budget cannot be implemented, which has implications for the expenditure level of the Community (limited to one-12th of the previous year's budget per month). Secondly, a 'conciliation committee', consisting of the Council and representatives of the European Parliament, is established to try to resolve the disagreement. The European Commission assists the work of the committee.

Ultimately, the Parliament may reject the budget outright under **Art 272** of the **EC Treaty** by a vote cast by a two-thirds majority of its members. This has now happened on four occasions, in 1980 by the newly directly elected Parliament, eager to use its budgetary powers, and in 1982, 1986 and 1988. Although it may reject it, the Parliament cannot increase the total amount of the budget beyond the maximum rate of increase set by the Commission, unless the alteration is agreed by the Council. The disagreement is generally, therefore, centred on the distribution of the budget. Such disagreements sometimes erupt into the public domain and have been subject to proceedings before the ECJ, as in *EC Council v European Parliament* (1986). In 1988, in an attempt to improve the budgetary procedure, an institutional agreement was entered into by the Council, Commission and the European Parliament. While recognising the varying competencies of the institutions in the budgetary field, it fixed new rules for co-operation between the institutions. However, the Council successfully obtained the annulment of the adoption of the budget by the European Parliament because the Parliament had exceeded its powers regarding compulsory expenditure (*Council of the European Union v European Parliament* (1995)).

The normal authority of a parliament is that the national government is dependent upon confidence and continued support to remain in office. There is no such relationship between the European Parliament and the main political decision-making body in the Community, the Council of Ministers. The ministers who form the Council are representing their national governments, who in turn must retain the support of his national parliaments. Therefore, any vote cast by a minister at Council meetings must be supported by their national parliament. Is this the main democratic control over European legislation? Are the national Members of Parliament, representing the same constituents as the MEPs, exercising democratic control? In theory, this could be possible, at least for major issues. However, it has one major drawback, in that the national parliaments rarely have the procedures or time necessary for clear debate of issues before they are discussed and agreed at the Council of Ministers. Although attempts are being made to ensure better information and debate in national parliaments on European issues, this is not happening at the moment. The only really genuine and consistent debate takes place in the European Parliament, but what authority does that have? As indicated above, it has some important powers, and there is pressure for these to be extended. Since the

TEU, both the **Treaty of Amsterdam** and the **Treaty of Nice** have extended the area of EU policy subject to the co-decision procedure. The **Constitution Treaty 2004** proposed to increase the scope of the co-decision procedure and give more involvement to national parliaments but it has not yet been ratified by all Member States.

Question 2

'The European Court of Justice is unlike any English court.'

Discuss.

Answer plan

This illustrates a common type of essay question on the ECJ. The task is to discuss the special features of the Court. This has a special impact for the UK because it is very different from the national courts, including the House of Lords.

The main points of the question are:

- function of the ECJ as defined by **Art 220**;
- personnel, term of office, function – judges and Advocates General;
- procedures and languages;
- form of judgments; and
- comparison with the English courts.

Answer

The ECJ is one of the main institutions of the European Community. It provides the independent judicial function necessary to ensure, as **Art 220** states, 'that in the interpretation and application of this Treaty the law is observed'. The main influence on the characteristics of the ECJ was the French legal system, notably the highest administrative court in France, the Conseil d'Etat. However, this is not the only reason why the Court is different from any English court. Another important factor is that the Court was established to work not within a State, but within a community which brought together a number of States in a new relationship, which had implications for their own legal systems.

There are 27 judges on the ECJ, with each Member State providing one judge. Appointed for a term of six years, the judges elect their own President of the Court, who serves in that post for three years. Like all posts within the Court, it is possible for the period in office to be renewed. Although this fixed but renewable term of office is not found in English courts, the attributes the judges should have are the same. **Article 223** specifies that they should be independent and qualified for the highest judicial office within their respective countries. However, an important difference is that, whereas English judges are selected from barristers and, to a lesser extent, solicitors, judges in some Member States are chosen from a much wider field, including academic lawyers. Thus, when the judges in the European Court deliberate, they are bringing together a variety of legal backgrounds which would not be found in an English court.

Perhaps a striking difference about the ECJ is the role given to Advocates General, a post derived from the French legal system and unknown in English law. There are eight Advocates General appointed to the Court. They have the same backgrounds as judges, the same term of office and, perhaps most importantly, the same status. Therefore, Advocates General should not be seen as inferior to judges, as the precedence within the Court for both depends upon the date of appointment, and not the designated office. Advocates General are given a specific role under **Art 222**, which states that 'it should be the duty of the Advocate General, acting with complete impartiality and independence, to make, in open court, reasoned submissions on cases brought before the ECJ, in order to assist the Court in the performance of its tasks'. Unlike in senior English courts, where a full judgment is given, including dissenting views, only one judgment is given by the ECJ. All the judges must agree to the one judgment, which is why they appear so terse and lacking in any real discussion of the law. They do not contain the *obiter dicta* or the *ratio decidendi* found in the common law tradition.

The importance of the Advocate General is that he hears and reads all the evidence as a judge would do, but he gives his opinion to the Court as to what the judgment should be before the judges themselves reach their decision. In his opinion, the Advocate General can range over the case law of the Court or, if appropriate, the jurisprudence of the Member States. In this way, some insight is given as to the direction European Community law may take in the future. Obviously, the judges do not have to follow the Advocate General's opinion, but if they do not it can be just as illuminating as when they do!

The workload of the ECJ has increased tremendously since the Court was established in 1957. To help the Court deal with cases, the 27 judges sit in chambers of up to five judges, but always with an odd number, so that there can be a clear decision in a case. In 1989, the Court of First Instance was set up to assist the ECJ by taking a specific jurisdiction with the safeguard of appeal to the ECJ itself. This is not unusual, as all Member States have a hierarchy or structure for their courts. The ECJ itself has a general jurisdiction with regard to Community law, only fettered by the types of action specified in the Treaty. There are a number of direct actions available which include judicial review (**Art 230**), actions against a Member State for failure to fulfil an obligation (**Arts 226** and **227**) and illegality (**Art 241**). It is also possible to obtain interim measures under **Art 243**, such as interlocutory injunctions.

In addition, there is the special procedure for preliminary references under **Art 234**. Under this procedure, courts in the Member States can ask the ECJ questions regarding the interpretation of the Treaty or validity and interpretation of Community Acts. This does not amount to an appeal relationship, but is the recognition of a 'co-operation' between the national courts and the ECJ. The nearest procedure to this in English law is appeal by case stated in criminal cases, but this is insignificant compared to the preliminary reference procedure. With regard to the doctrine of precedent so familiar to common law systems, such as in the UK, there is no such rigid adherence in the ECJ. There is, however, the Community law general principle of certainty and therefore it is unlikely that the ECJ would depart from its previous decisions without good reason.

As indicated above, the greatest influence on the ECJ has been the French judicial system. Perhaps it is to be expected, therefore, that although cases may be brought in any of the 23 official languages recognised by the Court, the working language of the Court is French. Whenever a case is brought to the ECJ, whether as a direct action which is heard in its entirety only by the Court or a request for a preliminary reference from a Member State under **Art 234**, it is processed by the Court Registry to ensure that the progress of the case can be recorded. This is especially important with preliminary references, where the whole procedure is dominated by the 'file' of written documentation sent by the national court. The procedure is that on receipt by the Registrar, the President of the Court will assign the case to one of the six chambers and nominate one of the judges to act as *rapporteur*. The First Advocate General will, at the same time, designate the Advocate General for the case.

The role of the judge *rapporteur* is that, although all the papers will go to every judge hearing the case, only he will have studied them closely in order to produce a preliminary report. This report, together with any views expressed by the Advocate General, will help the Court decide what the relevant issues are. It may be decided that the case should be heard by the full Court, as normally happens with cases between the Member States or Community institutions. These early stages, covering the written proceedings and the preparatory inquiry, are held in private. Where oral proceedings follow as with direct actions, these are held in open court in Luxembourg. The next stage is for the Advocate General to deliver his opinion to the Court. Some time after this, the Court will deliver its judgment. If it is a preliminary reference, the answers given by the Court to the questions raised by the national court will be sent back to that court so that it can complete its hearing. If it is a direct action the Court will deliver its judgment, which may take the form of a declaration, as with **Art 228**. However, if the judgment needs to be enforced, for example against a company, the Court itself has no mechanism for enforcing its judgments. Any enforcement has to be left to the appropriate judicial machinery of the Member State.

▌NOTE

See Chapter 4 on Direct Actions and Chapter 5 on Indirect Action before the ECJ and the Court of First Instance.

Question 3

Briefly describe the role of at least two of the following:

- the Committee of Permanent Representatives;
- the Court of First Instance;
- the Economic and Social Committee.

Answer plan

This question follows the tradition, mentioned above, of essay questions on the institutions. However, instead of asking a narrower question on only one institution, this question gives you the opportunity to exercise some choice. It must be remembered that this type of question is not as easy as it looks with regard to obtaining marks!

Answer

(a) The Committee of Permanent Representatives (COREPER)

The Council of Ministers is the main political power within the Community, bringing together the government ministers of the 27 Member States. However, such ministers are busy individuals with many demands upon their time. They are members of their national parliaments and governments. They do not have the time to spend in long debate on routine Community matters. To assist them, COREPER, an acronym from the name of the Committee in French, was established first under the Council's Rules of Procedure but then formally under the **Merger Treaty 1965**. The Committee of Permanent Representatives is composed of individuals of ambassador rank who are accredited to the European Community. Their main task is to carry out work preparatory to Council meetings and other work delegated to them by the Council.

The Committee works very closely with the Commission, as it seeks to represent the views of its governments in the discussion of Commission proposals. In order to carry out this task effectively, it is very important that there is very good liaison between members of COREPER and the appropriate national government departments. Thus, in discussing draft Community legislation, national viewpoints can be aired. This is not just a one-way transmission of information, in that the views of the representatives of other governments can be channelled back. In this way, disagreements can usually be ironed out before the proposal comes before the Council to make its decision.

When the Council of Ministers meets to discuss Commission proposals, there are two agendas, A and B. Items on the A agenda are those upon which provisional agreement has been reached in the course of the preparatory COREPER meetings. This allows the Council to concentrate on the items on the B agenda, where there is still disagreement and where political compromise is needed.

As the activity of the Community has increased, so the workload on COREPER has led to it being divided into two. COREPER 1 is composed of deputy Permanent Representatives, who generally discuss matters of a more technical nature, and COREPER 2 is composed of the Ambassadors, who discuss politically important matters.

(b) The Court of First Instance (CFI)

This Court was established under the **Single European Act (SEA) 1986** and came into operation in 1989. The ECJ, which had been established by the **Treaty of Rome**, had experienced increasing difficulties in coping with the workload, as the number of Member States had increased and the policy area had expanded. The solution finally accepted by the Council of Ministers was to 'attach' the CFI to the ECJ and to give it a limited jurisdiction with a possible appeal to the ECJ itself. As the CFI has been very successful in its operations, the scope of its jurisdiction has been widened.

Although it is quite common for judicial structures in the Member States to form a hierarchy of courts, the SEA uses the word 'attach' quite deliberately. The CFI is not a separate institution. It shares not only the building in Luxembourg with the ECJ, but also other facilities, such as the library. It appoints its own Registrar, but other administrative services are shared.

The CFI is based on **Art 225**. There are 27 judges appointed to the Court, one from each Member State. Although there are no Advocates General specifically appointed to the CFI, the need for such a role to be fulfilled is recognised. Where an Advocate General is required in a particular case, one of the judges will be requested to carry out this role. This will not happen in every case before the CFI.

11

The Court may sit in chambers of three or five judges in order to hear cases brought before it.

Like the judges appointed to the ECJ, those appointed to the CFI have a six-year term of office, which is renewable. Unlike their colleagues, the criteria for selection as a judge in the CFI are not so high as in the ECJ. In the ECJ, prospective judges must possess the ability for appointment to high judicial office. **Article 225** states that for the CFI, judges are to be chosen 'from persons whose independence is beyond doubt and who possess the ability required for appointment to judicial office'.

As already indicated, the ECJ's workload increased dramatically in the 1980s, and concern was expressed about the effect this was having on the time it was taking it to deal with cases. The resultant jurisdiction of the CFI indicates that one of the problems encountered by the ECJ was those cases which required a long examination of questions of fact. These are very time-consuming and involve sifting through a great deal of evidence. Originally, there were three categories of case which came before the CFI. These were: staff cases, where employees of the Community have a dispute with regard to their employment; cases brought under the **European Coal and Steel Community Treaty**, concerned with production and prices; and, most importantly, competition cases. In 1994, this jurisdiction was extended to include any action brought by any natural or legal persons against an act of a Community institution. If these cases also contain a claim for damages, the CFI can hear that claim as part of the action. However, the CFI itself now has a 30-month wait for cases to be heard. This is unsatisfactory for the individual concerned. Therefore, the **Treaty of Nice** reduced some aspects of the CFI's workload, for example by setting up specialist chambers to deal with staff cases. In November 2004 the Council adopted a decision to establish the EU Civil Service Tribunal, with an appeal to the CFI on points of law only. However, it also added others to relieve the pressure on the ECJ, such as giving the CFI some requests for preliminary rulings.

Appeals from the CFI are to the ECJ and have to be brought within two months. The appeal will only be heard on points of law and not of fact. Some writers believe that large companies involved in competition cases will always seek to appeal to the ECJ and therefore the reduction on the ECJ's workload envisaged by establishing the CFI will not materialise. It is something which only experience will tell, but the time-consuming factual aspects of the case will not be something which can be raised on appeal and will not therefore take up the time of the ECJ. The three grounds of appeal mirror the grounds of annulment under **Art 230**, namely, lack of competence, breach of procedure or infringement of Community law by the CFI.

(c) The Economic and Social Committee (ECOSOC)

The Committee is established under the **EC Treaty**, but it is not an institution of the Community. It is in fact an advisory committee appointed under **Arts 257 and 263**.

It consists of representatives of the various sections of economic and social life of the Community. It provides a sounding board for informed and general opinion of matters relating to the policies of the Community and this helps the Council and Commission as they develop European legislation. Although the opinions of the Committee are not binding, they do appear to have influence. The Commission has a very good working relationship with the Economic and Social Committee. This is perhaps reflected by the fact that generally, the Committee supports the proposals put forward by the Commission. The relationship with the Council has not been so well developed, although attempts have been made in recent years to improve this. Since 1987, it has become a regular practice for the person holding the office of President of the Council to address the Committee on matters discussed at the European Council. This has spread to ministers from the Member State holding the presidency to address meetings of the Committee.

Although advisory, the Commission or Council consults the Committee when it considers it appropriate, in addition to those instances where it is obligatory to do so under some Articles of the Treaty. An example of this is **Art 71**, which deals with international transport within the Community and the common rules established to implement the policy.

There is a total of 344 members of the Economic and Social Committee. These are allocated to the different Member States to reflect their size, with the large countries such as France, Italy, Germany and the UK having 24 each, down to five for Malta. The Committee reflects three particular groups of people: the Employers' Group, which is made up of representatives of employers' organisations and chambers of commerce; the Workers' Group, which represents trade unions, and a group of 'Other Interests', which includes small businesses, family, environmental and similar representatives. Within these groups can be found the representatives of the various categories of economic and social activity specified in **Art 257**. It is impossible, given the limited number of members from each country, for all the interest groups within that country to be represented. This is recognised by the obligation placed on the Council to ensure that the total Committee at Community level reflects the requirement of **Art 257** as stated in the case of *Confederazione Italiana Dirigenta di Azienda v EC Council* (1988). In order to achieve this, each Member State submits a list of potential members amounting to twice its actual allotted members. The Council appoints the members on the basis of unanimity. Once appointed, the members of the Economic and Social Committee act in their personal capacity, and not as representatives following instruction from their Member State or interest group. In preparation for enlargement of the EU, the **Treaty of Nice** had set a ceiling of 350 members to the Committee.

Question 4

Critically review the tasks and powers of the Council of Ministers. What procedures does it have in order to carry out its tasks under the Treaty?

Answer plan

This question allows you to draw upon other parts of the syllabus to look critically at the work of the Council of Ministers. The main points to cover are:

- Arts 202–210 – Treaty source for the Council;
- membership and procedure of the Council;
- relationship of the Council of Ministers with the European Council;
- support given by COREPER;
- the voting procedures of the Council; and
- the co-operation and co-decision procedures and the European Parliament.

Answer

The task of the Council is to ensure that the Community's objectives set out in **Pt 1** of the Treaty are attained. These objectives are generally specified in economic terms with a commitment to improving the standard of living and closer relations between the Member States. In order to achieve this, the Council is given authority under the Treaty to play a very important part in the legislative process of the Community. The Council of Ministers is specified in **Arts 202–210**. This is the main political institution of the EU. Its membership is made up of one representative of each Member State, so there are 27 members. Although the main representative is the foreign minister of each member, the actual minister varies according to the main business of the meeting. Thus, if the Common Agricultural Policy is being discussed, it will be the agricultural ministers who will attend, and so on.

The Presidency of the Council is held in rotation by each Member State for a period of six months. The minister representing the Member State holding the Presidency takes the chair of meetings of the Council and has an important role with regard to setting the agenda and progressing Community business. This causes problems for the small Council secretariat as the focus of the political element of the EU moves around Europe. It has also been criticised on the grounds that the period is too short for individual ministers to acquire expertise in the role. The formal reference to the role of the Presidency in the Treaties and the Council's Rules of

Procedure are extremely brief. The Presidency's basic duty is simply to get results. Each Presidency usually begins with the holder making a statement to the European Parliament with regard to what he or she hopes to achieve during his or her six months in office. The Presidency of the Council of Ministers coincides with the Presidency of the European Council where the procedural framework is less rigid, but the need for good conduct and organisation of business is even more pressing in view of the potential importance of the results.

The sheer burden of business now coming before the Council of Ministers causes problems. This was affected by two developments in the 1980s. The Community had basically achieved the objectives it had originally set itself and was operating in a less economically favourable time. This had led to discussions in the Council becoming more narrowly national in character, with the members of the Council negotiating more strongly within an inter-governmental forum. Secondly, the Council's position as the main seat of political authority was eroded by the establishment of the European Council. When the European Council, composed of the Heads of Government, was first introduced in 1974, it was to provide political initiatives to deal with policy deadlock. However, it now seems to deal with many of the major decisions facing the Community. It was formally recognised in the **Single European Act 1986**.

However, is it realistic to expect government ministers to play a significant role in the Council of Ministers in developing policy at Community level, as against making decisions to adopt such policies or legislation? For example, any British minister who may be involved in a meeting of the Council of Ministers is in charge of a government department, and takes part in debates and answers questions in the House of Commons or, in exceptional cases, the House of Lords. As an MP, there are also constituency problems and interests to deal with. How much time is there for EU matters? Obviously, there has to be some time, because this is part of his job, but a great deal of the work of the Council of Ministers is undertaken by the Committee of Permanent Representatives (COREPER). This group of diplomats represent the views or interests of their particular government. They liaise with the various government ministries and bring these views to the discussions which take place in Brussels. The idea is that when the Council of Ministers meets, much of the preliminary discussion has taken place and the ministers can concentrate on those issues which may require a political compromise or are politically sensitive.

Recently, the main discussion and action involving the Council of Ministers has centred on its voting procedures. In **Art 205**, it was envisaged that the Council would move, after the transitional period, to majority voting, except for those specific matters identified by the Treaty as requiring unanimity. This was not to be a simple majority, but generally a qualified one on the basis of **Art 205**. This Article gave each Member State a number of votes depending roughly upon the size of its population, ranging from 10 for the largest Member States to two votes for the smallest country, Luxembourg. On any issue before the Council, it requires a combination of the larger and smaller Member States to accumulate the necessary votes to adopt the measure. This seeks to ensure that no interest group in the Council can dominate the voting and encourages a compromise in the sense that the measure must be acceptable to a range of Member States. The necessary voting majority was 62 votes in favour of the measure. The intention of the Treaty was hindered by the events of 1966 that led to the **Luxembourg Accord** or Compromise, which was instituted to obtain the co-operation of the French Government in the working of the EU. This recognition of a 'veto', in the sense that unanimity was required on particular issues not specified as requiring unanimity under the Treaty, slowed down the actions of the Council, in that it could not proceed faster than its slowest participating government. Governments who joined in the 1970s and 1980s assumed that they did so with a power of veto on issues they considered important to them, although they were politically shocked on occasions when they tried to exercise it. It was not until the **Single European Act 1986** that attempts were made to speed up the decision-making process of the Council of Ministers to meet the target of completing the Internal Market by 1 January 1993. Although academic debate still continues on whether the veto still exists, it is important to recognise the political nature of the Council. If the President of the Council is aware of the political implications of calling for a vote where a minority of the Council have strong objections, it is likely that such a vote will be postponed for further discussion. Under **Art 11(2)**, the matter can be referred to the European Council.

The Inter-Governmental Conference (IGC) at the end of 2000 in Nice was dominated by the implications for voting in the Council of Ministers of the planned enlargement of the EU to 27 members. Under the **Nice Treaty**, the larger Member States such as the UK have 29 votes, down to Malta with just three votes. The number of votes needed for adoption of a measure was raised to 255 votes. However, the **Nice Treaty** also introduced the idea of a 'dual majority' in the voting procedure. In addition to these votes where a qualified majority is needed, a Member State may require that the qualified majority represents at least 62% of the total population of the Union. This arrangement maintains the balance between the large and smaller Member States, whilst respecting the democratic rights of the majority.

The Treaty now recognises that the Council of Ministers no longer has the final say on legislation and concluding treaties or agreements with third countries. Also the Council can only act on the basis of a proposal from the European Commission. **Article 7** of the **Single European Act 1986** replaced the original **Art 149** of the **Treaty of Rome** and introduced the co-operation procedure, which gives the European Parliament greater involvement in the legislative process on certain issues. If the Council wishes to ignore Parliament's amendments to its common position, it must do so by unanimity. Likewise, if it wishes to amend the proposals from the Commission, it must do so unanimously. The **Treaty on European Union** extended the involvement of the European Parliament so that it shares power equally with the Council on some matters, to the extent that the Parliament can prevent the adoption of the proposal. As the European Parliament exercises more authority in the legislative process, it has to correspond to a reduction of that held by the Council. However, as the powers of the Community institutions are being reviewed in the context of enlargement, the Council of Ministers remains the main political power within the Community, although the scope of the co-decision procedure was extended in the **Treaty of Nice**.

▌NOTE

See Chapter 12 on the possible impact of suggested reforms on the relationship between the Council and the European Parliament.

Question 5

What is the role of the Commission? Is it sufficiently accountable?

Answer plan

This question allows you to draw upon the other areas of a European Law syllabus to illustrate the powers and functions of the European Commission. The main points to cover are:

- **Art 211 EC** and the general duties of the Commission;
- the appointment and organisation of the European Commission;
- the role of the Commission and Community legislation;
- the Commission's role in external relations;
- the enforcement powers of the Commission under **Art 226 EC**;
- the powers of the Commission with regard to competition policy; and
- elements of the **Constitutional Treaty 2004** dealing with the relationship between the Commission and the European Parliament.

Answer

The main roles of the European Commission are given in **Art 211 EC**, and indicate the key functions envisaged for it by the Treaty. Perhaps the most important role given to the Commission is its power to initiate European laws in the form of draft regulations and directives, and as the executive arm of the Community once those laws are passed. Although the main political power of the Community rests with the Council of Ministers, the Council is dependent upon receiving a proposal from the Commission before it can act. These proposals cover the full range of Community policy specified in the Treaty and the general power under **Art 308 EC**. In exceptional cases the Council, and more latterly the European Parliament, can request proposals under **Art 208 EC**, but even here a proposal must come from the Commission. The introduction in 1993 of the co-decision procedure whereby the European Parliament's legislative role in certain policy areas was greatly increased requires the involvement of the Commission. If the European Parliament wishes to amend the Council's common position, such amendments are first considered by the European Commission which can either adopt them or give reasons for their refusal to the Council. The role of the Commission in directing and stimulating the development of the EU cannot be underestimated.

Following the passing of Community Acts, such as those mentioned in **Art 249 EC**, it is for the Commission to ensure that they are applied. Some observers refer to this as the policing role of the Commission, but it goes further than this. The Commission is acting in an executive role, implementing the agreed policy of the Community. In order to ensure that Member States implement the Community Act and generally fulfil their obligations under the Treaty, the Commission is granted a power under **Art 226 EC**. This power can lead to an 'enforcement action' before the ECJ but first the Commission has to deliver a reasoned opinion to any Member States which it feels is failing to fulfil an obligation. If the Member State is unable to satisfy the Commission that it is not failing to do so, the Commission can bring the matter before the European Court of Justice. If the Court agrees with the Commission's view it can make a declaration under **Art 228 EC** requiring the Member State to comply with its judgment and, if appropriate, imposing a fine. This is a very powerful weapon given to the Commission, which has led to it being called 'the guardian of the Treaties'. The Commission has complete discretion as to whether to bring an action under **Art 226 EC**, but this has to be seen within the context of its overall duty under **Art 211 EC** to ensure that the Treaty and the associated measures taken are applied. Therefore there is a mixture of legal and political pressure on the Member State to comply.

There is no 'EU government' in the sense that one would associate with a sovereign national state, but the Commission does play some of the roles of a government. The Commission is seen as the body representing the Community interest as a whole and therefore it is understandable that the original treaties gave a special role to the Commission with regard to the Community's external relations. The Community is a large economic trading area and as such belongs to a number of international organisations, such as GATT. International trade is an area of policy that was transferred to the Community when the **EEC Treaty** was signed in 1957 and so there is a division of 'sovereignty' between the Member States and the

Community. In addition the Community is party to bilateral and multilateral agreements with countries or trading blocs. Under **Art 301 EC** such international agreements are to be negotiated by the Commission, although they are concluded by the Council of Ministers after receiving the approval of the European Parliament.

Given that the free market is seen as a fundamental principle of the EU, the important area of competition policy provides an example of the wide powers of the Commission. The competition policy of the Community is founded upon **Arts 81, 82** and **86 EC** covering both the private sector and the activities of governments of Member States. The authority of the Commission with regard to the private sector is not restricted to those undertakings which are based in the European Community but includes all those who are involved in an economic activity within the Community. This was a lesson learnt by ICI, before the UK became a member of the Community, in the *Dyestuffs* case in 1972. As indicated above, the Commission is involved in the Community Acts specified in **Art 249 EC**. In the specific area of competition policy this results in decisions being taken which are binding upon those to whom they are addressed. Thus the Commission, exercising its powers under **Regulation 1/2003**, can investigate restrictive practices or abuses of a dominant position affecting the Community and if the competition policy has been breached, it can impose very large fines. Many of the undertakings involved in such cases complain that the Commission's powers are excessive in that they are 'prosecutor, judge and jury'. However, there is the possibility of appeal to the Court of First Instance. The Commission's role with regard to mergers was also increased by the **Merger Regulation 4064/89** and now **Regulation 139/2004**. Under **Regulation 4064/89** the Commission must approve such mergers between undertakings with a worldwide turnover of more than 5,000 million euros, where at least two of the firms have a combined turnover of more than 250 million euros in the European Community. Actions by governments of Member States which may affect undertakings by providing subsidies or other unfair treatment are also subject to the powers of enforcement of the Commission, much to the annoyance of the Member States concerned.

It can be seen that the roles and powers of the European Commission are very wide. Without the European Commission, the European Community could never have been constructed and developed to the extent it has. Although it should operate on a collegiate basis, the increased number of Commissioners and the policies of the Community make this difficult. With enlargement in May 2004 and January 2007 there are now 27 Member States, each with one Commissioner. The **Constitutional Treaty 2004** proposed that the number of Commissioners from 2014 should be reduced in size and consist of Commissioners corresponding to two-thirds of the number of Member States, based on a system of rotation. Such a system was designed to meet the problems of an ever larger number of Commissioners but it was always a sensitive issue and was considered to be a factor in the Irish vote against the **Lisbon Treaty** in June 2008. As the **Constitutional Treaty** and the **Lisbon Treaty** have not been ratified, each Member State will continue to have the power to nominate a Commissioner.

The Commissioners are not 'elected' but nominated by the Member States. Even though they have to be approved or confirmed in office by the European Parliament since the **Treaty of Amsterdam**, the question arises as to how accountable they are. They are not to be 'mandated' by their Member State or to be seen favouring one Member State or organisation, so once in office there is no control by the Member State, which is in line with the functions of the Commissioner envisaged by the treaties. The term of office of the Commission is synchronised with the European Parliament elections. They can only be removed as a group by the European Parliament and the ECJ, under **Arts 213 and 216 EC**, only deals with individual Commissioners who breach their obligations under the Treaty. Neither of these possible actions has ever been taken. Since the problems in 1999 of the Santer Commission, the President of the Commission has gained in authority and there is an arrangement whereby Commissioners agree to resign from office if requested to do so by the President. There is also the possibility of the President of the Commission changing the portfolio or area of responsibility for a Commissioner, a form of 'reshuffle'. But again, this gives more authority to the President of the Commission, and how accountable is she? Also the nomination of Commissioners by Member States will take place in 2009 after the elections to the European Parliament so that the strength of particular parties will be known and presumably be reflected in the nominated Commissioners. The President of the Commission will be 'elected' by the European Parliament to emphasise the responsibility of the President to the Commission but it is unlikely to increase accountability.

NOTE

You should look at Chapter 4 on Direct Actions, where **Art 226 EC** actions are dealt with in more detail, and Chapter 7 on Competition Policy.

CHAPTER 2

SOURCES OF LAW

INTRODUCTION

As you are no doubt aware, the European Union is based upon treaties which, under international law, have a special significance. They form the basis not only of the institutions, but also of the powers which can be exercised by those institutions and the procedures under which they must operate. Therefore, it is no wonder that the starting point for any discussion of the legal basis of the European Community is the treaties upon which it is founded. The treaties are considered to be the primary source of Community law. The basis of any legal action must be founded on a treaty provision.

Although it is perhaps an over-simplification to use this analogy, if you think of the treaty as an enabling Act, then what is required is the equivalent of delegated legislation to provide the structure and detail necessary to produce an effective measure upon which individuals can base their actions and which the legal system can enforce. Hence we come to what are generally called secondary sources of Community law. These are listed in **Art 249** as regulations, directives and decisions. Although recommendations and opinions are mentioned, these are not legally binding. This Article provides the key definitions of these Community administrative acts which are so important to the study of European law.

As every student of a common law system is aware, the judiciary, in their deliberation and judgments on the law, create rules or principles which are followed in subsequent cases. Although the European legal system does not have such a rigid adherence to precedent as found in the common law, the judges in the European Court of Justice (ECJ) have provided an additional secondary source of law to add to the administrative acts found in **Art 249**. Examples of this will be found in specific questions throughout the later chapters of this book, but a few points can be made now to show the impact of this source of law. As will be discussed in Chapter 3, there is a clear acceptance within the Community that the ECJ provides definitive and authoritative judgments on points of European Community law which are followed by the courts of the Member States.

Checklist

You need to have a good understanding of the role of the EC Treaty as an authority for Community Acts or judgments of the ECJ. When you are tracing the authority of a particular Community Act, you will generally go back to a Treaty Article. In addition, you should cover the following points:

- primary and secondary sources of Community law;
- administrative acts defined in **Art 249**;
- general principles of Community law; and
- methods of interpretation used in Community law.

Question 6

Critically review the development of general principles of law as part of the law of the European Community.

Answer plan

Generally, questions covering only general principles of Community law are essay questions, similar to this one. However, you must be prepared to deal with this topic within problem questions, where a particular general principle may be the ground which will allow a remedy to be granted to one of the parties. The most common question where these occur asks you to deal with an action for judicial review under **Art 230**. You should look at Chapter 4 to see how the topic of general principles can be integrated into a problem question drawing upon a number of topics in the syllabus.

With regard to this question, the main points for discussion are:

- the role of general principles within a legal system;
- authority for the development of general principles within the EC legal system; and
- specific examples of Community general principles, including the most important ones.

Answer

General principles of law are found in all legal systems, including the common law system. Within the common law system of England, they are seen as a device to hide judge-made law, whereby a judge seeks to show that his ruling was derived from a principle of sufficient generality so as to command common assent. In this way, a firm legal base could be provided for the judgment. Within the legal systems of the Member States, the development of general principles has taken place over a number of years and has been cloaked in historical respectability or authority. However, the European Community was facing the possible development of general principles in a modern era and therefore had to be more conscious of what it was undertaking. The ECJ has developed a doctrine that rules of Community law may be derived from general principles of law in addition to treaties and Community legislation.

The ECJ has pointed to three Articles of the EC Treaty to provide some justification for general principles as a source of law. These are:

(a) **Article 220**, which states that 'The Court of Justice shall ensure that in the interpretation of the Treaty the law is observed'. In view of the word 'law' being used, it is considered that it must refer to something over and above the Treaty itself, and it is not unreasonable for this Article to oblige the judges of the Court to take general principles into account;

(b) **Article 230** deals with judicial review and specifies the grounds upon which an annulment can be based. The first paragraph of the Article includes the words 'infringement of this Treaty, or of any rule of law relating to its application . . .'. The phrase 'any rule of law' must refer to something other than the Treaty itself. This has been used by the ECJ as a basis for the principle that a Community Act may be quashed for the infringement of a general principle of law; and

(c) **Article 288** is concerned with non-contractual liability (tort), and expressly provides that the liability of the Community is based on the 'general principles common to the laws of the Member States'.

Given this authority from the Treaty, three points should be noted before going on to specific general principles:

(a) the Court is prepared to apply principles of law, even if they are not found in the legal system of every Member State;

(b) whatever the factual origin of the principle, it is applied by the ECJ as a principle of Community law and not of national law. This is very important, as can be noted by the development of the general principle of protection of fundamental rights given below;

(c) there is little doubt that the ECJ would have applied general principles of law even if none of these Treaty provisions existed, because of the function of such general principles.

PROPORTIONALITY

This principle is derived from German law, where it underlies certain provisions of the German Constitution. 'A public authority may not impose obligations on a citizen except to the extent to which they are strictly necessary in the public interest to attain the purpose of the measure' (*Internationale Handelsgesellschaft* (1970)).

Thus, if the burdens imposed are clearly out of proportion to the object in view, the measure will be annulled. Proportionality is important in economic law and therefore has a wide application within the EU. It frequently involves imposing taxes, levies, duties, etc, in the hope of achieving economic advantages. The ECJ will not interfere unless there is a very clear and obvious infringement of the principle.

An example is the *Skimmed Milk Powder* case (*Bela-Muhle Josef Bergman v Grows Farm* (1977)), where the Council had sought to reduce a surplus of skimmed milk powder in the Community by forcing animal feed producers to incorporate it in their product in place of soya, which was the normal protein element used. The drawback to the producers was that the skimmed milk was three times more expensive than the soya. The ECJ held that the regulation embodying the scheme was invalid, partly because it was discriminatory and partly because it offended against the principle of proportionality. The effect of making animal feed producers use skimmed milk was to increase the price of animal feed and thus harm all livestock breeders. The imposition of the obligation to purchase skimmed milk powder was not necessary in order to diminish the surplus. On the other hand, the benefits of the policy were felt only by dairy farmers. Therefore, the policy worked in a discriminatory fashion between different categories of farmers.

NON-DISCRIMINATION OR EQUALITY

Specific reference to this principle can be found in the Treaty, notably in the original **Art 7**, which dealt with discrimination on the grounds of nationality, and **Art 141** which deals with equal pay. However, the ECJ has gone beyond these provisions in holding that there is a general principle of non-discrimination in Community law. This does not mean that Community institutions must treat everybody alike, but that there must be no arbitrary distinctions between different groups within the Community. For an example concerning a business, see *the Skimmed Milk Powder* case, above. The case of *Sabbatini v European Parliament* (1972) illustrates how the principle applies to discrimination between the sexes. The Court went further in the case of *Prais v Council* (1976), where it held that the principle also covered discrimination on the basis of religion.

PROTECTION OF LEGITIMATE EXPECTATIONS

According to this principle, derived from German law, Community measures must not, in the absence of an overriding matter of public interest, violate the legitimate expectations of those concerned. Thus, a business, holding a reasonable expectation which it has acted upon in the normal cause of business and having suffered a loss, may seek to have the Community measure annulled. The ECJ sometimes seeks to avoid annulment by adopting a strained interpretation of the measure concerned.

In *Deuka v EVGF* (1975), the German intervention agency (EVGF) was the national authority concerned with the payment of premiums to processors who made wheat unfit for human consumption and only suitable for animal feed. In order to qualify for a premium, Deuka had to obtain the prior agreement of EVGF and to carry out the process under their supervision. A European Commission regulation increased the premium payable as from 1 June 1970, that is, during a crop year. Deuka processed a quantity of wheat which had been purchased before 1 June, and thus claimed they were entitled to the increased premium. This was refused. Following legal proceedings in the German courts, a reference was made to the ECJ. The regulation was not declared invalid, but the Court stated that, in view of the principle of legal certainty, it should be interpreted so that the increase was payable, even if processing took place after 1 June, provided that the wheat was purchased and the relevant authority approved before 1 June. Therefore, this interpretation gave full protection to the legitimate expectations of the processors (see also *Commission v Council* (1973), which is concerned with salary payments to Community staff).

FUNDAMENTAL RIGHTS

It was not until the case of *Stauder v City of Ulm* (1969) that the ECJ recognised this general principle. The refusal to do so earlier had created pressure between the Court and some of the Member States, notably Germany and Italy, where such rights had been enshrined into the respective constitutions. The matter was resolved when an administrative judge in Stuttgart asked the ECJ whether a particular requirement was compatible with the general principles of Community law. The result was that the ECJ expressly included the protection of 'fundamental human rights enshrined in the general principles of Community law and protected by the Court'. In the later case of *Internationale Handelsgesellschaft* (1970), the Court stated that 'fundamental rights form an integral part of the general principles of the law, the observance of which it ensures; [and] in safeguarding those rights, the Court is bound to draw inspiration from constitutional traditions common to the Member States . . .'. The European Convention on Human Rights was recognised in the Preamble to the **Single European Act 1986** and the ECJ has accorded a special significance to the Convention (*ERT* (1989)). At the IGC held in December 2000 in Nice, it was decided not to include the **Charter of Fundamental Rights** in the Treaty.

Although a joint proclamation by the Council, Parliament and the Commission was made in support of the Charter, there is legal uncertainty as to its status. It was included in the **Constitution Treaty 2004**, but this treaty has not yet been ratified.

PROCEDURAL RIGHTS

These rights have been developed to fill the gaps where EC legislation does not provide specific safeguards for a person's rights. Examples include:

(a) *the right to a hearing* – this is drawn from the tradition of English law and was first used in *Transocean Marine Paint Association v Commission* (1974), where Advocate General Warner submitted that there was a general rule that a person whose interests are perceptibly affected by a decision taken by a public authority must be given the opportunity to make his views known. As the Commission had failed to do so in this competition case, its decision was annulled;

(b) *the right to due process* – in the case of *Johnston v Chief Constable of the Royal Ulster Constabulary* (1986), Mrs Johnston claimed that she had been subject to sex discrimination by her employer, contrary to **Directive 76/207**. A certificate issued by the Secretary of State sought to provide conclusive evidence that the derogation from Community obligations was on the grounds of national security. The Court held that such a provision was contrary to the 'requirement of judicial control stipulated by [**Art 6** which] reflects a general principle of law which underlies the constitutional traditions common to the Member States'.

The advantages of general principles are the same for the Community legal system as for Member States. They help to fill the gaps which always arise when it is not possible to have a written text to cover every legal eventuality. They constitute the unwritten law of the Community. Also within the Community, the characteristic role of general principles as limiting the power of the administration to take measures affecting the citizen has been continued.

General principles of law are relevant in the context of EC law in a number of ways:

(a) they may be invoked as an aid to interpretation in the sense that 'the measure should not conflict with general principles';

(b) general principles may be invoked by both Member States and individuals in order to challenge Community Acts;

(c) general principles may also be invoked as a means of challenging action by a Member State, where the action is performed in the context of a right or obligation arising from Community law; and

(d) general principles may be invoked to support claims for damages against the Community (**Art 288**).

Question 7

Explain the nature and legal effect of regulations, directives and decisions made by the Council of Ministers, the European Parliament and the Commission of the European Community.

Answer plan

Most questions on sources of law are essay questions like this one. However, you must remember that a good understanding of these topics can be invaluable when answering problem questions, which come up in later chapters. The best example is that of cases brought under **Art 230**, where the ability to discuss what is meant by a regulation is very important.

This question is looking for a clear understanding of the definitions in **Art 249** and the legal effect of a regulation, a directive and a decision!

Answer

The forms of EC legislation or administrative acts are listed in **Art 249**. This provides the basic definitions for a regulation, directive and decision. **Article 249** does not give the authority to issue such legislative measures, as they have to be authorised by specific Articles of the Treaty. However, where the Council or the Commission, in order to carry out their tasks, do need to issue a legally binding act, it is to **Art 249** that attention must be given.

Under **Art 249**, the definition of a regulation is that it shall have general application and be binding in its entirety and directly applicable in all Member States. It does not mean that a regulation necessarily has to apply to all Member States. It could be applicable in only one Member State. However, as long as it retains its character of being applicable to an abstract group of persons it will still be a regulation. This is important if an individual is seeking to challenge the validity of a regulation by using the **Art 230** procedure, as was discussed in *Zuckerfabrik Watenstedt* (1968).

Under **Art 253**, it is a requirement that certain formalities be completed in order for a valid regulation to be made. The reasons upon which the regulation is based must be given and any proposals or opinions which were required by the Treaty to be obtained must be referred to. The next Article, **Art 254**, requires that regulations are published in the Official Journal of the Community. The Council's Rules of Procedure for regulations require them to be numbered, dated and signed. Regulations also carry a formula describing their legal effects, that is, 'this Regulation is binding in its entirety and directly applicable in all Member States'.

This formula raises two points about the effects of regulations. The first is whether national legislation is required by the Member State to implement the regulation. The view of the ECJ is that regulations have a mandatory effect and have the force of law in the Member States without the need for transformation or confirmation by their legislatures. The Court went further in the 1972 case of *EC Commission v Italy*, when it stated that 'all methods of implementation are contrary to the Treaty which would have the result of creating an obstacle to the direct effect of Community regulations and jeopardising their simultaneous and uniform application in the whole of the Community'. Although there are exceptional cases where such national legislation is required, in such cases, the national law must not disguise its Community character by altering the wording of the regulation or its date for coming into force.

The second point concerns the meaning of 'directly applicable in all Member States'. 'Directly applicable' means that the regulation does not require a national measure to become binding upon the citizens and also that national authorities and national measures cannot prevent its application. There is often confusion between 'direct applicability' and the term 'direct effect', especially as the ECJ itself seems to use the terms interchangeably. The Treaty and other sources of Community law can have direct effect, but only regulations are directly applicable. In *Politi v Italian Ministry of Finance* (1971), the ECJ held that, under **Art 249**, 'Regulations shall have general application and shall be directly applicable in Member States . . . Therefore by reason of their nature and their function in the system of the sources of Community law, regulations have direct effect and are as such capable of creating individual rights which national courts must protect'. Therefore, not only may individuals rely on specific provisions as against other individuals and Member States, they may invoke the general objective and purpose of regulations as against national legal provisions. Thus, in *Amsterdam Bulb BV v Producktschap voor Siergewassen* (1977), it was stated that 'the moment that the Community adopts regulations under **Art 40** of the Treaty establishing a common organisation of the market in a specific sector, the Member States are under a duty not to take any measure which might create exemptions from them or affect them adversely'.

Question 8

Critically review the methods of interpretation used by the European Court of Justice (ECJ).

Answer plan

This question is seeking an answer which shows knowledge and understanding of how the ECJ goes about the process of interpreting Community law.

The main points raised by this question are:

- purpose of methods of interpretation;
- influences on the ECJ; and
- methods used by the ECJ – teleological, contextual, literal, historical.

Answer

With regard to EC law, the ECJ is the final arbiter. There are no appeals against judgments it gives. Under the preliminary ruling procedure of **Art 234**, the ECJ can be requested to provide a definitive interpretation of the Treaty or of a Community Act. This can be extended under other Articles of the Treaty to include other sources of law which are legally binding in the European Community. In order to carry out its tasks, the ECJ has developed a number of tools of interpretation. The European Court 'tool box' is not unlike the English methods of literal, golden, mischief, etc, but with the very important difference that it has been developed in the context of influence of domestic law (mainly France and Germany) and international law. However, like English judges, the judges of the ECJ very rarely use one method of interpretation in a particular case. They use a variety of rules of interpretation and then decide, as part of the judicial art, which is the most appropriate in the circumstances. Given the authority of the ECJ, this gives the judges a great deal of influence over the character and effectiveness of Community law.

Whatever method or approach to interpretation the Court may utilise, it must be remembered that they are operating in a legal system which has a strong linguistic dimension. There are 11 official languages, so all the Community texts written in the languages of the Member States are recognised as having equal validity. The main approaches to interpretation are characterised by the teleological approach, which is increasingly favoured by the ECJ. The teleological approach requires the judge to look to the purpose or object of the text before him. As Lord Denning observed in *Bulmer v Bollinger* (1974): '. . . the **[EC] Treaty** is quite unlike any of the enactments to which we have become accustomed . . . It lays down general principles. It expresses its aims and purposes . . . But it lacks precision.' Faced with a body of law couched in such terms, the ECJ uses the teleological approach. In the **Art 82** competition case of *Continental Can*, the ECJ referred to the 'spirit, general scheme and wording of **Art 86**, as well as to the system and objectives of the Treaty'. In the *Colditz* case, certain social security regulations were before the Court, which declared that 'the solution to this question . . . can only emerge from the interpretation of those regulations in the light of the objectives [**Arts 39–42**] of the Treaty'.

The contextual approach involves the Court placing the provision, whether from a treaty or a Community Act, within its context and interpreting it in relation to other provisions of Community law. Given the lack of precision in many Community provisions, it is no wonder that frequent reference is made to the 'framework of Community law', as in *Costa v ENEL*, or 'one must have regard to the whole scheme of the Treaty no less than to its specific provisions', in the *ERTA* case. Contextual interpretation is also used for Community legislation.

In the important case of *Defrenne*, the ECJ was considering whether the **Equal Pay Article**, now **Art 141**, had direct effect. It brought together a teleological approach when looking at the socio-economic purpose of the Article, but within a particular context (or contextual approach), in that **Art 141** has a close relationship with **Art 136** (**Art 117** at the time of the case), which concerned the need to promote improved working conditions and an improved standard of living for workers.

Although not stated in the judgments of the Court, writings of retired members of the ECJ indicate that they favour the teleological and context approaches to interpretation because they reflect the way that the Community is changing as it seeks to fulfil its aims and objectives in the future.

The literal interpretation is an approach which every court takes when faced with the question 'What does this mean?' The ECJ is no exception, but whereas the national judge may feel that his task is then at an end, the ECJ may decide that the plain meaning of the words should not be followed, but preference should be given to allow for the aims and objectives of the treaties to be achieved. In other words, the teleological or contextual approaches are given priority. In the ERTA case, the Commission sought to have the Council decision to co-ordinate the Member States' negotiations under the European Road Transport Agreement annulled. The Council argued that the action under **Art 230** (then **Art 173**) was not valid, in that the Community Acts mentioned were those found in **Art 249** (then **Art 189**), namely, regulations, directives or decisions. Despite the clear wording of **Art 249**, the ECJ held that the purpose of **Art 230** was to subject to judicial review all those measures which had legal effect. They declared: 'It would be inconsistent with this objective to interpret the conditions under which the action is admissible so restrictively as to limit the availability of this procedure merely to the categories of measures referred to by **Art 189** [now **Art 249**].' In *Stauder v City of Ulm*, the ECJ had to consider the different wording of a Commission decision permitting the sale of cheap butter to those in receipt of welfare benefits. Stauder was a German national who, under German law implementing the decision, was required to give his name when purchasing the butter, something which he claimed was contrary to his fundamental rights. The Dutch text followed the German text, but the Court referred to the French and Italian texts, which only stipulated that a coupon referring to the person concerned needed to be presented. The Court adopted this more liberal version of the decision, which would enable its objectives to be achieved without any breach of fundamental rights.

Historical interpretation is associated with the attempt to ascertain the subjective intention of the author of the text before the Court. It is not used very often, because of the lack of documentation available to help the Court. The negotiations surrounding the original treaties are shrouded by secrecy and thus the *travaux preparatoires* are not available. However, the Official Journal publishes all legislative proposals by the Commission as well as formal opinions of the European Parliament. In addition, the legislative Acts of the Community are required, under **Art 253**, to state in their Preamble the reasons on which they are based and to refer to any proposals or opinions which were required by the Act. These Preambles give some assistance to the Court, as they did in *Markus v Hauptzollamt Hamburg-Jonas* (1969).

CHAPTER 3

EC LAW AND NATIONAL LAW

INTRODUCTION

One of the central principles established by the European Court of Justice (ECJ) is that of the supremacy of Community law over national law. Having gained acceptance for this, the Court went on to establish the principle or doctrine of direct effect, which gives rights to individuals which can be enforced in the courts of the Member States. Both of these developments were signalled in the early cases of *Van Gend en Loos* and *Costa v ENEL*.

However, it is also important to note that the Court has built upon these principles in other topics, such as preliminary references, which are dealt with in Chapter 5. Generally, the specific questions on this topic are essay types, but aspects of the principles associated with the relationship of Community law and national law also arise in questions on other topics which can be in both essay and problem format.

Checklist

You should understand the principle of supremacy of Community law and direct effect developed in the following cases: *Van Gend en Loos, Costa, Simmenthal SpA (No 2)* and *Internationale*. In addition, the following specific points should be covered:

- the principle of direct effect in relation to direct applicability;
- the direct effect of treaty provisions, regulations, directives and decisions;
- the test for direct effect; and
- vertical and horizontal direct effect.

Question 9

Critically discuss the development of the principle of supremacy of EC law.

Answer plan

This essay question requires a discussion of the supremacy of Community law over national law and how it has come about. The main points for this question are:

- the Treaty basis used to justify supremacy of Community law, notably **Art 10**;
- the foundations of the Community referred to in *Van Gend en Loos, Costa, Internationale and Simmenthal*;
- how Community law is incorporated into national law;
- the reaction of the Member States to this development.

Answer

When the EC was established, it required a transfer of sovereignty for certain specific areas of policy from the Member State to the Community. This meant that some legal matters that had been the sole prerogative of a Member State were no longer within its control. This inevitably led to a situation of conflict between national and EC law. Yet if the Community was to fulfil its aims, it was necessary that such conflicts were speedily resolved, with a minimum of uncertainty. However, this question raised constitutional problems of varying magnitude for all Member States.

The primary source of Community law, the Treaties, contains no specific mention of any priorities in the relationship between national and EU law. However, in the view of the ECJ, the legal basis on which the Community rests necessarily presupposes the supremacy or primacy of Community law. Under international law, the question is resolved by the constitutional rules of the Member State concerned. Principally, it will depend on the means by which international law is incorporated into the domestic law of that Member State. There are two approaches to this incorporation, in that the legal systems of States are generally either monist or dualist in their approach to international law. In monist States, such as France, all law is treated equally, in the sense that national courts can apply international treaties, as long as the appropriate constitutional procedures have been followed. In cases of conflict with national law, monist countries usually recognise the supremacy of Treaty provisions. However, in dualist States, such as the UK, international law and national law are considered to be fundamentally different. As such, international treaties can never be applied by national courts, but only domestic legislation can be brought about by the international treaties. Thus, the **EC Treaty** has to be specifically incorporated into domestic law. In the UK, this was achieved by the **European Communities Act** 1972, specifically **ss** 2 and 3. However, whatever the method of incorporation used by the Member State, this does not in itself settle the question of priorities.

The ECJ has placed great importance upon the uniformity of application of Community law in the Member States, and the desire to see that the Community was not weakened by diversity in interpretation or application. Therefore, it is understandable that the Court would develop its own constitutional rules to ensure that where there was a conflict between EU and national law, it would be EU law which prevailed. It was in the case of *Van Gend en Loos* that the ECJ took its first tentative steps in this process. The case was an **Art 234** (then **Art 177**) preliminary reference from the Dutch courts on whether **Art 25** (then **Art 12**) of the Treaty had direct effect. The Court took the opportunity of declaring that 'the Community constitutes a new legal order in international law, for whose benefit the States have limited their sovereign rights, albeit within limited fields'. In *Costa v ENEL*, the Court went further when asked a specific question by the Italian court on the priority of EU law and national law. With the transfer of sovereignty mentioned in *Van Gend* 'comes . . . a clear limitation of their sovereign rights upon which a subsequent unilateral law, incompatible with the aims of the Community, cannot prevail'. Thus, by establishing a European Community, now the EU, with real powers, the Member States created a body of law which applies to their nationals as well as to themselves.

In the important case of *Internationale Handelsgesellschaft mbH*, the Court was concerned with a conflict between an EC regulation and provisions of the German Constitution protecting fundamental rights. Under German law, the Constitution was superior to a statute. As a country with a mitigated dualist legal system, it was necessary for the **EC Treaty** to be incorporated into the national legal system and the vehicle used to do this was a statute. Thus, given that there was no provision in the Constitution to allow it to be overridden by EC law, the plaintiff claimed that the regulation should be nullified. Which should prevail: the regulation or the Constitution? The ECJ took a very strong view and insisted that the legality of a Community Act cannot be nullified by national law. The German Constitutional Court was concerned about the lack of protection for fundamental rights within the Community. Until this changed, the fundamental rights provision of the German Constitution would take priority. This would not mean that they would rule on the validity of a Community Act, but rather they would conclude that such a measure could not be applied in Germany. This did not happen in the *Internationale* case or in any subsequent German case, but it does indicate a possible conflict in particular circumstances. A similar conclusion occurred in the *Frontini* case, only here it was the Italian Constitution's protection of fundamental rights which was involved. The

Constitutional Courts in both Germany and Italy were not happy with the hard line taken by the ECJ. The important difference is that the Italian Constitutional Court has repeated the possibility of declaring that a Community measure may not apply in Italy. This was in the *Fragd* case in 1990.

Thus, as far as the ECJ is concerned, all EU law, regardless of whether it is a Treaty provision, a Community Act or an agreement with a third country, must take priority over all conflicting domestic law. This applies whether the national law is enacted prior or subsequent to Community law. In the absence of any specific Treaty provision, how can this be justified? It in fact reflects the approach of the Court, which is pragmatic and pro-Community based on the purpose, the general aims and the spirit of the Treaty. In its view, Member States apply to join the Community and must therefore take the necessary measures to comply with EU law. The Community was established with its own institutions which have powers under **Art 249**, with no qualification or reservation, to make laws binding upon all Member States. Regulations are specifically said in **Art 249** to have 'binding force' and to be directly applicable in all Member States. To the Court, this shows a clear indication of the supremacy of the legislative provisions conferred on the Community. If a State could unilaterally nullify its effects by means of domestic legislation overruling Community law, Community legislation would be quite meaningless.

The ECJ has repeatedly used **Art 10** to emphasise the fundamental obligation upon Member States to implement Community legislation, so that it receives uniform application throughout the Community. Under **Art 10**, Member States are required to abstain from any measure that could jeopardise the attainment of the objectives of the Treaty. Where Member States fail to fulfil their obligations, **Art 226** EC gives authority to the Commission to instigate enforcement procedures. The Community would not survive if States were free to act unilaterally in breach of such obligation. If the aims of the Community are to be achieved, there must be uniformity of application of Community law throughout all the Member States. This will not occur unless all States accord priority to EU law. In fact, all new members of the Union must accept the principle of *acquis communautaire*, which requires them to accept not only the Treaties, but the whole body of Community law.

A final case provides guidance to national judges faced with a case that shows a conflict between a national law and EU law. In *Simmenthal SpA (No 2)*, an Italian judge was faced with a conflict between a Council regulation on the common organisation of the market in beef and veal and the Italian veterinary and public health laws. Under Italian law, domestic legislation contrary to EC regulations may be held unconstitutional, but only by the Constitutional Court and not by the ordinary courts. Should the Italian judge of first instance disregard inconsistent national legislation without waiting for its repeal or a declaration from the Constitutional Court making it invalid? The instructions given in answer to the **Art 234** (then **Art 177**) reference were that a national court was under a duty to give full effect to Community law, even if there was a conflicting provision of national law, and without waiting for a higher court to rule on the matter. This is similar to the *Factortame* case in the House of Lords, where it was accepted that directly effective Community law must prevail over any inconsistent subsequent domestic legislation. Any incompatible national law is automatically inapplicable, because, unless Community law is given priority over conflicting national law at once, from the moment of its coming into force, there can be no uniformity of application throughout the Community.

Within a short space of time, the courts of the Member States, despite their different constitutional rules and traditions, have adapted to the principle of supremacy of EU law. This is perhaps due in part to the persuasive judgments of the ECJ and the attitudes of the courts of the Member States. They have accepted that Community law, stemming as it does from the Treaty, has an independent source. It cannot be challenged by judicial process on the basis of any national provisions, however framed, without being deprived of its character as Community law and, more importantly, without the legal basis of the Community itself being called into question. The supremacy of Community law stems from the Treaties and not from the national constitutions. The special and original nature of Community law requires that its supremacy over national law is acknowledged. The ECJ recognised the importance of this and, as Lord Bridge stated in the House of Lords' judgment in *Factortame (No 2)*: 'If the supremacy within the European Community over the national law of the Member States was not always inherent in the **EC Treaty**, it was certainly well established in the jurisprudence of the Court of Justice.' The decision of the House of Lords was subsequently confirmed in *R v Secretary of State for Employment ex p EOC* (1994), when it was stated that in judicial review proceedings in UK courts, an Act of Parliament can be declared incompatible with EU law.

Question 10

Critically examine the development of the doctrine of direct effect.

Answer plan

This is an important topic and it is very likely that in any question where advice is required on enforcing a Community right, it will be appropriate to discuss the topic of direct effect. This question is an essay question, but it is not uncommon for problem questions to be asked on this topic. The main points that should be discussed in this essay are:

• what is meant by direct effect;

- the difference between direct effect and direct applicability;
- the test for direct effect;
- the direct effect of Articles of the Treaty, regulations, directives and decisions; and
- the difference between vertical and horizontal direct effect.

Answer

When a State joins the European Union, all Community law becomes part of its own legal system or, to use the international law phrase, 'directly applicable'. However, the ECJ has also developed a principle of direct effect whereby a provision of Community law may confer rights upon an individual which are required to be directly applied by national courts at the suit of individual litigants, without the need for domestic implementing legislation. Not all EU law is directly effective. This will depend upon the construction of a particular provision, its language and purpose, although there is often confusion because of the phrase in **Art 249** which describes regulations as directly applicable. This does not mean that only regulations are capable of direct effect. Many categories of EU law are capable of direct effect as long as they satisfy the test established by the ECJ. This began with the case of *Van Gend en Loos* (1963), which concerned a preliminary reference made by a Dutch court about **Art 25** obliging Member States to refrain from setting new customs duties. The view of the Dutch Government and other Member States was that this was a matter which did not allow an individual to bring an action enforcing rights, but should rather be left to an enforcement action under **Art 226 or 227**.

The ECJ set out the basic requirements for direct effect to be identified when it said in *Van Gend*: 'Art 25 [formerly Art 12] sets out a clear and unconditional prohibition, which is not a duty to act, but a duty not to act. This duty is imposed without any power in the Member States to subordinate its application to a positive act of internal law. The prohibition is perfectly suited by its nature to produce direct effects in the legal relations between the Member States and their citizens.' However, the Court has not restricted direct effect to prohibitions. In *Alfons Lutticke's* case, which concerned **Art 90**, it was established by the ECJ that a positive obligation to repeal or amend discriminatory provisions was directly effective.

Subsequent to this case, many Articles of the Treaty have been declared to have direct effect, thus giving the citizen the ability to claim and enforce a right under the Treaty which the government of the Member State concerned has failed to provide. A good example of this development is *Defrenne v Sabena (No 2)*. This case involved a claim made by a Madame Defrenne for equal pay with male stewards. She based her claim upon **Art 141** (then **Art 119**). Whereas Van Gend was seeking to enforce a right against the Dutch State, Madame Defrenne was seeking to enforce a right against her employer, Sabena Airlines. This was an important point, because before it was thought that direct effect was limited to relationships with State bodies, that is, vertical effect. The judgment in *Defrenne* said that the direct effect of **Art 141** extends to all agreements which are intended to regulate paid labour collectively, as well as to contracts between individuals. Thus, many Treaty provisions have now been successfully invoked vertically and horizontally. The fact of their being addressed to States has been no bar to their horizontal effect.

It was more surprising for Member States when the ECJ took a similar line with directives. Under **Art 249**, 'a directive is binding, as to the result to be achieved, upon each Member State to which it is addressed, but shall leave to the national authorities the choice of form and methods'. They are not described as 'directly applicable', as are regulations. This, the Member States argued, was an indication that they should not produce direct effects. In addition, they required further action by the Member State and thus could not meet the test for direct effect indicated in *Van Gend*. However, in *Grad*, the ECJ ruled that a directive and a decision could be directly effective. The directive, in this case on VAT, specified a limit for its implementation, as is common with all directives. These directives, addressed to Member States, impose an obligation to achieve the required result. As the ECJ said in *Becker*, another case involving VAT, 'wherever the provisions of a directive appear . . . to be unconditional and sufficiently precise, those provisions may, in the absence of implementing measures adopted within the prescribed period, be relied upon as against any national provision which is incompatible with the directive or in so far as the provisions define rights which individuals are able to assert against the State'.

If the time limit given for the implementation of the directive has not expired, it cannot have direct effect, as was stated in *Ratti*. Ratti was an Italian who ran a firm selling both solvents and varnishes in Italy. Two directives had been adopted covering the packaging and labelling of these products. Ratti complied with these directives, but they had not been implemented in Italy, with the result that he was prosecuted for failure to comply with the provisions of the Italian law. At the relevant time, the deadline for the implementation of one of the directives had expired, but that for the second had not. On an **Art 234** reference, the ECJ held that the directive for which the time for implementation had expired was directly effective, but the other was not. This gave Ratti a defence to the charges relating to the packaging and labelling of the solvents, but not for those concerning the varnishes. It must be remembered that in all cases when an individual is seeking to enforce direct effect, the test must be satisfied.

Even if the Member State has introduced the required legislative act, it may be that what they have done is defective. In this type of situation, the directive may still be directly effective, as was held in the *Verbond van Nederlandse Ondernemingen (VNO)* case. However, unlike Articles of the Treaty, directives cannot have horizontal effect. They cannot have direct effect as against another individual or company. This type of horizontal direct effect is felt to be contrary to the principles of equality. This was stated in *Marshall v Southampton and South West Hampshire AHA* (1986), where Marshall was said to be employed by a 'public' body in the form of the Health Authority and thus able to enforce the direct effect of the *Equal Treatment Directive 76/207*. However, the ECJ in *von Colson* put an obligation on the courts of Member States to 'take all appropriate measures to ensure fulfilment of a directive'. Under the *von Colson* principle, the courts of Member States should interpret national law so as to ensure that the objectives of the directive are achieved. In *Lister v Forth Dry Docks* (1990), the House of Lords took this line by interpreting the UK domestic regulation on safeguarding employees whose employer's business was transferred on the basis that it had been introduced for the purpose of complying with an EC directive. This has obviously greatly extended the possibility for an individual to obtain the benefits of the direct effect of a directive, even though the State (or any emanation of the State) is not the defendant to the action. In the *Marleasing* case, the ECJ took the *von Colson* principle a step further when it held that the principle could be applied, even if the necessary national legislation had not been introduced to comply with the directive.

As in other circumstances where the ECJ has developed the scope of its interpretation, there is one important limitation to the *von Colson* principle. This is in relation to criminal proceedings, as in *Kolpinghuis Nijmegen*, where the Dutch authorities sought to prosecute Kolpinghuis for breach of a Water Purity directive which had not been implemented in the Netherlands. The ECJ held that, when interpreting national law to comply with Community law, regard must be had to the general principles of the Community, notably that of legal certainty and non-retroactivity (see *Arcaro* (1997)).

In addition to regulations and directives, the other source of law specified in **Art 249** is decisions, which are legally binding on the person to whom they are addressed. The Court stated in the *Grad* case that these can have direct effect. With regard to international agreements, the ECJ has not taken a consistent approach. Some, like the GATT Treaty in *International Fruit Co*, were held not to be directly effective, whereas others were, such as the **Yaounde Convention**, under the ACP policy of the EU, in *Bresciani*. It would appear that each agreement must be considered by the ECJ on its own merits.

The test for direct effect requires three criteria to be passed by the provision concerned. The provision must be sufficiently clear and precise; it must be unconditional; and it must leave no room for the exercise of discretion in implementation by the Member State or Community institution. Each criterion is given a broad interpretation by the ECJ, so that some provisions which are not particularly clear or precise have been found to produce direct effects. The interpretation skills of the ECJ can always be used to clarify the meaning of the provision. It is also important to note that, if the provision should not yet have been implemented by the Member State, it will not have direct effect. Obviously, you cannot enforce an obligation until the time has expired for that obligation to have been fulfilled. However, the development of the doctrine of direct effect has been an important one for the Community, but more importantly for the individual.

Question 11

'Directives are addressed to the governments of Member States and therefore cannot give rights to individuals of Member States.'

Discuss.

Answer plan

Although there are general questions on direct effect, like the previous question, a topic which has dominated in the last few years is the direct effect of directives. Problem questions are generally not asked specifically on this topic, but it does lend itself to being included in particular situations, for example, where an individual is seeking to enforce a right based upon a directive which has not been incorporated in national law. However, it is essay questions, like this one, which allow for a discussion of the diverse points arising from the development of the principle of direct effect as applied to directives. The specific areas which need to be discussed are:

- the doctrine of direct effect generally, based on *Van Gend en Loos*;
- the application of direct effect to directives (*Van Duyn v Home Office*);
- the response to the direct effect of directives (*Cohn-Bendit case*);
- the *von Colson* principle; and
- developments in State liability (*Francovich v Italian State*).

Answer

It is true that directives are clearly defined in **Art 249** as being addressed to the governments of Member States, but the Article also adds that they are binding as to the result to be achieved. There is an obligation on the Member State to fulfil this requirement, even though it has discretion as to how this is achieved. Thus, directives are a source of European Community law and are part of the new legal order which developed with the establishment of the Community. As the ECJ stated in the important case of *Van Gend en Loos*, this new legal order is for the benefit not only of the Member States themselves, but also their nationals or citizens. The Court went on to say that, in this way, obligations and rights would be conferred on individuals. How does this apply to directives? Presumably, there is no problem if the government of the Member State receiving the directive fulfils it by selecting an appropriate domestic mechanism, such as an Act of Parliament or Statutory Instrument, to implement it. In this way, any rights associated with the directive will become available to the individual and recognised and enforced by the national courts. However, what if the government of the Member State fails to implement the directive, or does so in such a way as to deprive the individual of some of the rights associated with the directive? It is in this context that this statement has been made, and will now be discussed.

The principle of direct effect was established by the ECJ in the case of *Van Gend en Loos*, which concerned **Art 25** (then **Art 12**). The judgment stated that, if certain criteria were satisfied, the provisions in question would give rise to rights or obligations on which individuals may rely before their national courts, that is, they would be directly effective. The criteria are that the provision must be clear and unambiguous, it must be unconditional and it must take effect without further action by the EU or Member State. Could this principle apply to directives? There are obvious questions to be asked because, by definition, directives do require further action, in that Member States have the choice as to the form and methods to be used to implement the directive. The Court did not find this a hindrance.

In the case of *Van Duyn v Home Office* (1974), the ECJ held that provisions of directives could be directly effective on their own. Before this case, questions about directives were always linked with Articles of the Treaty or decisions, so no clear principle could be established. In the *Grad* case, involving a decision and the directive introducing the VAT system, the Court held that, although regulations under **Art 249** (then **Art 189**) were directly applicable, it did not follow that other categories of administrative acts could not have similar effects. They added that this was particularly the case where the Community had imposed an obligation on Member States to act in a certain way, as *l'effet utile* of such a measure would be weakened if they did not fulfil that obligation. It would mean that the nationals of that State would not be able to invoke it before the courts, and the national courts would not be able to consider it as part of Community law.

In *Van Duyn*, the Court had to consider in an **Art 234** (then **Art 177**) reference whether a private individual could invoke an Article of a Council directive dealing with the personal conduct of an individual and the derogation allowed to a Member State on the grounds of public policy – specifically, whether the UK Government could refuse leave to enter the UK to a Dutch Scientologist because of the UK Government's policy towards the Church of Scientology. The Court repeated its judgment in *Grad*, only making the specific reference to directives instead of a decision, as it had done in that case. Thus, Van Duyn could ask the national courts to enforce the individual rights given to her by the directive.

This judgment did not go without criticism, notably by the French *Conseil d'Etat* in the *Cohn-Bendit* case (1979). Cohn-Bendit wished to challenge a decision taken by the French Minister for the Interior expelling him from French territory on the grounds of **Directive 64/221**. An Article in this Directive requires the person against whom such measures are ordered to be informed of the reasons, for example, public security, public policy, etc. In the *Rutili* case (1975), this Article had been declared by the ECJ to be directly effective. However, even though the minister had decided not to oppose Cohn-Bendit's entry into France and thus remove the substance of the case, the *Conseil d'Etat* went on to give judgment. They had not made an **Art 234** (then **Art 177**) reference, but gave their clear view that directives cannot be invoked by the nationals of Member States, that is, they cannot have direct effect when challenging an administrative decision of the State. This was completely contrary to the case law of the ECJ.

The judgment in *Cohn-Bendit* prompted the European Court to clarify its ruling on the possibility of individuals involving the provisions of directives. It considered that if a Member State had not adopted the implementing measures required by a directive in the prescribed periods, that State should not be able to rely upon its own failure to deprive individuals of seeking to enforce rights before the national courts. This was clearly stated in *Ratti*. However, direct effect as applied to directives was to have some limitations. Unlike Articles of the Treaty and, to a certain extent, regulations, directives were to be limited to vertical direct effect and not encompass horizontal direct effect. If it was the government which had not fulfilled its obligations arising from the directive, it should be against the government that rights arising from the directive should be enforced. In *Becker* (1982), a German credit broker successfully claimed the benefit of a provision of the sixth **VAT Directive** against the German VAT authorities. However, it was also made clear in this judgment that there was no question of a directive being involved to impose obligations on individuals, or to have an incidence on mutual relations between individuals, that is, horizontal direct effect. The contrast between the UK cases of *Marshall* (who was employed by an area health authority) or *Foster* (who was employed by the pre-privatisation British Gas corporation) on the one hand, with *Duke* (employed by GEC Reliance Ltd, a public company) on the other, clearly shows how a right can be enforced by some, but not by others, under the principle of direct effect of directives. It would appear, therefore, that unless the individual is able to show that there is some relationship with the State, the quotation forming this question is correct.

It is also correct that every directive involves a timescale for implementation. This period, normally two years, is to give the government of the Member State time to formulate and pass the appropriate domestic measure. Until this period has elapsed, the directive cannot, as was confirmed in *Ratti*, have direct effect.

In *Emmott v Minister for Social Welfare* (1991), Mrs Emmott brought an action against the Irish Minister for Social Welfare on the basis that she received less benefit than a man would have done in equivalent circumstances. Under a directive issued in

1979, all discrimination on the grounds of sex in matters of social security are prohibited. The directive should have been implemented by 1984, but was not implemented in Ireland until 1988. Mrs Emmott brought her action in 1987, when another case before the ECJ had led to it, declaring that the directive had direct effect. The vertical relationship between herself and the Irish Government satisfied the case law of the Court. The Irish Government, however, claimed that her action was statute-barred, because it had not been brought within the three months required by Irish law for judicial review. Could this national procedural requirement be used to deny Mrs Emmott a remedy? The Court held that directives had a particular nature, imposing an obligation on Member States to adopt, within the framework of their national legal systems, all the measures necessary to ensure that the directive is fully effective. Thus, Community law precludes the competent national authorities from relying on national procedural rules relating to time limits to stop an action by one of its citizens seeking to enforce a right that that Member State has failed to transpose into its domestic legal system. The time limit does not run until the date when the national implementing legislation is correctly adopted.

In *Francovich v Italian State*, the ECJ extended the impact of the law regarding directives by stating that 'Community law lays down a principle according to which a Member State is liable to make good damage to individuals caused by a breach of Community law for which it is responsible'. Mr Francovich was owed 6 million lire by his insolvent employers. However, because he was unable to enforce a judgment against them, he brought an action against the Italian Government for compensation. Under a Council directive aimed at protecting employees in the event of the insolvency of their employers, Member States were required to ensure that payment of employees' outstanding claims arising from the employment relationship and relating to pay was guaranteed. Unfortunately, the Italian Government had not set up any Italian system to act as a guarantor in these circumstances, hence his claim against them. The ECJ held that, subject to three conditions, damages are available against the State for failure to implement EC directives. The conditions specified are that the result required by the directive includes the conferring of rights for the benefit of individuals; the content of those rights is identifiable by reference to the directive; and, lastly, there exists a causal link between the breach of the State's obligations and the damage suffered by the person affected.

The ECJ has further developed this idea of indirect effect in its judgments in *Brasserie du Pêcheur* (1996) and *Dillenkofer* (1996). It is clear now that failure by a Member State to take any measure and transpose it as required into national law will constitute a serious breach of Community law per se. It will give rise to a right to damages for those individuals who suffer injury and there is a causal link between the breach of the State's obligation and the loss and damage suffered.

The ECJ has continued to evolve its principles with regard to providing the individual with the possibility of enforcing a right derived from a directive. In the *von Colson* and *Harz* cases in 1984, the Court developed an approach to interpretation based on **Art 10** (then **Art 5**), which requires Member States to take all appropriate measures to ensure fulfilment of their Community obligations. Under this principle, the national courts should interpret national legislation so as to ensure that the objectives of the directive are achieved. This assists those litigants who are unable to satisfy the test for direct effect, or who are bringing an action against a private employer, rather than the State or an emanation of the State. This method of interpretation has maximised the impact of directives for individuals. As a further development of the *von Colson* principle, the Court held, in *Marleasing* (1990), that the principle could be applied even if the necessary national legislation had not been introduced to comply with the directive.

The development of the ECJ's approach to directives conferring rights upon individuals has continued throughout the last 20 years. It has been a true reflection of the comments made by the Court in *Van Gend en Loos* and subsequent cases that, when establishing the European Community, the Member States were creating a new legal order which has given rights to the citizens of the Member States and which must be recognised by their courts. In some circumstances, the Court has applied the principle of direct effect to achieve this and in others it has extended its approach to interpretation. It is clear that although directives are addressed to the governments of Member States, they do confer rights on those who live within the Community.

Question 12

Do the decisions of the English courts assist an individual seeking to enforce a Community right?

Answer plan

This essay question provides an opportunity to trace through English judgments the approach taken to direct effect of directives and the interpretation of domestic legislation. You should cover the following points:

- direct effect of directives – *Marshall* (1986);
- vertical and horizontal effect of directives;
- **European Communities Act 1972**;
- *von Colson* (1984);
- *Marleasing* (1992);
- *Pickstone v Freemans plc* (1989);

- *Lister v Forth Dry Dock and Engineering Co Ltd* (1990);
- *Francovich* (1990); and
- the *Brasserie du Pêcheur* and *Factortame* cases (1996).

Answer

When a Member State joins the Community, it undertakes to fulfil all the obligations arising from the Treaties and other binding sources of Community law. This is achieved by accepting that Community law overrides any conflicting national law (*Simmenthal* (1978)). However, there were problems for the individual who tried to enforce a right arising from Community law not recognised in the national courts, for example, if the conditions associated with identifying direct effect, such as the measure being precise and unconditional, were not satisfied. More importantly, he or she may not be able to use direct effect to enforce the right against another private individual (*Marshall* (1986)). In circumstances where the government was at fault, the European Commission could bring an action before the ECJ under **Art 226** for failing to fulfil a Community obligation. It would also be open to the government of another Member State to use **Art 227**. However, both Articles lead to the same remedy under **Art 228**. This is mainly declaratory, although under the **Treaty on European Union (TEU) 1992**, the Court can impose a fine, but this provides no redress for the individuals affected by the Member State's action.

Articles of the Treaty and regulations have been held by the ECJ to have direct effect in both vertical and horizontal terms (see *Defrenne (No 2)* (1976)). Thus, in such circumstances, the individual can enforce the right against the government or another individual. However, the other main source of Community law, directives, was in a much weaker position, even though such measures are important in creating rights under Community law. The ECJ has sought to redress this imbalance by making directives come within the principle of direct effect. In *Van Duyn* (1975), the ECJ relied on the binding effect attributed to a directive under **Art 249** (then **Art 189**), coupled with the civil law doctrine that a legal measure must be presumed to have an *effet utile*, or useful effect. Furthermore, the Court thought it was inequitable to allow a Member State to rely on its own failure to implement a directive as a defence (*Ratti* (1979)). This view was strengthened by **Art 10**, which requires a Member State to take all appropriate measures to ensure fulfilment of the obligations arising out of the Treaty or resulting from action taken by the institutions of the Community. In this way, it became impossible for the Member State to evade an obligation imposed by a directive.

However, the Court limited the impact of this extension of the principle of direct effect to directives by limiting it to vertical relationships. Thus, the individual who was employed by the State or an emanation of the State (see *Marshall* (1986) and *Foster v British Gas* (1990)) could enforce a right arising from Community law in a national court and obtain the appropriate remedy. Those who could not prove such a relationship with the government were unable to do either, as was confirmed in the case of *Kampelmann* (1997) involving the **Employee Directive 91/533**. *Duke v GEC Reliance* (1988) provides a good example of the division that vertical and horizontal application of direct effect of directives brought about. Unlike Mrs Marshall or Mrs Foster, Mrs Duke was unable to enforce her rights under the Equality Directives.

There is a potential conflict between the doctrine of parliamentary sovereignty in UK law and the principle that Community law takes priority over inconsistent national laws. The **European Communities Act 1972** attempts to deal with this problem by making all provisions of Community law which are directly effective part of English law. Lord Denning, in *Macarthys Ltd v Smith* (1979), suggested that English courts would give effect to a directly effective provision of Community law, notwithstanding any subsequent enactment by Parliament, unless Parliament had made it clear that it intended to override any inconsistent provisions of Community law. Lord Diplock, in *Garland v BREL* (1982), stated that the words of a statute passed after the adoption of a Community measure dealing with the same subject were to be interpreted, if they were reasonably capable of bearing such a meaning, as being intended to carry out the UK's obligations under the Community measure and not as being inconsistent with it.

Mrs Duke, in 1988, maintained that the **Equal Treatment Directive**, as interpreted in *Marshall*, required Member States to prohibit discrimination in relation to retirement ages and that s 6(4) of the **Sex Discrimination Act 1975** had to be interpreted in a way consistent with that requirement. Lord Templeman, giving the main judgment in the House of Lords, rejected this argument. He held that, although the **Equal Treatment Directive** had been adopted subsequent to the **1975 Act**, s 2(4) of the **European Communities Act 1972** did not require the courts to give it priority over the 1975 Act in Mrs Duke's case, because the directive was not directly effective as between her and her former employers. **Section 2(4)** only required the court to construe an Act of Parliament in accordance with directly effective provisions of Community law. This judgment has been criticised as taking too narrow a view of the **European Communities Act**. However, in *Pickstone*, Lord Templeman made the point in his judgment that the **Sex Discrimination Act** had not been passed to give effect to the directive. But, in *Pickstone*, the 1983 **Regulations** had been introduced to meet the obligations of the directive and the rulings of the Court against the UK Government.

The division between vertical and horizontal direct effect of directives was circumvented to a certain extent by the judgment in the *von Colson* case (1984). This required national courts to construe national law to give effect to the provisions of a directive. In this way, the provisions entered into domestic law and could be relied upon before national courts. The provisions of the directive become an aid to construction of the national law and in this way are enforced by the national court. The *Marleasing* judgment (1992) extended this principle by requiring a national court to construe national law in the light of the wording and purpose of any relevant Community directive, whether the national law originated before or after the adoption of the directive.

This approach has been taken up by the UK courts. In *Pickstone v Freemans plc* (1989), the House of Lords said that English courts must adopt this interpretation, even if to do so would involve departing from the normal canons of construction. This could amount to reading certain words into the relevant national legislation in order to achieve a result compatible with Community law. The Court of Appeal encountered difficulties in the appeal by Mrs Webb against her dismissal by her employer when she became pregnant (*Webb v EMO Air Cargo (UK) Ltd* (1992)). The national legislation that the Court of Appeal had to interpret was the **Sex Discrimination Act 1975**. Judgments of the ECJ on the **Equal Treatment Directive** appeared to indicate that dismissal on the grounds of pregnancy was automatically contrary to the Directive. However, the Court of Appeal held that the **Sex Discrimination Act** did not automatically forbid the dismissal of a woman on the grounds of pregnancy and to give it that meaning would be to distort, rather than construe, English law. On the subsequent appeal to the House of Lords, it was indicated that national law had to be open to an interpretation consistent with the directive if the duty of construction were to apply. Following a further reference to the ECJ, it was stated that Mrs Webb's dismissal could not be justified on the grounds of pregnancy (1994).

The House of Lords cited *Pickstone* with approval in *Lister v Forth Dry Dock and Engineering Co Ltd* (1990), where a claim had been made against a private party. The judgment suggests that, where legislation has been introduced specifically in order to complement an EC directive, UK courts must interpret domestic law to comply with the directive. In some circumstances, this may require supplying the necessary words by implication, in order to achieve a result compatible with EC law. In the *Lister* case, no reference was made to the fact that the directive in question was not directly effective.

However, there is some inconsistency in approach. The judgment in *R v British Coal Corp ex p Vardy* (1993) indicated a reluctance to apply the *Marleasing* principle. In this case, Glidewell J found it impossible to follow the House of Lords' approach in *Lister* since the wording of the statute, the **Trade Union and Labour Relations Act 1992**, was clearly at odds with the directive. In such circumstances, the wording of the statute approved by Parliament was to be followed. An action by the European Commission under **Art 169** would have seemed until recently to be the only possibility. However, the ECJ has developed a remedy by stating that it is a principle of Community law that the Member States are obliged to make good any loss and damage caused to individuals by breaches of Community law for which they were held responsible (*Francovich* (1990)). In the *Brasserie du Pêcheur* and *Factortame* cases

(1996), the ECJ held that, provided the conditions for State liability were satisfied, the principle could and did apply to all Community law as a whole, whether or not directly effective. Therefore, if there is not a manifestly serious breach by the Member State, it is not required to compensate for any loss suffered (*R v HM Treasury ex p BT* (1996)). Where there is liability, it is up to the national court to assess the amount of damages, provided that the domestic law does not treat breaches of EU law less favourably than similar domestic claims (*Sutton v Secretary of State for Social Security* (1997)). In *Levez v Jennings*, the UK rule that damages for sex discrimination should not go back further than two years was considered. Although the rule itself was not criticised, the ECJ indicated that there may be circumstances where its application would be incompatible with the principles of EU law, for example, where there had been deceit by the employer. In the House of Lords' judgment in *Factortame 4* (1999), the UK's breach of its Community obligations was sufficiently serious to entitle the Spanish owners of the vessels to substantial damages.

CHAPTER 4

JUDICIAL REMEDIES AND REVIEW (1): DIRECT ACTIONS

▌INTRODUCTION

As part of its jurisdiction, the ECJ can hear cases brought before it by individuals, Community institutions or governments of Member States. These actions must be brought under specific Articles of the Treaty and are heard solely by the Court, hence the term direct actions as compared with indirect actions or preliminary references made under **Art 234**. These are covered in the next chapter. This area of Community law lends itself to both problem and essay questions, as the 'popular' areas are suitable for both question formats.

Checklist

You should have a general knowledge of how the European Court operates.

In particular, you must be familiar with the following areas:

- enforcement actions brought by the European Commission under **Art 226**, including both the formal and informal stages of the procedure;
- enforcement actions brought by Member States under **Art 227**;
- the remedy available by **Art 228** to actions under **Arts 226** and **227**;
- the action for annulment under **Art 230**, especially the question of *locus standi* and grounds for annulment;
- the possible action under **Art 232** and its relationship with **Art 230**;
- the remedies provided for under **Arts 230** and **232**; and
- the plea of illegality – **Art 241**.

Question 13

What enforcement actions are available against a Member State in breach of its obligations? Are such actions effective?

Answer plan

This is typical of questions set on this topic. It should be noted that it is in two parts, both of which must be answered in the essay that follows if good marks are to be gained. It is not sufficient merely to describe the possible actions, as some evaluation must also be included. The main points to be raised are:

- direct actions under **Arts 226** and 227;
- the remedies available under **Art 228**;
- the role of the Commission under **Art 226**; and
- possible action available in a Member State.

Answer

The **EC Treaty** allows two types of direct enforcement action under **Arts 226** and 227. The most usual action taken against a Member State is by the European Commission under **Art 226**. Although Member States have a possible action under **Art 227**, which allows them to take another Member State before the ECJ, as in *France v UK (Re Fishing Net Mesh Sizes)* (1978), this is rarely used. It is therefore **Art 226** which is the predominant enforcement action used against Member States that are in breach of their obligations, although it is possible for action to be taken in the national courts of the Member State in certain circumstances.

It is appropriate that **Art 226** should give the Commission power to bring an action against a Member State in breach of its obligations, as it has a duty to make sure that Community law is applied. This duty is found in **Art 211**, which lays down the general duties of the Commission. The instigation of the **Art 226** procedure may be due to an act or omission, such as national legislation contrary to Community law or a failure to implement Community law. Therefore, a Member State's failure under the Treaty can be sufficient grounds, as can an action contrary to Community law. However, the procedure under **Art 226** is lengthy and does not provide a speedy process for getting the breach rectified. Whether it is a failure of a positive or negative act, the consequence of a successful action under **Art 226** is for a declaration by the Court under **Art 228** requiring the Member State to take action to fulfil its obligations and the possible imposition of a fine.

The first stage of the **Art 169** procedure is often described as the administrative stage. The ECJ has stated that the purpose of this stage is to allow the Member State either to comply with its obligations under Community law or to put forward an effective defence to the complaints made by the Commission. Initially acting on a complaint, perhaps from a trade association, MEP or another government, the Director General responsible for that sector of Community policy will write to the Member State concerned. These informal communications with the Member State will attempt to ascertain the facts and if possible reach a settlement. They are conducted with discretion, so as to avoid any embarrassment that might result for the Member State. The Commission, having fully investigated the possible breach, will consider whether there is sufficient evidence to justify the commencement of formal proceedings. If the Commission has taken the view that a Member State is in breach of its obligations, the Commission will write to the Member State under its powers in **Art 169**, indicating the breach and inviting the Member State's observations. The Member State then responds to this letter with its own view, which is generally that they are not in breach of this particular obligation. If a settlement acceptable to the Commission is not possible, this administrative stage of **Art 226** will end with the Commission issuing a Reasoned Opinion. This Opinion is very important, as it provides the Member State with a final opportunity to remedy its failure and to this end informs the Member State of what, in the Commission's view, needs to be done to accomplish this. If the Commission decides to go on to the judicial stage of the **Art 226** procedure, the Opinion defines the matters which the Court will be requested to adjudicate on.

It could be argued that the matter could end before the judicial stage, especially as the number of contraventions of Community law is large. To take all the matters further under the procedure would require a large staff. There is also the fact that many Member State governments resent the initiation of the formal enforcement procedure. Does the Commission have to take the matter further? Some writers argue that the Commission has a discretion as to whether it takes further action. However, this ignores the duty given to the Commission under **Art 211** to ensure that Community law is applied. This duty requires the Commission to take the most appropriate action in the circumstances to ensure compliance with Community law. In the EURATOM case of *Commission v France* (1971), Advocate General Roemer indicated that, in some circumstances, the Commission might be justified in not initiating the enforcement procedure. These included situations where an amicable settlement may be achieved if formal proceedings were delayed, or where a major domestic political crisis could be aggravated if proceedings were commenced concerning matters of secondary importance.

An attempt is made to reach a satisfactory settlement without resorting to litigation and in the great majority of cases this has proved possible. If this is not possible, an action by the Commission can be brought before the European Court. The aim of the action is to obtain a declaration that the Member State has failed to fulfil its obligation. The Member State will be bound under **Art 228** to take the necessary measures to comply with the judgment. At one time, the only sanction available to the Commission was to institute a further action against the Member State if it did not comply. The **Maastricht Treaty** made an important amendment to **Art 228** in relation to an action brought under **Art 226**. This now allows the Court to impose a lump sum or penalty payment on any Member State failing to fulfil its obligations, based upon a sum specified by the Commission when it brings the matter before the Court. The basic penalty is fixed at 5,000 euros per day multiplied by factors reflecting the gravity and duration of the non-compliance as applied in the case of *Commission v Greece* (2000).

A common form of infringement by Member States has been the adoption of measures that restrict the free movement of goods within the Community, contrary to **Art 228**. Such measures are against one of the fundamental principles of the Community and are often disguised under legitimate derogations allowed by **Art 30**. Action taken by the Commission in these circumstances is seeking effective rather than purely formal compliance with the Treaty obligations, that is, with the spirit rather than just with the letter. For example, in the *Turkey* case (1982), the UK Government had imposed a ban on the importation of poultry not vaccinated against Newcastle disease. Although ostensibly to protect animal health, which is possible under **Art 30**, its effect was to protect the British poultry industry against imports, notably from France. Although the Court held that such restrictions were contrary to the UK's obligations under the Treaty, the measure did give the British poultry industry some limited protection before the UK Government complied with the **Art 228** (then **Art 171**) order. There are many such examples involving all Member States where, perhaps for domestic political reasons, national measures have been adopted, only to be repealed when judgment has been given by the Court against them. In this sense the **Art 226** action is ultimately effective, but it does take time.

The action available to a Member State under **Art 227** is very similar to that used by the Commission under **Art 226**. However, the Member State must inform the Commission, which is given three months to investigate the matter and deliver a Reasoned Opinion. Here, the Commission is acting more as an umpire and conciliator than an accuser. After the Reasoned Opinion has been given by the Commission, or if three months have elapsed without its doing so, the complainant Member State can bring the matter before the Court. The burden of proof is on the complainant Member State, with the Commission intervening in support of one side or the other. This procedure is very unpopular with the Member States, who generally leave such enforcement actions to the Commission, unless there is a strong political or other reason for them to do otherwise.

In the early years, the Commission did not pursue defaulting Member States with vigour. However, in 1977, the Jenkins Commission decided that, in future, more rigorous use would be made of the **Art 226** procedure. Nevertheless the volume of work places a heavy burden upon the staff of the Commission, which now encourages complainants to seek remedies in the national courts where appropriate. In the landmark case of *Van Gend en Loos* (1963), the Court had recognised that individuals should be able to protect their rights themselves in addition to relying on the Commission. This has become much easier with the development of the principle of direct effect. For example, in *Schoenenberg* (1978) and *Meijer* (1979), individuals were able to claim that national legislation was contrary to obligations imposed by the Treaty in the Member State concerned. This was achieved by the courts concerned using the preliminary reference procedure provided by **Art 234** (then **Art 177**). This happened at the same time as the Commission was taking action against the Member State under the **Art 226** (then **Art 169**) procedure. However, while the **Art 226** procedure has its value in bringing the Member State into line for the future, action in the national courts coupled with an **Art 234** reference does concentrate the mind of the Member State involved! The developments of the law relating to the award of damages has given new emphasis to the possibility of using the national courts for enforcement purposes. In *Francovich v Italian State*, the European Court stated that: 'Community law lays down a principle according to which a Member State is liable to make good damage to individuals caused by a breach of Community law for which it is responsible.'

It can be seen that, although the Treaty only specifies enforcement action under **Arts 226** and **227**, these are not the only possibilities. Action under **Art 226** by the Commission does achieve the desired result, but its main drawback is the time it takes to achieve this, although it is possible to obtain interim measures under **Art 243** where proceedings are being taken under **Art 226** against a Member State. For example, both the UK Government, in relation to a temporary subsidy to pig farmers, and the Irish Government, over its fisheries conservation measures, were brought before the Court in 1977 and appropriate orders were made to stop their infringements immediately. However, the most effective actions are those indirect actions brought in the courts of the Member State concerned.

Question 14

In response to calls to encourage healthy eating among young children, Vegnon has developed a process to puree vegetables to make them attractive to children. They are one of only five producers in the EC to produce such a mixture of vegetables in puree form, and anticipate huge demand from both the private purchaser and also the public sector from schools, hospitals, etc. To meet this demand Vegnon has opened a new plant in Scotland to handle the range of bottled and tinned pureed vegetables.

Last month the Council, following representation from the meat extract industry, adopted a regulation to reduce the quantity of vegetables going forward for pureeing.

In an annex to the regulation there was a list of the five producers, including Vegnon, who were subject to the regulation and limiting their production to that of the last year. This meant that the production anticipated for the Scottish plant could not now take place and would result in a big financial loss to Vegnon.

Vegnon seek your advice as to how they may challenge this regulation and what remedy would be available.

Answer plan

This problem question is the kind of practical scenario question often set on this topic, regardless of the actual product or process used to provide the framework. This question requires you to advise Vegnon, who wish to challenge this regulation. Keep to the points raised in the question and do not merely describe all you know about the subject! Questions on **Art 230** often cause difficulty for students, but one way of solving this is to break the problem down into a number of small questions, pose them and then answer them as if you were advising someone in front of you.

The main points to be raised for Vegnon are:

- the procedure under **Art 230**, including the time limit;
- whether the measure is a 'true' regulation (what is a 'true' regulation?);
- the Court's interpretation of 'direct and individual concern';
- possible action in the national courts if *locus standi* for **Art 230** is not accepted by the European Court; and
- possible action for damages under **Arts 235** and **288**.

Answer

Vegnon wishes to challenge the regulation so that it can be declared invalid. There are two ways under Community law that this can be done. The Treaty allows for actions for annulment or judicial review under **Art 230** but there is also the possibility for a challenge to be brought before a national court. If the challenge under **Art 230** is successful, the remedy provided by the Treaty will be the annulment of the regulation, thus allowing Vegnon to bring the Scottish plant into production. There may also be the possibility of a claim for damages against the Council under **Arts 233** and **288**. However, it is very rare that a successful action can be brought under **Art 230** by non-privileged applicants like Vegnon. In order to advise Vegnon, careful consideration must be given to the wording of **Art 230** and the interpretation given by the ECJ.

Under **Art 230**, any legal person may bring an action against a decision addressed to that person or against a decision which, although in the form of a regulation or a decision addressed to another person, is of direct and individual concern to the former. For Vegnon it is a regulation that they wish to challenge, and to do this they must show that it is not a true regulation but a 'bundle of decisions'. When approaching this question, the ECJ is not restricted by the title of the Community measure as merely because it is called a regulation is not conclusive. In *Calpak* (1980), it was pointed out that this is to prevent Community institutions choosing to issue a decision in the form of a regulation so as to deny the opportunity to an individual to challenge the measure. In *Royal Scholten-Honig v Intervention Board for Agriculture*, the ECJ said: 'In examining this question (re Regulation) the Court cannot restrict itself to considering the official title of the measure, but must first take into account its object and context.' A starting point is the definitions given to various Community measures in **Art 249**, where regulations are described as the main legislative instrument of the Community.

A regulation under **Art 249** should apply to objectively determined situations and produce legal effects with regard to categories of persons regarded generally and in the abstract. This means that it should have a 'normative' character. As long as the regulation maintains these objective characteristics it will still be considered a regulation, even though the number or even identity of the persons to whom it applies can be ascertained. In *Royal Scholten-Honig* the Court insisted that an individual cannot challenge a true regulation, so Vegnon must get over this hurdle if the proceedings at the ECJ are to be admissible. It is not always easy to state clearly that a particular Community measure is a true regulation but, in the *Fruit and Vegetable* case (1962), the Court said: 'A measure which is applicable to objectively determined situations and which involves immediate legal consequences in all Member States for persons viewed in a general and abstract manner cannot be considered as constituting a decision, unless it can be proved that it is of individual concern to certain persons within the meaning of **Art 230**.' There have been relatively few cases where the applicants have satisfied the Court on this point.

A case which may assist Vegnon is *CAM SA v Commission* (1975), where a fixed number of traders were held to be individually concerned because of a factual situation which differentiated them from all other persons and distinguished them individually. Here there were a fixed and known number of cereal traders, because the regulation affected those who had already applied for export licences. This factual situation differentiated them from all other persons and distinguished them individually from others affected by the regulation. Thus the action was admissible, since he was individually concerned because the applicant was one of a fixed and identifiable category. Vegnon may only challenge a regulation if the 'regulation' is really a decision. Decisions are characterised by the limited number of persons to whom they are addressed. In order to determine whether or not a measure constitutes a decision, one must inquire whether that measure concerns specific persons. Can this be linked to the named five producers in the regulation? In Vegnon's case the number of producers is limited and in fact they are named. They can be said to be directly concerned, in that the regulation leaves the Member State no discretion in implementation, but are they individually concerned as is required by **Art 230**? Applicants can only claim to be individually concerned if the decision being challenged affects them by reason of certain attributes which are peculiar to them, or by reason of circumstances in which they are differentiated from all other persons, and by virtue of these factors distinguishes them individually, just as in the case of the person addressed. It will not be sufficient for Vegnon to prove that its business interests will be adversely affected. In the cases where it has been successfully pleaded, such as the *Toepfer* case (1965), the decision being challenged referred to a fixed list of importers which could not be amended. In Vegnon's case there is not this fixed list, although the companies are named in the regulation. However, it could be argued that anyone could enter this business activity, so the requirement of 'individual concern' in **Art 230** is not met. In *Zuckerfabrik Watenstedt* (1968), a producer of raw beet sugar asked for an Article of a regulation to be declared void, with no success. The Court said that a regulation does not lose its characteristics as a regulation simply because it may be possible to identify the persons to whom it applies, as long as it fulfils the objectivity of a regulation.

More importantly the ECJ has taken a very narrow view of what is meant by individual concern and follows the principles stated in the *Plaumann* case. In that case involving clementines, the ECJ stated that the applicant must show that it was affected by reason of certain attributes or circumstances which differentiated if from all others and which distinguished it as individually as if the decision had been addressed to it. There have been exceptions such as in the *Japanese Ball Bearing* cases, where four major Japanese producers of ball bearings were held entitled to challenge a regulation. Although the measure was of general application, some of the Articles specifically referred to the applicants. Even a 'true' regulation can be of individual concern to some persons if it is referable expressly to their particular situation, either alone or as a member of a known or closed class: for example, the Japanese manufacturers. However, this seems to have been an exception to the general approach of the Court. The ECJ in *Union de Pequeños Agricultores* (2002) reaffirmed its case law on the conditions for access of individuals to an action under **Art 230**. Vegnon must fulfil all the criteria if the action is to be admissible. As it cannot challenge a regulation, it must prove that it is a decision which is of direct and individual concern to it.

The fact that Vegnon is listed makes it, arguably, directly and individually concerned, as there is a close and specific relationship between it and the measure being challenged. However, the ECJ has not always been consistent on this point. The Court has laid more emphasis on the requirement of individual concern. If the Court can be satisfied on this, the requirement of direct concern is often assumed.

All this advice has centred on the question of *locus standi*, as this is the major hurdle for any applicant in Vegnon's situation. It must be remembered that the proceedings under **Art 230** must be instituted within two months from the date of publication of the regulation, and from the facts in the problem this is still possible. Having obtained the Court's agreement that the action is admissible Vegnon would have to prove one of the grounds for annulment specified in **Art 230**. There are four such grounds, covering lack of competence, infringement of an essential procedural requirement, infringement of the Treaties or of any rule of law relating to their application and finally, misuse of powers. It is not clear from the problem which particular grounds Vegnon may plead, but the most general one is infringement of the Treaties or of any rule of law relating to their application as this would include general principles of Community law such as legitimate expectations. If successful, the remedy under **Art 231** is for the regulation to be declared void or *erga omnes*.

It is possible to challenge the validity of a regulation in the national courts of a Member State. However, if a company knew that it had a right under **Art 230** and failed to take up that right, the ECJ may refuse to give a preliminary reference on validity (*TWD Textilwerke Deggendorf GmbH v Germany* (1994)). Assuming that this is not the situation for Vegnon, it would have to be a party to an action in a Member State and the court hearing the case would have to make a request for a preliminary ruling under **Art 234(1)** concerning the validity of the regulation. As Vegnon will suffer financially because of the regulation they may bring an action for damages for 'normative injustice' where the regulation constitutes a sufficiently flagrant breach of a superior rule of law protecting individuals under **Art 288**. In *Schoppenstedt* (1971), the Court held that the plaintiff company could sue the Council for damages on the basis of an allegedly illegal regulation even though as a 'natural or legal person' they would have no *locus standi* to seek its annulment under **Art 230**. The advantage of an action under **Art 288** is that it is not restricted to the two-month time limit which applies to challenges under **Article 230**. The disadvantage is that the Court has adopted a very restrictive view of the three elements identified in the *Schoppenstedt* as being necessary to satisfy for Community liability in tort to be imposed.

Question 15

Critically review the ability of an individual to challenge the validity of a Community Act under **Art 230(4)**.

Answer plan

This essay question reflects the discussion that is taking place with regard to the remedies provided by the Community Courts for individuals. Although the national courts can make a request for a preliminary ruling under **Art 234**, the restrictive tests used by the ECJ have raised criticisms from academics and practitioners. This developing area of EU law gives rise to many discussion questions and it is important to deal with the basic principles but then go on to discuss the issues.

The main points to be raised are:

• the procedure under **Art 230**;

• the ECJ's interpretation of 'direct and individual concern';

• the *Plaumann* test;

• the challenges to the case law of the ECJ on **Art 230**.

Answer

The case law of the ECJ acknowledges the principle that an individual who considers himself wronged by a Community measure must have access to a remedy and be able to obtain complete judicial protection. There are a number of ways in which this can be achieved, including an action for annulment under **Art 234**. There is also a possible action for damages under **Arts 235** and **288** or an action before a national court where the question of validity can be raised.

However, there is an argument that proceedings before the courts of a Member State may not provide effective judicial protection for individual applicants because such courts cannot declare Community Acts invalid. Where an applicant can raise the question of validity before a national court, that court may make a request for a preliminary ruling from the ECJ. Advocate General Jacobs in *Union de Pequeños Agricultores* argued that this strictly limited competence of national courts does not provide the individual with the rights identified in the **European Convention on Human Rights** and the **Charter of Fundamental Rights**. **Article 6** of the **European Convention** requires a fair trial and **Art 13** refers to an 'effective remedy'. More recently, the **Charter of Fundamental Rights**, although not legally binding, states in **Art 47** that 'everyone whose rights and freedoms guaranteed by the law of the Union are violated has the right to an effective remedy before a tribunal'.

Also, under **Art 234** the right to make a request for a preliminary ruling is with the court and not the parties to an action. Therefore, the national court may, using its discretion, refuse to make a request for a ruling and delay may occur if the individual appeals that decision through his national legal system. If no implementing legislation is required of the national authorities of a Member State, there may be no basis for an action before the national courts. Even if there is such legislation, Advocate General Jacobs stated in his Opinion in *Union de Pequeños Agricultores* (2002) that it is wrong to expect someone to 'breach the law in order to gain access to justice'. Such actions are both expensive and time-consuming for the individual who wishes to challenge a Community Act.

On the other hand, there is the advantage under an **Art 230** challenge that the institution that adopted the measure in dispute is a party to the proceedings from the beginning. However, the difficulty arises in the question of *locus standi*, or the right to bring the action before the Court. If individuals wish to challenge a decision addressed to themselves there is no problem, other than meeting the time requirements under **Art 230(5)**. Given the substance of most Community measures that may be challenged, it is desirable for reasons of legal certainty that this happens as soon as possible. Where the decision is addressed to another, or where the challenge is against a decision disguised as a regulation, the individuals must show that the measure is of direct and individual concern to them.

This has been very restrictively interpreted by the ECJ, and it was in this context that the remarks of Advocate General Jacobs arose in *Union de Pequeños Agricultores*. The Union de Pequeños Agricultores, a trade association that represents and acts in the interests of small Spanish agricultural businesses, wished to have annulled a regulation that set up a common organisation in olive oil. As the regulation in question had the normative characteristics associated with a regulation, it could not be challenged by the Union under **Art 230(4)**. This follows the case law identifying that the general rule to be applied is that if a decision is not of individual concern to an undertaking, that undertaking cannot challenge it even though it may be adversely affected by it (*Plaumann v Commission* (1962)). If that condition is not satisfied, then a natural or legal person does not have, under any circumstances, the standing to bring a challenge before the Community Courts (*CNPAAP v Council* (1996)). Is there a compelling reason to read into **Art 230(4)** a requirement that individual applicants must be differentiated from all others, in the same way as an addressee? In Jacobs' opinion, the key factor is whether an individual is likely to be adversely affected by the measure. Such an interpretation would improve judicial protection and greatly simplify the application of **Art 230(4)**, but it was rejected by the ECJ.

In *Jégo-Quéré et de SA v Commission* (2002), the Court of First Instance had to consider whether the plaintiff could challenge a regulation concerned with the size of fishing nets used off the Irish coast. The regulation established emergency measures to protect fish stocks and as such it would be hard to show it to be of individual concern under the case law of the ECJ. However, taking up the points made by Advocate General Jacobs in *Union de Pequeños Agricultores*, the CFI said that the interpretation of **Art 230(4)** should be reconsidered in the context of the EC establishing a complete system of legal remedies and procedures so that the Community Courts could review the legality of measures adopted by the institutions.

However, the ECJ has rejected these requests to reconsider the way that **Art 230(4)** is applied. The ECJ has taken the view that general measures in the form of regulations may be challenged by individual applicants in such cases as *Extramet* (1991).

The Court has also recognised that a factual situation may arise which differentiates the applicant from other persons and may be regarded as individually concerned, as in *Codorniu* (1994), but the Court will not go further. In the discussions leading up to the **Treaty of Amsterdam**, the Court itself raised the issue of whether **Art 230(4)** is sufficient to guarantee effective protection against infringements of fundamental rights arising from the legislative activity of the institutions.

In this context, though, the view of the ECJ is that it is for the Member States to establish a system of legal remedies and procedures, which ensure respect for the right to effective judicial remedy. For the ECJ itself to adopt the views of the Advocate General in the case would go beyond the jurisdiction conferred by the Treaty on the Community Courts. However, the ideas in the courts of the Member States on increasing the ability of an individual to bring an action for judicial review have not been mirrored by the ECJ when applying **Art 230(4)**. Under the **Treaty of Nice**, it will be the Court of First Instance that will generally hear actions for annulment, subject to the possibility of appeal to the European Court of Justice, and that may maintain the pressure for reform.

Question 16

Critically discuss the development of State liability in damages in the national courts for violation of Community law.

Answer plan

This essay question is looking at the availability of damages in actions before a national court. This is in contrast to **Art 288**, which is more restrictive. The main thrust of any answer is the *Francovich* case (1992), and the implications of the case in future proceedings before national courts. The ECJ has developed the principles of State liability since this case and this development needs to be analysed.

Answer

The ECJ recognised, in the *Francovich* case (1992), that individuals may have a right to damages in the national courts against the national authorities where they have suffered loss as a result of the non-implementation of a directive by a Member State. The *Francovich* case involved **Directive 80/987**, which provided for the approximation of the laws of the Member States relating to the protection of employees in the event of the insolvency of their employer. The Italian Government had not implemented the directive, with the result that, when Francovich's employer became insolvent, the employees had substantial arrears of salary.

Consequently, the parties brought an action against the Italian State for failing to fulfil the obligations incumbent on it under **Directive 80/987**. The European Court, responding to an **Art 234** reference, developed its analysis of direct effect of directives from *Costa v ENEL* (1964) to deal with the question of damages. It identified three criteria which would have to be satisfied. The Court began by restating the criteria for the application of direct effect. These are that the provision must be clear and unambiguous, it must be unconditional and, finally, its operation must not be dependent on further action being taken by Community or national institutions. In applying these criteria to the facts of the *Francovich* case, the provisions of the Directive were insufficiently precise and were not unconditional, and so did not have direct effect. Thus, Francovich and the other employees involved could not rely on the Directive as against the Italian Government in order to recover their lost wages.

In the *Francovich* case, the ECJ considered the question of the circumstances in which a Member State could be held liable in damages for its violation of Community law. Until this case, the approach taken by the Court had been to state that it was left to national law to determine in which courts an action could be brought and what procedural rules should govern the action. On this basis, the general rule was that Community rights were to be treated no less favourably than analogous domestic law rights. In this way, it was assumed that domestic law would fully protect Community rights by providing a remedy obtainable in national courts. The Court stated that the effectiveness of Community law could be called into question, and the protection of rights would be weakened, if individuals could not obtain compensation when Community rights were undermined by violation of Community law.

The Court emphasised the principle that national courts are obliged to give full effect to Community law to protect rights which individuals derive from Community law (*Simmenthal* (1978), *Factortame* (1991)). It also referred to the obligation imposed on a Member State by **Art 10** (then **Art 5**) to take all appropriate measures to ensure fulfilment of Community law. Arising from these considerations, the Court stated that, as a general principle, Member States are obliged to make good damage caused to individuals by a violation of Community law for which they are responsible. In those cases where there has been a failure to implement a directive, three conditions are required to be satisfied. These are that the contents of the directive were intended to confer rights on individuals, that the contents of the rights can be identified from the provisions of the directive and, lastly, that there was a causal link between the damage suffered by the individual and the State's breach of its obligations. It was for national law to determine the courts dealing with such claims and the procedures to apply.

In his Opinion, Advocate General Mischo had given weight to the fact that the European Commission had already taken action against the Italian State under **Art 226** (then **Art 169**) for its failure to implement the Directive. This had resulted in a declaration by the Court against Italy under **Art 228** (then **Art 171**). However, the Court did not make this point in its judgment. The ECJ held that all the conditions necessary to give a right of action in damages for non-implementation of the Directive were present and, therefore, Francovich and the other applicants had a right to compensation from the Italian State.

Directives only have vertical direct effect and can be enforced only against the State. In the *Francovich* case, the applicants could not rely upon the principle of direct effect as against the State, as the State was not the body responsible for protecting the substantive right to payment of unpaid wages. However, if the Directive had been implemented, the Member State would have designated a body responsible for respecting the substantive right. Italy had failed to implement the Directive, and the Court recognised a right of action based on the responsibility of the Member State for damage caused by its failure to give effect to substantive Community rights in its legislative capacity.

Although *Francovich* involved the non-implementation of a directive, a broad interpretation of the Court's judgment could be that there is a general right to compensation where an individual has suffered loss as a result of a breach of Community law. Thus, the right to damages in the future might be understood as extending more broadly than the facts of *Francovich* would suggest. For example, in *Kirklees MBC v Wickes Building Supplies Ltd* (1992), the House of Lords held on the basis of *Francovich* that if the ECJ considered s 47 of the **Shops Act 1950** to be invalid as being in conflict with **Art 28** (then **Art 30**), the UK might be obliged to make good the loss caused to the individuals by the breach.

In *Bourgoin SA v Minister of Agriculture, Fisheries and Food* (1986), the Court of Appeal was dealing with a situation where a public authority had exercised its public law powers in a way that contravened Community law. The minister had imposed a ban on the import of turkeys contrary to **Art 28** (then **Art 30**), which was directly effective. The Court of Appeal had held that the appropriate remedy was a public law remedy, obtainable by way of judicial review. Only if the public body had been guilty of misfeasance in a public office would the public body be liable in damages. This is difficult to prove and would result in damages not being available. In *Kirklees*, the House of Lords doubted whether, in the light of *Francovich*, the *Bourgoin* case was correctly decided and considered that the UK might be potentially liable in damages for a breach of **Art 28** (then **Art 30**).

Francovich clearly represents a further development in Community law on remedies. Further references were made to the ECJ under **Art 234** (then **Art 177**), in order to obtain clarification of the implications for individuals who have suffered loss through a breach of Community law. The ECJ subsequently elaborated on the *Francovich* criteria in *Brasserie du Pêcheur* and *Factortame (No 3)* (1996), where the

Court developed the prerequisites for the application of the principle of State liability. The Court held that, provided the conditions for State liability were satisfied, the principle applied to all Community law as a whole, whether or not it was directly effective. In *Dillenkofer* (1996), there had been a total failure to implement a directive and the question of discretion was raised. The ECJ held that the Member State had manifestly and gravely disregarded the limits on its discretion, which gave rise to an individual right to a claim for damages provided the stated preconditions were satisfied. The Court took the view that difficulty in implementation of a directive was no defence.

In *Sutton v Secretary of State for Social Security* (1997), the ECJ stated that it is up to the national court to assess the amount of damages, provided that the domestic law does not treat breaches of EU law less favourably than similar domestic claims. In *Factortame* (No 4) (1999), the Court of Appeal held that the breaches of Community law identified in *Commission of the EC v UK* (1989) were sufficiently serious to give rise to liability for any damage that might subsequently be shown to have been caused to individuals. As a result of this judgment, it is likely that Spanish trawler owners will receive in excess of £80m in damages. It would seem that State liability as a principle can be seen as an effective mechanism for safeguarding the rights of individuals who can meet the three criteria.

Question 17

Analyse TWO of the following cases which came before the ECJ and explain their importance in the development of Community law:

(a) *Plaumann* – Case 25/62;

(b) *Roquette Frères v Council* – Case 138/79;

(c) *Schoppenstedt* – Case 5/71.

Answer plan

When approaching a question like this, the temptation is to produce too descriptive an answer. The facts are important, but are only one element of the answer. You should deal with the following:

- the facts, the legal points raised and the decision of the Court.
- the kind of case it was? – whether a preliminary reference or a direct action and which Article of the Treaty it was based upon.

- the cases chosen for this type of question have usually played their part in developing or reinforcing European Court judgments – what part has this case played?

Answer

(a) Plaumann v Commission – Case 25/62

This was an action by one of 30 German importers of clementines against a refusal by the Commission to grant a request by the Federal Republic of Germany for permission to suspend the customs duties on the import of fresh clementines from non-EC countries. The refusal by the Commission had been made in a decision under the now repealed **Art 25(3)**. The implication for Plaumann was that it had to pay a customs duty of 13%, whereas the German Government had asked the Commission to reduce it to a 10% duty.

The main importance of this case concerned whether Plaumann could challenge this decision by the Commission. It was open to the German Government to challenge the decision because it was addressed to them. But could Plaumann as a 'private individual' bring the matter before the ECJ? An action for annulment can be brought under **Art 230**, but as far as individuals are concerned this Article has been restrictively interpreted by the Court. It is possible to challenge a decision addressed to oneself, but if it is addressed to another, the applicant must show that it is of direct and individual concern to them.

The Commission contested the case by claiming that it was inadmissible under **Art 230** (then **Art 173(2)**) because the decision addressed to the government of a Member State was of a special nature and therefore not susceptible to challenge by private persons. It also said that Plaumann was not directly and individually concerned. Thus, the argument before the Court concentrated on this issue of inadmissibility.

The Court accepted that **Art 230** (then **Art 173(2)**) does allow an individual to bring an action against decisions addressed to another person if they are of direct and individual concern, but the Article neither defines nor limits the scope of these words. The words should be given their natural meaning and the broadest interpretation. As the provision provides a right for interested parties to bring an action, it must not be interpreted restrictively. Therefore, the Commission's argument was not considered to be well founded.

On the question of 'direct and individual' concern, the Court decided to look at whether the applicant was individually concerned, because if the answer is negative it will be unnecessary to inquire whether he is directly concerned. On this question of 'individually concerned', the decision must affect applicants by reason of certain attributes which are peculiar to them, or there must be certain circumstances which differentiate them from all other persons. As a result of these factors, the applicant is distinguished individually, just as if they were the person to whom the decision was addressed.

In the *Plaumann* case, the decision affects Plaumann as an importer of clementines, a commercial activity which may be practised by any person. Thus, he is not distinguished sufficiently to show individual concern. Therefore, the Court declared the action for annulment to be inadmissible on the second point put forward by the Commission. This case was followed by a number of cases decided on a similar basis, to the detriment of the applicants – for example, *Spijker Kwasten BV v Commission*, which involved a six-month import ban on Chinese brushes where Spijker was the sole importer into the Netherlands.

(b) Roquette Frères v Council – Case 138/79

This case arose in the wake of a successful challenge to **Regulation 1111/77** in the *Isoglucose* case of *Royal Scholten-Honig* in 1978. The result was that the regulation was declared to be invalid on the ground of discrimination. The regulation had sought to control the sugar market. Isoglucose is a direct substitute for liquid sugar, of which there was a surplus. As this surplus had to be exported at a loss, it was felt that the isoglucose manufacturers should contribute to export costs by paying a levy. As the regulation imposing the levy was invalid, no such levy was being collected. Therefore, a new regulation was needed which imposed a levy, but did not discriminate between the producers. Under the Common Agricultural Policy, such a regulation required that the Parliament should be consulted before being adopted by the Council.

The problem was a matter of time. The new regulation was needed to come into force at the same time as the sugar scheme, namely July 1979. By March 1979, the Commission had drafted the regulation, which was based on the one which applied to sugar. Therefore, the new regulation did not discriminate between the two products. However, the regulation contained an annex which gave precise methods of calculation.

The draft regulation came before the Parliament in April, but no final decision was made. June 1979 was the first time that direct elections were to be made to the European Parliament. The old Parliament 'died' before it could give its opinion, although the specialist Agricultural Committee was in the process of reconsidering the regulation. The regulation was urgently needed, but there was no Parliament. In the recitals to any regulation the words 'having regard to the opinion of the European Parliament . . .' are usually included. This regulation said that the Parliament had been consulted, but had not delivered its opinion! The Council believed that the judgment of the Court in the *Isoglucose* case had to be implemented before too long and that the regulation be adopted before the beginning of the sugar year on 1 July 1979.

Who could challenge the regulation? At that time, the Parliament was considered not to have *locus standi* under the then **Art 173**, although, following *Les Verts v Parliament* (1983), this would not be the situation today. Therefore, the only possibility was for an individual to bring an action for annulment under **Art 230** (then **Art 173(2)**). However, no individual can challenge a true regulation. There was something special about this regulation, in that it contained the annex which applied the scheme set up by the regulation to particular firms. Therefore, as far as these firms were concerned, the measure affected them 'like a decision'. Such firms could also count on the Parliament intervening in the action on their support, as they are entitled to do under the Court Statute.

The Council challenged the firms' action under **Art 230** (then **Art 173**), but the Commission observed that if the action was declared inadmissible, there would surely be a reference on the matter under **Art 234** from a court of a Member State. The Court agreed that the action was admissible. The ground under **Art 230** (then **Art 173(1)**) which was successfully pleaded was the breach of an essential procedural requirement, in that the Parliament had not been consulted. This raised the question as to what amounted to consultation? As the Parliament had received the draft regulation, was this sufficient? The Court found that it was not, as Parliament was allowed, under the Treaty, to play an actual part in the legislative process. This reflects the fundamental democratic principle of the Community.

Having found that the regulation was faulty, the Court had to declare it void under **Art 231** (then **Art 174**). This case provides a good example of a decision which, although in the form of a regulation, is of direct and individual concern under **Art 230**. The importance of the case goes further in its effects on the balance of power of the Community institutions. Since the case, the **Single European Act 1986** has introduced the co-operation procedure for certain policy areas, but this case shows that the Court recognised the importance of the democratic principle and the role it gives to the European Parliament.

(c) Schoppenstedt – Case 5/71

The undertaking Aktien-Zuckerfabrik Schoppenstedt brought an action in 1971 on the basis of **Art 288** (then **Art 215(2)**), claiming damages from the Council caused by **Regulation 769/68**. This regulation laid down the measures needed to offset the difference between national sugar prices. The European Court is given jurisdiction in disputes relating to compensation for damage by **Art 235**. However, this jurisdiction is linked to **Art 288**, which states that, in the case of non-contractual liability, the Community shall make good any damage caused by its institutions. The case is to be judged in accordance with the general principles common to the laws of the Member States.

The Council contested the admissibility of the application on the grounds that the applicant was claiming compensation for the removal of the legal effects arising from the contested regulation and not for any wrongful act or omission. Secondly, if the action was recognised as admissible it would undermine **Art 230** (then **Art 173**), under which individuals are not entitled to bring applications for the annulment of regulations.

On the substance of the case, the Court said that the non-contractual liability of the Community presupposes at the very least the unlawful nature of the act alleged to be the cause of the damage. No non-contractual liability will arise involving measures of economic policy unless a sufficiently flagrant violation of a superior rule of law for the protection of the individual has occurred. Having set this principle, the Court had to decide whether such a violation had actually occurred in this case.

Analysing this sentence, 'a superior rule of law for the protection of individuals' includes any general principle of Community law. This would include such examples as equality or proportionality. The requirement that there should be a 'sufficiently flagrant' or serious violation has been narrowly construed by the Court. In the case of *Bayerische HNL Vermehrungsbetriebe GmbH v Council and Commission* (1978), the Court stated that no liability would be incurred by the Community institutions unless the institution concerned had manifestly and gravely disregarded the limits on the exercise of its power. In subsequent cases, the Court's view has been that the breach must be both serious and inexcusable.

The applicants contended that by adopting different criteria for the right of compensation of sugar producers, the regulation infringes **Art 37(3)**. However, the Court rejected this argument, as the prices must be governed by market forces. Therefore, the applicant's action failed on the substance, because the condition mentioned above was not satisfied. The impact of the case has been the test set by the Court in actions under **Art 288** in the field of legislative economic policy. Cases which have followed have been regularly rejected.

CHAPTER 5

JUDICIAL REMEDIES AND REVIEW (2): INDIRECT ACTION – PRELIMINARY REFERENCES

INTRODUCTION

This type of action has proved very important for the development of Community law. It has been used by the European Court of Justice (ECJ) as a vehicle for establishing many of the fundamental principles covered in other chapters of this book. It is very important, therefore, to have a good understanding of this topic, which can arise in both problem and essay questions.

Checklist

You should have a general knowledge of the reasons for such a procedure being incorporated into the Treaty and, in particular, you must be familiar with the following areas:

- the matters for referral under **Art 234**;
- the difference between interpretation and validity questions;
- what is a court or tribunal within the Article;
- the difference between courts which have a discretion and those which have an obligation to refer;
- the impact of the *CILFIT* case;
- the guidelines and procedures used in English courts; and
- the impact of a reference on the parties and subsequent cases.

Question 18

What are the objectives of the system of preliminary references? Has the ECJ extended the use of **Art 234** beyond these objectives?

Answer plan

This type of essay question allows you to use your knowledge of areas of Community law to illustrate how the ECJ has extended the role of **Art 234** within the Community. The following points should be covered:

- objectives of the **Art 234** procedure (formerly **Art 177**; new numbering should generally be referred to, as in this answer);
- the relationship between the ECJ and national courts under the procedure;
- the role of policy in the ECJ;
- the extension of the scope of **Art 234**;
- the development of direct effect;
- the development of *acte clair* in the context of **Art 234**.

Answer

In the early stages of the European Community, the ECJ made it clear that a new legal order had been established. It was recognised by the authors of the Treaties establishing the Community that a court was necessary to ensure that there was a uniform interpretation and application of Community law throughout the Member States. It would undermine the new Community if the effect of its law varied from one Member State to another, especially in the economically sensitive areas associated with the European Economic Treaty. It was necessary to give ultimate authority to one court, whose jurisdiction extended over the whole Community. This was the ECJ. However, the relationship between the ECJ and the national courts was not to be on a hierarchical appellate basis associated with national court structures. It was important that the relationship should be seen to be based on co-operation, with the shared objective that all courts wished to apply the law, whether it be of national or Community origin. It was the ECJ which was granted the power to give definitive judgments on the validity and interpretation of Community law.

Thus, from the beginning, there were seen to be two clear differences between the procedure under **Art 234** and the action of appellate courts. First, it is the parties to an action who normally decide whether to appeal or not. Secondly, when a case goes to appeal in a national context, it is normally the appeal court which decides the case and it may either uphold, amend or overturn the decision of the lower court. Neither of these applies to the **Art 234** procedures. It is the national court which decides whether a reference should be made, and only specific issues are referred to the ECJ in the form of questions. Once the ECJ has answered these, they are sent back to the national court for a final decision. This suggests that national courts are not subordinate to the ECJ, but co-equal.

Given this need for uniformity in the Community, **Art 234** specifies the initial boundaries of the role of preliminary references. Under **Art 234**, the Treaty specifies that references can be made requesting: (a) interpretation of the Treaty; (b) the validity and interpretation of acts of the institutions of the Community; and (c) in appropriate cases, the interpretation of the statutes of bodies established by the act of the European Council. It is (a) and (b) where the important developments have been made in Community law by the use of **Art 234** references. In the early cases of *Van Gend en Loos* (1963) and *Costa v ENEL* (1964), the ECJ took the opportunity to stress the relationship between national law and Community law and the legal implications of the transfer of sovereignty when Member States established the Community. Both of these very important cases were brought before the Court via **Art 234** references from their national courts. However, perhaps the best example of how the Court has used **Art 234** to develop Community law is direct effect. Having established the supremacy of Community law over national law, the ECJ introduced the concept of direct effect. This was the result of the Court's view that a new legal order had been established with the Community and that this gave rights to individuals which their national courts had to uphold. Subject to three requirements being satisfied, this meant that an individual could claim a right under the Treaty, administrative act or other act treated as *sui generis* by the Court. This very important development was not expressly mentioned in the Treaty, the primary source of Community law. It was implied by the ECJ under its powers of interpretation and within its role in explaining what Community law was. Thus, it was possible to identify three issues which could be referred for a ruling under **Art 234**, namely, interpretation, validity and direct effect.

As a policy decision, the Court has developed the principle of direct effect of Treaty Articles, regulations and directives. However, this is not the only example of how the ECJ has extended the jurisdiction of **Art 234**. As mentioned above, the Court has extended 'acts' of the institutions to include not only those specified in **Art 249**, but also those acts which are *sui generis*. In the *ERTA* case (1971), the Court held that such acts of the Council could be an act for the purposes of judicial review under **Art 230** (then **Art 173**) and thus likely to fall within **Art 234** procedures. This was taken further in the *Haegeman* case (1974), where the Court held that the Association Agreement between the Community and Greece was covered by **Art 234** (then **Art 177(1)(b)**). As agreements between the Community and non-Member States are normally concluded by the Council, this was sufficient grounds for the

Court to regard such agreements as Community Acts. It could be argued that, as the agreement was concluded by means of a Council decision, this was correct. However, it was not the decision which was interpreted by the Court, but the agreement itself. Obviously, the non-Member State was not bound by the Court's interpretation, but Member States were. As international agreements between the Community and non-Member States are part of Community law and binding on Member States, it is clearly important that uniform interpretations should be given to the agreement throughout the Community. The agreement had to be brought within **Art 234** if it was to be interpreted by the Court. Thus, the Court said that the agreement constituted an act of a Community institution in so far as it concerned the Community. Even if the agreement between the Community and a non-Member State is a mixed agreement in that there is a shared authority between the Community and Member States, this does not seem to have affected the ECJ's view of its jurisdiction to interpret the agreement. This approach is another example of the Court's policy-orientated interpretation, which has extended **Art 234**.

There are other examples of the impact of **Art 234** references on Community law as its scope has been broadened by the ECJ. It is seen by the Court as the best way of moving Community law forward within the teleological interpretation of the Court. The flow of cases on the direct effect of directives is perhaps a clear example of this, culminating in the *Francovich* judgment (1992). However, the constitutional impact of references on Member States should not be ignored. In the UK, the *Factortame* case challenged long-standing constitutional principles. However, if the objectives of the preliminary references system are to ensure uniformity and not to allow disparities due to legal traditions, it would appear that the ECJ is seeking to fulfil them. As the scope of Community action has increased, it is to be expected that the matters coming within **Art 234** references will also increase. How else can the ECJ provide the interpretation and validity necessary for uniform application throughout the Community? If the ECJ did not provide these, there would be no focus for the Member States and a danger of various interpretations undermining the Community itself.

Another objective of **Art 234** was to distinguish between those courts which had a discretion to refer under **Art 234(2)** and those which had an obligation to refer under **Art 234(3)**. Courts under the latter paragraph are those against whose decisions there is no judicial remedy under national law. This does not automatically mean the highest court in the judicial structure of a Member State, but the highest court hearing that particular case (*Costa v ENEL*). In the UK, some judges, such as Lord Denning, consider that only the House of Lords comes within the category of **Art 234(3)**.

However, whatever the arguments on this point, the ECJ has taken a policy decision to limit the obligation of such courts to refer. The *CILFIT* case (1982) is the most important development in this respect, where the ECJ held that final courts are in the same position as other national courts in deciding whether they need to refer a question of Community law before giving judgment.

If, for example, the ECJ had already given an authoritative interpretation under **Art 234**, there is no purpose in a further reference, although it could be made. However, the Court went further, to say that the correct application of Community law may be so obvious as to leave no scope for any reasonable doubt as to the manner in which the question is raised, thus enabling the **Art 234** court to refrain from making a reference. This echoes the principle of *acte clair*, so familiar to the French legal system. The ECJ may have felt that the national legal systems were now so well schooled in the principles of Community law that this development could take place. It may be that they felt this was a reasonable way of reducing the workload of the Court or to further the co-operation on which the relationship with national courts is based. However, to ensure that national courts did not remove this obligation as a matter of course, the Court indicated the special characteristics of Community law which had to be considered, for example, the linguistic nature of the Court's jurisdiction, the special terminology and the contextual approach of the ECJ. Only if the national court could satisfy itself on these matters could the obligation to refer be removed.

Given that the preliminary procedure was designed to deal with the danger of divergences in the interpretation of Community law in Member States (*International Chemical Corp* (1981)), it can be seen that the ECJ has extended the interpretation of **Art 234** itself. This is in three respects, namely, the scope of Community law covered, direct effect and the mandatory nature of **Art 234**. However, there have been limitations on this development, as can be seen in the *Firma Foto-Frost* case (1988), where the ECJ reiterated that national courts could not declare a Community Act invalid, but had to make a reference under **Art 234**.

Question 19

Christine is a secretary with Welch's Import Agency. On a recent visit to Amsterdam, Christine collected a number of boxes at the request of her employer and brought them back with her to England in her car. At Dover, she was stopped by customs officials and her car was searched for drugs. Although no drugs were found, the boxes belonging to her employer were opened and found to contain pornographic films and magazines, much to the embarrassment of Christine. She was subsequently charged with a criminal offence under the **Obscene Publications Act 1959**.

At the Crown Court hearing, Christine's counsel stated that the case raised a question of European law and requested that a reference be made to the ECJ. The judge said that he would make no reference, as the law was clear in his eyes and he did not wish to delay the case.

Can the judge refuse this request? What guidelines have been developed to assist English judges when deciding whether to make a reference?

Answer plan

This problem question on **Art 234** requires the application of basic principles, including:

- the procedure under **Art 234**;
- the difference between **Arts 234(2)** and **234(3)**;
- implications of *acte clair* and *CILFIT*;
- English guidelines produced by senior judges;
- the *Rheinmuhlen* case.

Answer

Christine's counsel has asked about a possible reference by the Crown Court judge to the ECJ. Under **Art 234**, it is possible for any court or tribunal to request a preliminary ruling from the ECJ on a matter of Community law in order for the national court to give a judgment in the case before it. This request can be on a question of interpretation of the Treaty, interpretation or validity of acts of the Community institutions or whether the principle of direct effect applies. The purpose is to provide the means for a definitive statement from the Court that will ensure that Community law is applied uniformly across all Member States. Thus, the Crown Court comes within the category of court which **Art 234** was designed for. However, within **Art 234**, there are two categories of court. Under **Art 234(2)**, courts or tribunals have a discretion in that they may make a reference.

Article 234(3) indicates that those courts or tribunals in Member States against whose decision there is no judicial remedy under national law have an obligation to make a reference. This obligation has been qualified by the case law of the ECJ, such as the *CILFIT* case. As Christine's case is being heard before the Crown Court, **Art 234(2)** clearly applies. However, in either instance, it is the court or tribunal which decides and not the parties to the action. Therefore, the judge hearing Christine's case can refuse the request for a preliminary ruling under **Art 234** to the European Court of Justice.

Given the importance of the decision to make a reference to the Court, a number of guidelines would appear to be desirable to assist a judge hearing a particular case to decide whether to exercise discretion to make a reference or not. The European Court itself has refrained from producing guidelines as to the circumstances in which this step should be taken, but it has indicated that it is essential for the national court to 'define the legal context' (*Irish Creamery* (1981)). However, national judges have attempted to fulfil this need. The first judge to do so in the UK was Lord

Denning, in the first case to come before the Court of Appeal involving Community law. This case was *Bulmer v Bollinger* (1974), an action over the use of the term 'champagne' when describing an alcoholic drink called Babycham. In this case, Denning indicated what he considered to be important factors. Perhaps the most important was that the point of Community law must be conclusive, in the sense that the case must turn on the point of Community law involved. In other words, if Community law was 'x', then the plaintiff would succeed, but if, on the contrary, it was 'y', then the defendant would defeat the action. It may be that, after hearing the evidence, the case could be settled on national law, thus making the reference unnecessary. The other factors he specified were associated with the time it took to get a ruling from the European Court, which required a stay of the English proceedings, which may have unfortunate results for the parties. Obviously, there was the expense of obtaining the ruling and the danger of overloading the European Court with too many references. He also felt that the wishes of the parties should be taken into account. Clearly, Christine wants a reference made, but this is not conclusive.

These guidelines have been criticised, in that they may fetter the English judge, contrary to the principle that national law cannot constrain the judge in the exercise of his discretion. This principle was stated by the ECJ in the German case of *Rheinmuhlen* (1974). In this case, the Court held that the power of a lower court to make a reference cannot be abrogated by any rule of national law. It also reiterated the importance of the **Art 234** procedure by stating that it is essential for the preservation of the Community character of law and ensuring that the law is the same in all Member States. However, the Court did recognise in *Rheinmuhlen* that, although the widest discretion was given to national courts regarding when to refer, **Art 234** does not preclude a decision to refer from remaining subject to the normal national law remedies. Thus, it would still be possible to appeal in these circumstances through the national court structure. Although in subsequent English cases, judges have been influenced by the words of Denning in *Bulmer v Bollinger*, they have repeated that they are only guidelines and do not fetter the discretion of the judge. However, one important point made by Lord Denning and repeated by subsequent English judges and the European Court itself is that it is important to ascertain the facts first, before the discretion to make a reference is considered.

In some civil cases, the facts may be agreed by the parties but, in criminal cases, such as Christine's, it is normally only after the case has been argued that conclusions can be drawn on the facts of the case. This is apparent in the context of deciding whether the point of Community law is conclusive. It may be that the case can be settled on the basis of national law. However, more importantly, it has a crucial role in framing the questions to be put to the ECJ in the request for a preliminary ruling.

MacPherson J, in *R v HM Treasury ex p Daily Mail and General Trust plc* (1987), provided a useful list of factors which consolidate those of previous English judges. His last point, that he did not find the point raised free from doubt, brings the wording of **Art 234** back into focus. The judge hearing Christine's case has a discretion to make a reference if he considers it necessary to enable him to give judgment. Although Christine's counsel has stated that a question of European law has been raised by the case, the judge clearly feels that he has the answer. This may be gleaned from the case law of the Court itself on the point raised, which was recognised in the *CILFIT* case (1981). However, English judges have been warned by Lord Diplock in *R v Henn and Darby* (1981) that just because the meaning of the English text seems plain, it does not mean that no question of interpretation arises. Where this is necessary, the ECJ, as Bingham J pointed out in *Commissioners of Customs and Excise v Samex ApS* (1983), is far better equipped than national courts to resolve issues of Community law. Later, as Sir Thomas Bingham MR, he confirmed this view and added that if there was any real doubt a court should make a reference (the *Stock Exchange* case (1993)).

It may be different for Christine if the hearing is before magistrates and thus without a jury to decide on questions of fact. In such courts, once questions of facts have been decided, it may be appropriate for the magistrates to make an **Art 234** reference if the guilt of the defendant turns on the interpretation or validity of Community law. This was followed in *R v Pieck* (1980), where the incompatibility of English law with Community law led to the defendant having the prosecution against him dropped. However, in *R v Plymouth JJ ex p Rogers* (1982), the Divisional Court dismissed the argument of the prosecution that no court or tribunal could refer questions to the Court of Justice unless all the facts had been admitted or found, because this would mean that, in criminal cases, there would not be an opportunity to request a ruling on the basis of no case to answer unless all the facts had been settled. On the other hand, it was better to call all the evidence so that there was no question of the defendant being acquitted on the facts, thus saving the expense and delay of a reference. A case before a judge and jury in a Crown Court highlights the problem of delay associated with making a preliminary reference. Lord Diplock stated in *Henn and Darby v DPP* (1981) that it can seldom be a proper exercise of a judge's discretion to hold up the proceedings for over nine months. The delay caused by a reference being made now would probably be at least double this length of time. The better course, he suggested, was to decide the case at first instance and allow an appeal against conviction through the hierarchy of national courts. This approach was subsequently adopted by the judge in *R v Tymen* (1981).

It would appear that the judge hearing Christine's case has complete discretion, but is there any appeal available to her? As mentioned above, the European Court recognised in the *Rheinmuhlen* case that **Art 234** references are subject to the normal appeal processes. If a reference had been made under the Crown Court equivalent of the High Court procedure in **RSC Ord 114**, there would be a two-week period before the reference was sent to the ECJ to allow for an appeal by one of the parties. However, in Christine's case, it is the decision not to make a reference that she is unhappy with. In these circumstances, the judge's refusal is interlocutory and leave to appeal is necessary either from the judge or from the Court of Appeal.

Question 20

To what extent does the system of preliminary rulings reflect a dialogue between the ECJ and the courts in the Member States?

Answer plan

This essay question is looking for a well-planned essay that develops the following points:

- purpose of **Art 234**;
- the *Foglia* cases;
- guidance provided by the ECJ;
- changing relationship with the national courts.

Answer

In the earliest cases coming before the ECJ in the 1960s, the creation of the European Community was said to have led to a 'new legal order', and such a Community needed a court which could give definitive judgments on question of European law that would be binding on all the Member States. **Article 234** provides a mechanism for such judgments to be given by the ECJ, and more recently by the CFI, on questions of European Community law. The relationship is not one of an appeal court jurisdiction commonly found within the judicial structures of the Member States, as the final judgment is made by the national court and not by the Community Courts. Some writers describe the relationship as a partnership, as there is a shared purpose to identify and apply the correct Community law to a given factual situation. The objective of the preliminary ruling procedure is to provide uniformity across the whole Community, so that Community law is applied in the same way in all Member States. Under **Art 234**, the Court of Justice is under a duty to supply all courts in the Community with the information on interpretation of Community law that is necessary to enable them to settle genuine disputes which are brought before them (*Foglia v Novello (No 1)* (1980)). Under **Art 225(3)** of the **Nice Treaty**, the Court of First Instance has gained jurisdiction to hear requests for a preliminary ruling. Before the Nice amendment, only the European Court of Justice had jurisdiction under **Art 234**.

The preliminary ruling procedure is available to any court or tribunal of any Member State. What constitutes such a court has been given a wide interpretation by the ECJ. It is not necessary that the body is recognised as a court by national law, neither must it be called a court. For the ECJ, the important question is whether the body concerned is performing a judicial function. The characteristic of such a function is the power to give binding determinations of the legal rights and obligations of individuals. The ECJ has used the mechanism of preliminary rulings to develop fundamental principles of Community law, such as supremacy and direct effect. However, **Art 234** has also been used to facilitate a dialogue between the national courts and the ECJ on issues where national law and Community law seem to be in conflict.

The preliminary ruling procedure recognised the different functions of the national courts and the Community Courts. It envisaged this relationship to be of equals as both were seen to be on a horizontal base. If the national court chose to ask a question it entered into a bilateral dialogue with the ECJ. The answers from the ECJ were sent back to that court, even though the answers were public and therefore available to everyone. The courts had different functions but a shared objective of applying the law. This is explicit in **Art 220 EC** but is mirrored in the national courts and the principle of the rule of law. Even though many now describe the relationship as more vertical as the importance of both Community law and the ECJ has increased, the Community Court still relies upon national courts to enforce Community law.

The wider recognition of the *acte clair* concept is perhaps a reflection of the developing dialogue between the ECJ and the national courts so that now even those national courts who were thought to be obliged to make a reference (**Art 234(3)**) need no longer do so (*CILFIT*). Although Advocate General Caporti in that case proposed that the concept should not be adopted, the Court rejected that opinion. However, while some commentators have suggested that they indicated restrictions or considerations so as to limit its use, the fact remains that *CILFIT* led to a much more relaxed, yet responsible, approach by those national courts. There are some commentators who say that the development was just pragmatic; too many requests for a preliminary ruling from those courts where there was no discretion under **Art 234(3)**. This may have been a factor but the development complemented the increasing role of the national courts in enforcing Community rights with the principle of direct effect or applying Community rules on competition.

In *Foglia (No 2)* the ECJ made clear that it would be the ultimate decider of the scope of its own jurisdiction. It would not answer hypothetical questions. If necessary it would have to examine the circumstances of the reference in order to determine whether the Court's jurisdiction had been properly invoked. In the *Foglia v Novello* cases in 1980 and 1982, the Court held that the reference was an abuse of **Art 234** as the case had been artificially constructed as a vehicle for obtaining clarification of Community law. There was, in the opinion of the Court, an absence of any real legal dispute between the parties. Novello, a French resident, had ordered some wine from Foglia, an Italian wine grower. The contract provided that Novello would not be liable for any French or Italian taxes which were contrary to the free movement of goods between the two countries. When a charge was subsequently levied by French customs, Novello claimed it was unlawful under **Art 90** (formerly **Art 95 EC**). The ECJ said that both parties agreed that the French law was incompatible with Community law, and the legal action had been a device to obtain a ruling that the French legislation was invalid. The Court went on to say that arrangements obliging such rulings would jeopardise the system of legal remedies available to protect private individuals against tax provisions which were contrary to the Treaty. A subsequent second reference by the Italian judge was an attempt to clarify the role of **Art 234** and the relationship between the national courts and the ECJ. However, the ECJ adhered to its earlier decision not to answer the question arising from the customs duty levied by the French law. It held that the **Art 234** procedure was not to be used to give abstract advisory opinions, but to contribute to the actual decisions of the cases. The ECJ believes that, like any court, it must be in a position to make an assessment to ensure that it has jurisdiction to hear the case. Normally the Court will rely on the assessment made by national courts but in exceptional cases it reserves the right to make its own (*Dias* (1992)).

The original division of the functions between national courts and the ECJ may have been separate, but it was equal – with the former deciding whether to refer, while the latter gave the ruling on the questions placed before it. *Foglia* represented a reshaping of that conception as the ECJ would now assert some control over the suitability of the reference. The ECJ refrained from reviewing the relevance even in cases like *Rewe-Zentrale v Hauptzollamt Emmerich* (1971) where the national court making the reference admitted that the questions raised were not relevant to the litigation. The questions were answered by the ECJ because the litigation was a test case for similar forthcoming cases. There have been a number of cases where the ECJ has made use of the *Foglia* principle, such as with the hypothetical nature of the questions. However, a practical problem is the fine line between hypothetical cases and test cases. In *Bacardi-Martini v Newcastle United FC* (2003) the ECJ refused to deal with a reference because a court in one Member State was asking about the compatibility of another Member State's law with EU law.

A second reason why the ECJ may not wish to give a ruling is that the questions raised are not relevant, as in the *Meilicke* case (1992). The third category where the ECJ may refuse a reference is where the questions are not articulated clearly enough for the Court to give any meaningful legal response, as in *AGS Assedic Pas-de-Calais v Dumon & Froment* (1995). Although the ECJ may tease out the real question the national court is asking, in this case they thought that it would be wrong to alter the substance of the questions asked. A fourth category is where the facts are insufficiently clear for the Court to be able to apply the relevant legal rules. In the *Telemarsicabruzzo* case (1993) the Italian court referred two questions to the ECJ concerning the compatibility of national provisions on the distribution of TV frequencies with

EC competition law. The national court provided almost nothing by way of explanation for these questions and therefore the Court decided that there was no need to answer the questions!

The Court incorporated the results of its case law into guidelines published in 1997 and subsequently updated in 2005 in its publication *Information Notes on References from National Courts for Preliminary Rulings*. The Court has recognised that there are limitations to its power to decline to take a reference and in fact has rejected very few. In *ICI v Colmer* (1996) the ECJ stated that: 'A request for a preliminary ruling from a national court may be rejected only if it is manifest that the interpretation of Community law or the examination of the validity of a rule of Community law sought by that court bears no relation to the facts or the subject matter of the main proceedings.' However, even though some argue that the dialogue between the ECJ and the national courts is one-sided, the preliminary ruling procedure has played the central role in the development and acceptance of concepts such as direct effect, supremacy and State liability.

Question 21

Crinkley plc are a large producer of potato crisps in the UK. Like all companies who are involved in manufacturing potato products, Crinkley have to purchase their potatoes from a national marketing organisation, as required by EU legislation. Under a recent Community regulation, all purchasers have to submit a tender together with a deposit of 10% of the total value of the tender.

Subsequently, Crinkley failed to take up all the supplies they had tendered for and were informed that they would, under the regulation, forfeit their deposit. This amounted to a substantial amount to Crinkley and could force them into liquidation. As a result, they are seeking to challenge the validity of the regulation, on the basis that it is contrary to the principle of proportionality. They are also suing the national potato marketing organisation to recover their deposit.

Advise Crinkley plc.

Answer plan

This problem question is seeking the application of **Arts 230** and **234** as a means of challenging a Community Act. In particular, the following points should be stressed:

- the requirements under **Art 230** for *locus standi* and the grounds for annulment;

- the procedures under **Art 234** and specifically the power of the ECJ under **Art 234** on questions of validity; and
- remedies.

Answer

There are two ways open to Crinkley to challenge the regulation which has affected them. One possibility is a direct action under **Art 230**, whereby they will bring an action before the ECJ and ask them to annul the regulation.

If they are successful, the Court could declare, under **Art 231**, the regulation *erga omnes* or, if appropriate, merely declare void that part of the regulation which is contrary to Community law and leave the rest of the regulation as lawful. Such a declaration would have an immediate impact on everyone within the Community. The alternative possibility is for Crinkley to seek to challenge the validity of the regulation in the English courts, probably in the action against the national potato marketing organisation to recover the deposit. In this situation, a successful challenge using the **Art 234** preliminary ruling procedure would have an immediate impact on Crinkley.

In order to bring an action under **Art 230**, it is necessary to satisfy the ECJ with regard to *locus standi*. Under **Art 230**, it is possible for an individual or company to institute proceedings against a regulation if it is in fact a decision and is of direct and individual concern to the individual or company. The measure in this problem is titled a regulation, although the name of the measure is not decisive in the view of the Court. A regulation under **Art 249** is of general application and has direct applicability throughout the Community. It is thus the main legislative or normative measure of the European Community. The main characteristic of a regulation is that it applies generally and objectively to categories of persons, whereas a decision binds those named individuals to whom it is addressed.

As far as the Court is concerned, a true regulation may not be challenged by an individual, as it stated in *Calpak* (1980). The problem for Crinkley is that the measure they are seeking to challenge does appear to satisfy the requirements of a regulation. Merely because it has had this financial impact on Crinkley, as against its effect on other potato product manufacturers, does not stop it being a regulation. In some cases, the Court has looked at the other requirements of **Art 230**, namely, that the measure is of 'direct and individual concern' to the applicant and, having concluded that it is, they have held that it cannot be legislative in character, that is, not a true regulation (*Sgarlata* (1965)). To satisfy the 'direct' requirement, it is merely necessary to show that there has been no exercise of discretion on the part of national authorities (*Toepfer v Commission* (1965)). However, 'individual concern' has been restrictively interpreted by the Court so as to make it very difficult for an individual to satisfy the Court on this matter.

In *Plaumann* (1963), a case involving the importation of clementines, the Court gives a good idea of the factors to be taken into account in deciding the criterion of 'individual concern'. If Crinkley could satisfy the requirement of *locus standi*, it would still have to satisfy the Court as to the ground for annulment specified in **Art 230**. Crinkley has already indicated that it wishes to challenge the regulation on the basis of proportionality. This is one of the general principles of Community law, initially derived from German law but now firmly recognised as being a Community principle. One of the most widely used grounds for annulment is 'infringement of this Treaty or of any rule of law relating to its application', which encompasses the claim that the principle of proportionality has been breached. The principle of proportionality requires that the means used must not be excessive in the context of the aim which it is intended to achieve. It has been successfully pleaded in a number of cases, including the *Skimmed Milk* case (1977). In this case, the ECJ had declared invalid an EC regulation which compelled producers of animal feeding stuff to add milk powder to their products in place of soya.

As an action under **Art 230** looks unlikely to materialise because of the problem of *locus standi*, it is necessary to look at an alternative possibility before the national courts. In order for Crinkley to use **Art 234**, a case must be brought before a court. This will be possible if the action is brought against the potato marketing organisation in an English court, probably the High Court. The judge hearing the action will have the discretion as to whether or not to make a reference to the ECJ. Under **Art 234**, the Court can give definitive answers to questions of interpretation and validity of Community Acts, which includes regulations. As the Court hearing the case will come within **Art 234**, the judge will have a discretion as indicated above. There are guidelines from previous cases heard in the UK to assist the judge in deciding whether to make a reference or not. The main one which is supported by the European Court is that it is important to ascertain the facts first. The Court prefers any reference to be set in the appropriate legal context. With regard to other factors, Lord Denning suggested, in *Bulmer v Bollinger* (1974), that time, cost, the workload of the European Court and the wishes of the parties should be taken into account. A number of references have been made by UK courts to the European Court on the validity of Community Acts, including regulations. In *R v Intervention Board for Agricultural Produce ex p ED and F Man (Sugar) Ltd* (1985), a large firm of sugar traders brought proceedings for judicial review of a decision based upon a Commission regulation. The grounds for the review included that the regulation was contrary to the principle of proportionality. On an **Art 234** reference, the Court answered that the regulation did contravene the principle and, to that extent, was invalid.

Does it make a difference to Crinkley that they probably do not have *locus standi* under **Art 230**? In the *Berlin Butter* case of *Ran v BALM* (1987), the Court stated, in response to an **Art 234** reference on the validity of a decision addressed to the German Government, that it is irrelevant whether the plaintiff would have *locus standi* under **Art 230**, or if, in fact, such an action had been initiated. Thus, it should not influence the judge in deciding whether to make a reference or not that an **Art 230** action is not possible. Is it possible, therefore, for the judge hearing the case in the national court to declare the regulation invalid without an **Art 234** reference? In the *Sugar* case (1985) mentioned above, the Divisional Court recognised that it could not make an order that the regulation was invalid. This view was clearly stated by the ECJ case of *Firma Foto-Frost* (1988). In this important case, the Court held that national courts could reject an argument based on invalidity of a Community measure, but they could not declare a measure invalid. National courts had a discretion whether or not to make a validity reference, but only the ECJ was competent to declare invalid the acts of Community institutions. One of the reasons given by the Court for this was that under the rules of procedure of the Court, Community institutions whose acts were being challenged were entitled to participate in the reference proceedings before the Court. Thus, they had the chance to defend their action before the Court before the measure was declared invalid.

What if the Court considers that Crinkley's view is well founded and agrees that the regulation is invalid? A special feature of invalidity rulings is the immediate consequence they may have outside the context of the actual case in which the question of validity is raised. In *International Chemical Corp SpA v Amministrazione delle Finanze dello Stato* (1981), the European Court held that, once an act had been declared void, a national court could not apply the act without creating serious uncertainty as to the Community law applicable. Therefore, although a judgment of the ECJ under **Art 234** declaring a regulation void is directly addressed only to the national court which referred the question, it is sufficient reason for any other national court to regard that act as void for the purposes of a judgment which it has to give. Thus, Crinkley will recover their deposit under national law if the regulation is declared invalid. However, the Court may decide to limit the retrospective effect of its rulings in order to leave previous transactions unaffected. The Court claimed jurisdiction to do this in proceedings under **Art 234**, by analogy with the power conferred upon it by **Art 231**, whereby the Court may state which of the effects of the regulation it has declared void (*Maize and Starch* cases (1980)).

My advice to Crinkley is that there is a presumption under Community law that a regulation is valid. Therefore, in order to defeat this presumption, an action must be brought which allows the European Court the opportunity to deliver its view on this matter. As an action under **Art 230** is unlikely, given its restrictive nature, a reference by a national court under **Art 234** seems the best way to challenge the regulation.

Although the national court under **Art 234** has a discretion as to whether or not it makes a reference, if a *prima facie* case can be made out by Crinkley, it is probable that a reference will be made. In the *Firma Foto-Frost* case, the ECJ suggested that a national court might grant interim relief even pending a ruling on validity, as happened in *Factortame Ltd v Secretary of State for Transport (No 3)* (1991). It has to be remembered that the national court cannot declare the regulation invalid, but merely uphold its validity. This issue was raised in *R (on the application of British American Tobacco) v Secretary of State for Health* (2003). If a reference is refused, Crinkley will have to be prepared to appeal, in the hope that a court which comes within **Art 234** will be obliged to make a reference to the European Court.

Question 22

Critically discuss the application of *acte clair* to Community law.

Answer plan

As well as appearing in problem questions concerning cases before courts within the **Art 234** definition, essay questions like this one can be set. You need to cover the following points:

- the role of **Art 234**;
- the specific interpretation of **Art 234**;
- the relationship between **Art 234(2)** and **234(3)** courts (formerly **Art 177(2)** and **(3)** respectively, but referred to throughout this answer using the new, post-**Amsterdam Treaty** numbering);
- the doctrine of *acte clair*;
- the impact of the decision in *CILFIT*; and
- the approach of UK courts.

Answer

The principle of *acte clair* is derived from French law. Its origin lies in the principle that the ordinary courts must seek a ruling from the Ministry of Foreign Affairs where a question of Treaty interpretation arises, unless the point of Treaty interpretation is clear. In such circumstances, no question of interpretation arises. It was not surprising, therefore, that the first courts to apply the doctrine to Community law were the French *Conseil d'Etat* and the *Cour de Cassation*. In *Re Shell-Berre* (1964), the *Conseil d'Etat* was concerned with the application by some oil companies for the annulment of a ministerial decree affecting garages selling petrol, contrary to

Art 31. The *Conseil d'Etat* refused to make a reference under **Art 234**, because that would only happen if there was any doubt as to the meaning or scope of the Treaty as it applied to the facts of the case.

The ECJ has accepted that a national court of last resort is not under a duty to make a reference under **Art 234** in certain circumstances. These are that the provision in question has already been interpreted by the Court, or where the correct application of European law is so obvious as to leave no scope for any reasonable doubt. This echoes the principle of *acte clair*. In *Da Costa en Schaake* (1963), the Court stated that the same question in this case had been referred in the case of *Van Gend en Loos* (1963) and had been answered to the effect that **Art 25** had direct effect. Therefore, the ECJ merely referred the Dutch administrative court to its previous decision. It went on to say that, if the Court had already pronounced on a question of interpretation, it may deprive the obligation to refer of its purpose and empty it of its substance. Prior to the case of *CILFIT SA v Ministry of Health* (1982), the ECJ had treated the obligation under **Art 234** as being a strict one, subject to only these derogations.

However, in the case of *CILFIT* (1982), the European Court appears to have accepted the principle of *acte clair*. The plaintiffs in this case were Italian companies which imported wool from non-member countries. Since 1968, they had been paying health inspection charges on those imports under Italian law. They now sought to argue that the Italian law was inapplicable by virtue of an EC regulation. The defendant, the Italian Ministry of Health, simply replied that the regulation did not apply to wool, as wool was not listed in Annex II to the Treaty. In spite of losing at first instance and on appeal, the plaintiffs took the case up to Italy's highest court, 'against whose decisions there is no judicial remedy under national law'. They claimed that this court was obliged by **Art 234(3)** to make a reference to the ECJ, although the Ministry of Health resisted the reference. They maintained that the solution was so obvious that it excluded any possibility of doubt as to the interpretation of the regulation and, hence, there was no need for a reference. In these circumstances, the Italian court did make a reference asking about the obligation to refer under **Art 234(3)**.

The Court said that, under **Art 234(3)**, the obligation to refer was based on co-operation between the national courts and the ECJ. This had been established with a view to ensuring the proper application and uniform interpretation of Community law in Member States and between national courts, in their capacity as courts responsible for the application of Community law. More particularly, it seeks to prevent divergences in judicial decisions on questions of Community law. The scope of the obligation to refer must be assessed in view of these obligations.

The Court went on to say that it follows from the relationship between **Art 234(2)** and **(3)** that courts and tribunals referred to in **Art 234** have the same discretion as any other national court or tribunal to ascertain whether a decision on a question of Community law is necessary to enable them to give judgment. Accordingly, these courts and tribunals are not obliged to refer to the ECJ a question concerning interpretation of Community law raised before them if that question is not relevant, that is to say, if the answer to that question, regardless of what it may be, can in no way affect the outcome of the case. The same effect, as regards the limits set to the obligation laid down by **Art 234**, may be produced where previous decisions of the ECJ have already dealt with the point of law in question, irrespective of the nature of proceedings which led to those decisions, even though the question at issue is not strictly identical.

Finally, the Court dealt with *acte clair*. It stated that the correct application of Community law may be so obvious as to leave no scope for any reasonable doubt as to the manner in which the question raised is to be resolved. However, before a court within **Art 234(3)** comes to the conclusion that such is the case, the national court or tribunal must be convinced that the matter is equally obvious to the courts and tribunals of other Member States and to the ECJ itself. It is only if these conditions are satisfied that the national court or tribunal may refrain from submitting the question to the ECJ and take upon itself the responsibility for resolving the point of Community law.

This apparent acceptance of the principle of *acte clair* must be treated with great circumspection. As the Court pointed out in its *CILFIT* judgment, the matter must be assessed on the basis of the characteristic features of Community law and the particular difficulties to which it gives rise. First, Community legislation is drafted in several languages and the different language versions are all equally authentic – interpretation, therefore, involves the comparison of different language versions. Secondly, Community law uses terminology which is peculiar to itself – also, legal concepts do not necessarily have the same meaning in Community law as in the law of various Member States. Thirdly, every provision of Community law must be placed in its context and interpreted in light of provisions of Community law as a whole, regard being had to the objectives thereof and to its state of evolution at the date on which the provision in question is to be applied.

In light of all these considerations, the Court concluded that the answer to the **Art 234(3)** question is that it is to be interpreted as meaning that courts and tribunals, against whose decision there is no judicial remedy under national law, are required, where a question of Community law is raised, to comply with their obligations to bring the matter before the ECJ, unless it was established that the question raised is irrelevant or the Community provision in question has already been interpreted, or that the correct application of Community law is so obvious as to leave no scope for any reasonable doubt.

In the UK, the House of Lords had adopted the approach recommended by the European Court in *CILFIT*. In *Henn and Darby v DPP* (1981), Lord Diplock stated that, in the light of the established case law of the European Court, which was so free from any doubt, there was no need for an interpretation of **Art 28** (then **Art 30**). However, because the interpretation of the Court of Appeal was contrary to this view, a reference was made to the ECJ. The Court of Appeal had held that a total import ban did not constitute a 'quantitative restriction on imports' within **Art 28** (then **Art 30**), because it did not relate to quantities! In fact, it was already well established in the case law of the ECJ that the term 'quantitative restriction' covered not only reductions in permitted levels of imports, but also outright bans. In *Garland v BREL* (1983), the House of Lords made a reference, not because of any doubt regarding the answer likely to be given by the ECJ, but because there was no consistent line of case law on **Art 266** (then **Art 199**) which would make the answer too obvious and inevitable.

There are dangers associated with the principle of *acte clair*, as the Court of Appeal aptly demonstrated in *Henn and Darby v DPP*. However, there are other examples where its possible misuse could lead to the misapplication or non-application of Community law by national courts. The case of *Cohn-Bendit* (1979) illustrates this point, where the *Conseil d'Etat* held, contrary to the case law of the ECJ, that a directive could not have direct effect. To counter such possibilities happening in Germany, the German Federal Constitutional Court emphasised in *Re Patented Feedingstuffs* (1989) that it will review any arbitrary refusal by a court subject to **Art 234(3)** to refer to the European Court.

Professor Rasmussen believes that the *CILFIT* judgment means something very different from what it *prima facie* establishes. For him, the real strategy of *CILFIT* is not to incorporate an *acte clair* concept into Community law, but to call the national judiciaries to circumspection when they are faced with problems of interpretation and application of Community law. 'The reins are not cut loose, although that might seem to be what the court ruled in *CILFIT*.' However, it must not be forgotten that, in all such circumstances, national courts and tribunals, including those in **Art 234(3)**, remain entirely at liberty to bring the matter before the ECJ if they consider it appropriate to do so. If the principle of acte clair is to be invoked in the context of European Community law, it must be on the basis of the criteria supplied by *CILFIT*.

CHAPTER 6

THE FREE MOVEMENT OF GOODS

INTRODUCTION

This is one of the fundamental freedoms of the European Community and is perhaps the most important one as far as examination questions are concerned.

Examiners set both problem and essay questions on this area of Community law and it is one which you are strongly advised to revise thoroughly. The benefit of this hard work is that many important principles have been developed through cases associated with the free movement of goods, so that you can use them as examples in answering questions on other topics, such as preliminary references or general principles of Community law.

Checklist

You should have a clear idea of the principles of a customs union (**Art 23**) and the following specific points:

- prohibition of import duties on imports and exports within the EU and of all charges of equivalent effect (**Art 25**);
- prohibition of discriminatory taxation (**Art 90**);
- prohibition of quantitative restrictions and measures having equivalent effect on imports (**Art 28**) and exports (**Art 29**);
- the *Dassonville* formula and *Cassis de Dijon* principles; and
- derogation from **Arts 28** and **29** via **Art 30**.

Question 23

Critically review the role played by the European Court of Justice (ECJ) in the removal of non-pecuniary barriers to trade between Member States.

Answer plan

This essay question requires an answer which covers the following points:

- **Arts 28** and **29**, as they affect barriers to trade;
- **Directive 70/50 EC**;
- the *Dassonville* formula;
- the first principle from *Cassis de Dijon* and the rule of reason and mandatory requirements; and
- the second principle of the *Cassis de Dijon* case on the marketing of goods in Member States.

Answer

The European Community is based upon free trade between Member States, brought about by the abolition of customs duties and charges of equivalent effect. However, there are other barriers to trade of a non-pecuniary nature which have to be removed. **Arts 28** and **29** are designed to eliminate these barriers. These Articles are addressed to the Member States, but neither the Community institutions nor individuals are free to act in breach of them. Even if the measure concerned is not binding, these Articles will apply. This was provided for by the European Commission in the **Preamble** to **Directive 70/50** and confirmed by the ECJ in the *Commission v Ireland* case (1982). The most important one is **Art 28**, which prohibits quantitative restrictions and all measures having equivalent effect on imports. 'Quantitative restrictions' was interpreted by the ECJ in *Riseria Luigi Geddo v Ente Nazionale Rise* (1974) to include any measures which amount to a total or partial restraint on imports, exports or goods in transit.

Measures having equivalent effect to quantitative restrictions is a wider concept than that of quantitative restrictions. More importantly, the concept has been given a very generous interpretation by both the European Commission and the European Court. It has been held to include not just those measures which are overtly protective or applicable to imports or exports, which are referred to as distinctly applicable measures, but also measures which are applicable to imports, exports and domestic goods alike. These measures are called indistinctly applicable measures, and are often introduced for the most worthy of reasons. They range from regulatory measures designed to enforce a minimum standard, such as weight, size, quality, price or content for products, to tests and inspections or certification requirements to ensure goods conform to the set standard. They also include activity capable of influencing the behaviour of traders, such as promoting goods by reason of their national origin. This occurred in the *Commission v Ireland* case (1987), where an agency of the Irish

Government promoted a 'buy Irish' campaign to promote Irish goods within the Irish Republic, which was held to be contrary to **Art 28**.

To assist Member States in the identification of measures having equivalent effect to quantitative restrictions, the Commission passed **Directive 70/50**. Although this Directive was aimed at the transitional period during which time such measures were to be abolished, the Directive has been seen as providing some non-binding guidelines to the interpretation of **Art 28**. The Directive was not intended to provide an exhaustive list of measures capable of having equivalent effect to quantitative restrictions. The Directive used the terminology indicated above by dividing such measures into two categories. The first was distinctly applicable measures, which hinder imports which could otherwise take place, including measures which make importation more difficult or expensive than domestic production (**Art 2(1)** of the Directive). The other category covers indistinctly applicable measures (**Art 3** of the Directive), which are only contrary to **Art 28** 'where the restrictive effect of such measures on the free movement of goods exceeds the effects intrinsic to trade rules', or where 'the same objective cannot be attained by other measures which are less of a hindrance to trade'. Thus, such measures appear to be acceptable if they comply with the Community's general principle of proportionality.

The ECJ has developed its own definition of measures having equivalent effect to quantitative restrictions. This was first achieved in the case of *Procureur du Roi v Dassonville* (1974), and has been applied consistently by the Court. The *Dassonville* 'formula' is that all trading rules enacted by Member States which are capable of hindering, directly or indirectly, actually or potentially, intra-Community trade are to be considered as measures having an effect equivalent to quantitative restrictions. From this formula, it can be seen that it is not necessary to show that the measure is an actual hindrance to trade between Member States, as long as it is capable of such effects. It is necessary, however, to show some proof of a hindrance to trade, because a measure which is not capable of hindering trade between Member States will not breach **Art 28**; for example, where the measure merely affects the flow of trade, as in the *Oebel Belgian Bakery* case (1981).

The measure in *Dassonville* was a requirement under Belgian law that imported goods should carry a certificate of origin issued by the State in which the goods were manufactured. Dassonville imported a quantity of Scotch whisky from France. Unfortunately, the seller did not have the required certificate, so he produced a 'homemade' one, and was subsequently charged with forgery. In his defence, he claimed that the Belgian law was contrary to Community law. The national court made a reference under **Art 234** (then **Art 177**) to the ECJ, which applied the *Dassonville* formula and found that the Belgian measure was capable of breaching **Art 28** (then **Art 30**).

The *Dassonville* formula was developed further in the *Cassis de Dijon* case, which identified two principles. Having applied the *Dassonville* formula to the facts of the case, the Court stated that obstacles resulting from disparities between the national laws relating to the marketing of products must be accepted in so far as they may be recognised as being necessary in order to satisfy mandatory requirements. Such requirements were listed as those relating to the effectiveness of fiscal supervision, the protection of public health, the fairness of commercial transactions and the defence of the consumer. This is known as the first *Cassis de Dijon* principle. Thus, certain measures may be within the *Dassonville* formula, but will not breach **Art 28** if they are necessary to satisfy such mandatory requirements. This principle has come to be known as the 'rule of reason'. Before the *Cassis* case, it was assumed that any measure which fell within the *Dassonville* formula was a breach of **Art 28**, and could only be saved by the permitted derogation under **Art 30**. Since *Cassis*, as far as indistinctly applicable measures are concerned, the rule of reason may apply and save them from **Art 28**. If the measure is necessary in order to protect mandatory requirements, it will not be a breach of **Art 28**. This is significant, since the mandatory requirements permitted under the *Cassis* principle are wider than the grounds provided under **Art 30**. For example, in *Commission v Denmark* (1986), regarding disposable beer cans, the protection of the environment was held to constitute a mandatory requirement. However, where the mandatory requirement falls under one of the specific heads of derogation provided by **Art 30**, the Court may prefer to rely on the express provision of that Article. This happened in *Commission v Germany Re German Sausage* (1989), where the derogation was on health grounds. In the *Cassis* case itself, it was felt that the derogation was not necessary.

The word 'necessary' has been interpreted to mean no more than is necessary and is subject to the principle of proportionality. Other measures could have been used to protect the consumer regarding the alcoholic content of Cassis, such as labelling, which would have been less of a hindrance to trade. It would also have been fair to the domestic producer. The second principle from the *Cassis* case has far-reaching implications. It is suggested that there is no valid reason why, 'provided that goods have been lawfully produced and marketed in one of the Member States, they should not be introduced into any other Member State'. This principle gives rise to the presumption that goods which have been lawfully marketed in another Member State will comply with the 'mandatory requirement' of the importing State. This can be rebutted by evidence that further measures are necessary to protect the interest concerned. It is hard to rebut this presumption. The burden of proving that the measure is necessary is a heavy one, particularly when, although justifiable in principle, it clearly operates as a hindrance to intra-Community trade. Any evidence submitted in support of the measure will be closely scrutinised by the Court. In the case concerning additives in beer (*Commission v Germany* (1985)), evidence was taken concerning the medical effect of such additives from the World Health Organization and the Food and Agriculture Organization.

The ECJ has played an important part in removing the barriers to trade associated with measures having an equivalent effect to quantitative restrictions. By the introduction of the 'rule of reason' to such measures and the extension of the two principles stated in the *Cassis de Dijon* case, the Court has to try to balance the need for applying **Art 28** with the need to respect the mandatory requirements justified under **Art 30**. Instead of the slow process of seeking Community-wide standards under the harmonisation procedures, where the interests of Member States could delay progress, the case law of the Court moved the Community forward in the direction of achieving its goal of a common market.

Question 24

Rodney is a farmer living in the Welsh mountains who specialises in breeding rare varieties of pigs and sheep. For some time Rodney sent the animals to the nearby market for sale to meat wholesalers, but he has now decided to change his marketing strategy. He felt that he was not getting the added value that his special sheep and pigs should command, so he decided to slaughter and market the animals himself, selling direct to the consumer. The internet has allowed him to sell a lot meat in the UK and he has now been approached by consumers in France who wish to buy his vacuum-packed joints of meat and special sausages. However, he has received a letter from the French meat marketing board, which raises the following objections to his sales in France.

They claim that as his packs of meat are not labelled in French, they cannot be sold in France; the price list he included with the meat indicated that he was selling his meat below the minimum price set in France, and thus contrary to French law; the sausages contain additives which, although permitted under English law, are banned under French law; the pre-packed joints of meat do not comply with French standards of consumer protection with regard to weight, and finally that the selling of meat by post is contrary to French law.

Rodney feels that the French love of good food will provide a profitable market for his meat and sausages, so he seeks your advice as to the points raised by the French authorities.

Answer plan

This question represents the typical problem associated with the free movement of goods. The approach you should take is to state the principles and then apply them to the individual aspects of the problem.

You should deal with the following points:

- **Art 28** and barriers to trade;

- definitions and examples of quantitative restrictions and measures having equivalent effect;
- the *Dassonville* formula;
- the principles of *Cassis de Dijon*;
- the distinction between **Article 28 EC** and the categories of selling arrangements following the *Keck* case; and
- remedies.

Answer

Article 14 underlines the importance of the free movement of goods in the context of the four freedoms associated with the objectives of the Community. The internal market is identified as an area without internal frontiers in which the free movement of goods is protected and all obstacles to trade are removed. It has been relatively easy for the Community to deal with the more obvious barriers to trade, such as tariffs. It has been the non-pecuniary barriers or measures that are equivalent to quantitative restrictions, which are more subtle and disguised, that have caused problems, such as those experienced by Rodney. **Article 28** provides that barriers to trade which amount to quantitative restrictions and all measures having equivalent effect are prohibited. Such quantitative restrictions were interpreted by the ECJ in *Riseria Luigi Geddo v Ente Nazionale Risi* (1974) to cover any measure which amounts to a total or partial restraint on trade between Member States.

The concept of measures having equivalent effect to quantitative restrictions has been given a wide interpretation by the ECJ. It is much wider than mere quantitative restrictions. To assist with the application of the concept, it is divided into those measures which are indistinctly applicable and those which are distinctly applicable. Indistinctly applicable measures are often introduced by governments for seemingly the most worthy of purposes. As such measures are applied to both imported and domestically produced goods alike, they are often thought by the government concerned not to discriminate in any way and not to fall within the prohibitions of **Article 28**. Such measures include regulatory controls designed to enforce minimum standards, such as price, which occurs in Rodney's problem. Distinctly applicable measures are those which are applicable only to imported goods.

In the problem, the French Government has introduced standards for packaging any meat product. This was introduced to protect consumers. This measure comes within the category of indistinctly applicable measures, as it applies to both French and imported products of this type. It was **Directive 70/50** which introduced the categories of measures having equivalent effect to quantitative restrictions in order to help Member States to identify and eliminate such measures in the transitional period. Although this period has passed, the Directive is still seen as providing non-binding guidelines to the interpretation of **Art 28**. It is **Art 3** of the Directive which deals with indistinctly applicable measures. Such measures are said to be only contrary to **Art 28** if they do not satisfy the principle of proportionality; that is, if the same objective cannot be attained by other measures which are less of a hindrance to trade.

However, it is the case law of the European Court which is of most importance to Rodney. Building upon the Directive, the Court has given some very important judgments in this area of Community law. The first case was *Procureur du Roi v Dassonville* (1974), which led to the development of the *Dassonville* formula. Dassonville had imported some Scotch whisky from France. Under Belgian law, it was necessary to have a certificate of origin from the State in which the goods had been manufactured. As the seller did not have such a certificate, he produced one of his own. When he was subsequently charged with forgery, he claimed that the Belgian law was contrary to Community law. The Belgian court made a request for a preliminary ruling under **Art 234**. In its reply the ECJ referred to the *Dassonville* formula, which stated that the Belgian measure was capable of breaching **Art 28**. The formula is that all trading rules enacted by Member States which are capable of hindering, directly or indirectly, actually or potentially, intra-Community trade are to be considered as measures having an effect equivalent to quantitative restrictions.

In *Cassis de Dijon* (1978), the *Dassonville* formula was extended. In this case, a German law required the minimum alcohol content of Cassis to be 25%, whereas that imported from France was 15–20%. When it was challenged by the importer, the Court applied the *Dassonville* formula and held that the German law contravened **Art 28** (then **Art 30**). In rejecting the claim that they were protecting public health and the consumer, the Court stated that this could be achieved by the alcoholic content of the different products being stated on the label. Under the first principle, certain measures may fall within the *Dassonville* formula, but will not breach **Art 28** if they are necessary to satisfy mandatory requirements of the public interest. These include protection of public health and the defence of the consumer, and are wider than those listed in **Art 30**. This principle has become known as the 'rule of reason'. However, the national measure must be proved to serve a purpose which is in the general interest and has to take precedence over the requirements of the free movement of goods. Thus, if the measure is necessary in order to protect mandatory requirements, it will not breach **Art 28**.

The second principle derived from the *Cassis de Dijon* case gives rise to a presumption that goods which have been lawfully marketed in one Member State will comply with the 'mandatory requirements' of the importing State. This presumption can be rebutted, but it is very difficult to do so. The burden of proving that the measure is necessary to protect the interest concerned falls on the Member State which imposed it. Although the measure may be justifiable in principle, such measures clearly operate as a hindrance to intra-Community trade.

For his business to prosper, Rodney needs to challenge the French law and obtain a judgment that it is contrary to Community law. The most direct way to do this is to seek to sell a quantity of his meat and sausages in France and to be charged with contravening the domestic legislation. Once the case is before a court, he can request them to declare the legislation to be contrary to the provisions of Community law. The court will probably be reluctant to do this without a reference being made to the ECJ under **Art 234**. The discretion to make such a request under **Art 234** belongs to the court alone, but having raised the matter of Community law, the court can either decide the point itself or make a reference. It may be in Rodney's interest for the court to decide the matter itself, as a reference can take up to 18 months. Whatever the court decides to do, it is the principles of Community law outlined above which will be applied. It will be necessary to apply the principle of proportionality to ensure that the measures that go beyond what is strictly necessary to achieve the desired end are held to be contrary to Community law. It is therefore important to see how the ECJ has dealt with cases similar to Rodney's, because, as in *Greenham and Abel* (2004), the onus is on the French to show that their rules are necessary.

The first issue is the requirement that labelling should be in French. The ECJ in *Colim NV v Bigg's Continent Noord NV* (1997) made a distinction between linguistic requirements imposed by Community law and information required by national law with regard to labelling. Applying the second *Cassis* principle, Rodney's meat must be admitted to the French market, as it is marketed in the UK. The second point raised in the letter refers to the minimum selling price for meat in France, and following the case of *Keck and Mithouard* (1993) this would not be covered by **Art 28** but would be seen as a selling arrangement. Such an arrangement would be outside **Art 28** if the rule applied indistinctly to all traders operating within the territory and affected the marketing of both domestic and imported products. The same point would be made about the sale of meat by post. In the case of *Deutsche Apothekerverband* (2003) the internet was used for the sale of pharmaceutical products by mail order. In clarifying its case law, the Court said that the application to products from other Member States of national provisions restricting or prohibiting certain selling arrangements was not such as to hinder directly or indirectly, actually or potentially, trade between Member States within the meaning of the *Dassonville* judgment. This was provided that those provisions applied to all affected traders operating within the national territory and affected them the same way, both legally and factually. Obviously those who wished to sell by mail order from outside the country were at a disadvantage.

Another point raised by the French official deals with the weight of the pre-packed joints of meat. This measure appears to be indistinctly applicable, and since the *Cassis* case, it is necessary for any court hearing the case to apply the rule of reason to **Art 28**. Is the measure necessary to protect the mandatory requirement of consumer protection? If it is, then it will not breach **Art 28**. However, the ECJ case law has shown that the word 'necessary' has been interpreted to mean no more than is necessary by applying the principle of proportionality. As indicated above, the German Government in the *Cassis* case did not succeed with their defence, because the consumer could have been protected by some other means. In *Commission v Germany* (1985), a case was brought against the German prohibition of additives in imported beer. The European Court held that the prohibition of marketing products containing additives authorised in the Member State of production, but prohibited in the Member State of importation, is permissible only if it complies with the requirements of **Art 30**. But, the Court emphasised the last sentence of **Art 30**, which states that such prohibitions should not constitute a means of arbitrary discrimination or a disguised restriction on trade between Member States. The Court concluded that the use of a specific additive which is authorised in another Member State must be authorised in the case of a product imported from that Member State. In *Commission v Germany* (1989), German law on the meat content of sausages could not be enforced against imported sausages where there was no threat to health to invoke the derogation allowed to Member States under **Art 30**. This was held to be in breach of **Art 28** because the objective could have been achieved by other means, such as labelling, which would be less of a hindrance to trade. Here again, it would seem that Rodney can defeat any attempt by the French Government to justify the measures as being a mandatory requirement.

Question 25

Some time ago, Robson Pharmaceutical plc developed a new product to relieve flu symptoms and granted the right to sell under the Robson trade mark to two companies: one in Germany and one in the Netherlands. Robson Pharmaceutical plc kept the UK market and exports outside the European Economic Area (EEA).

Three months ago, the German company reported to Robson that their products were appearing on the German market. The goods had been purchased in the UK and Malaysia from pharmaceutical wholesalers and transported to Germany, where the packaging had been altered to conform to German drug laws. The German price for the Robson product is 30% higher than the price in the UK.

Robson Pharmaceutical have discovered that an English company, PharmaJones Ltd, are responsible for the exports to Germany. They have complained to the UK Government, as have the German company to their Government, and a joint approach was made to the Commission to stop this movement under **Art 30**. Robson Pharmaceutical have also contacted PharmaJones Ltd direct, but their response was that any action against them would be contrary to the free movement of goods.

Advise Robson Pharmaceutical plc.

Answer plan

As you read this question, you should mark those passages which you feel cover the facts and are relevant to the law, and make sure that you deal with them in your answer. The main points to cover are:

- **Arts 28** and **29**, stating the policy of free movement for imports and exports;
- the principles from *Cassis de Dijon*;
- derogation under **Art 30**;
- rights associated with trade marks;
- the **Trade Mark Directive (89/104/EEC)**.

Answer

This question concerns the free movement of goods, one of the fundamental principles of the European Community. The Community is based upon a customs union which provides for a common customs tariff to goods coming from outside the EC and the removal of barriers to the free movement of goods within the EC. This applies to both imports (**Art 28**) and exports (**Art 29**) between Member States. These Articles are aimed at the governments of Member States, but have implications for individual business organisations. The EC does not want to have a situation where governments remove barriers, only for companies to organise their operations so as to set up new ones. If a number of companies operate in this way, competition policy under **Arts 81** and **82** may be involved. However, in this problem, Robson Pharmaceutical plc do not appear to be acting in agreement with other undertakings or in a dominant position, so I will not look at the competition aspects of this problem in detail. What is more applicable is **Art 30**, which allows derogation from **Arts 28** and 29 on specific grounds with the overall requirement that there is not an arbitrary discrimination or a disguised restriction on trade between Member States. The essential function of a trade mark is to guarantee to consumers the real origin of goods or services (*Arsenal Football Club plc v Reed* (2002)).

There is a presumption in favour of goods lawfully marketed in one Member State of the Community being accepted in another Member State. This was clearly stated in the second principle identified by the Court in *Cassis de Dijon* (1978). If a company or State is seeking to rebut that principle, it must prove that the conditions are such that **Art 30** is applicable. This Article gives a number of grounds that are only available to the government of a Member State, for example, where it is claimed that restrictions are justified on the grounds of public policy or public security. However, it is possible for a business to seek derogation under **Art 30** on the ground of 'protection of industrial and commercial property'. This includes such intellectual property rights as patents, copyright and trade marks. This supports the recognition given in the Treaty that property rights have not been affected by the establishment of the EC. **Article 295** states that the Treaty shall in no way prejudice the rules in the Member States governing the system of property ownership.

If Robson Pharmaceutical plc are to achieve a solution to their problem, they must seek assistance from **Art 30**. How much protection will this Article give to them?

In *Deutsche Grammophon* (1981), concerning copyright, the ECJ stated that **Art 30** (then **Art 36**) permitted prohibitions or restrictions on the free movement of goods only to the extent that they were justified for the protection of the rights that form the specific subject matter of the property. In other words, it is necessary to look at what the owner of the property right is seeking to protect. Given that **Art 295** (then **Art 222**) clearly states that property rights have not been affected by the Community, the Court could not dispute this. However, the Court went on to draw a distinction between the existence of industrial property rights and their exercise. It was this latter aspect of property rights which could interfere with the free movement of goods and which the Court wanted to ensure was not in conflict with the integration of the 'common market'. This principle does not only apply to copyright, but to all intellectual property.

In the pharmaceutical case of *Centrafarm BV v Winthrop BV* (1974), a claim was made by Winthrop that their trade mark had been infringed. What right did the trade mark holder have? The Court held that they had the exclusive right to use the trade mark for the purposes of putting into circulation products protected by the trade mark for the first time. They might either do this themselves or transfer that right to a third party by way of licences, etc. Once the protected product has been put onto the market in a particular State by or with the consent of the owner, he can no longer be allowed to rely on his national property rights to prevent the importation of that product from that State into other Member States. The rights that are associated with the trade mark are exhausted. This doctrine of exhaustion of rights has been applied by the court to all types of property rights, including trade marks, patents and copyright – for example, see *Pharmacia & Upjohn SA v Paranova SA* (1997).

In this problem, Robson Pharmaceutical are the owners of the trade mark and therefore have the rights described above. They exercise these rights themselves in certain countries, but have consented to two companies exercising this right on their behalf in Germany and Holland. If a product like flu remedy has been lawfully put onto the market with the owner's consent in one Member State, the importation of that product into another Member State cannot be restricted. This will apply even if, as in Robson Pharmaceutical's case, the purpose is to prevent parties taking advantage of price differences in different Member States. This is, after all, what was attempted in *Centrafarm v Winthrop*. (The emphasis in that case was to ask what makes a trade mark valuable – the reservation to the owner, through his exclusive right to put marked products into circulation, or the goodwill associated with the mark.)

There have been cases where importers have sought to take advantage of the price differentials which apply in different Member States and the exhaustion principle, but the product has had to be repackaged or labelled to meet the requirements of that particular market. This is what has happened in this problem to meet the specification of the German drug laws. In the case of *Hoffman-La Roche v Centrafarm* (1978) a similar situation arose regarding the product 'Valium'. In the UK a subsidiary of the Roche group marketed the product in packages of 100 or 500 tablets at lower prices than in Germany.

Centrafarm purchased these UK products and repackaged them in 1,000 tablets, affixed the Hoffman-La Roche trade mark and sold them in Germany. Obviously, Hoffman-La Roche sought to protect what they saw as an infringement of their trade mark. In this important case, the ECJ laid down certain conditions which, if met by the importer, mean that the repackager cannot be restrained by the trade mark holder from importing the product. The conditions illustrate the possibility that the holder of the trade mark may seek to organise the marketing of his product so as to constitute a disguised restriction on trade between Member States. In *Centrafarm v American Home Products* (1978), the Court recognised this danger even though the use of different marks in the UK and the Netherlands could be justified under **Art 30** (then **Art 36**). The importer in *Pfizer Inc v Eurim-Pharm GmbH* (1981) followed these guidelines when importing Vibramycin tablets manufactured by Pfizer in the UK into Germany. In this case, the Court held that the plaintiff company could not rely on its trade mark and **Art 30** (then **Art 36**) to prevent the importation under these circumstances.

However, the principle of 'exhaustion of rights' only applies within the Community. The ECJ has been concerned that individual Member States cannot create their own rules regarding exhaustion of rights where the goods are imported from outside the EC. In the important case of *Silhouette International* (1998), the ECJ stated that the exhaustion of rights does not and cannot apply where goods placed on the market outside the EEA are brought into and sold within the EEA, which obviously includes the EC. The only exception to this appears to be where the trade mark owner can be said to have consented to the importation, circulation and sale. This was the view applied by the High Court in *Zino Davidoff SA v A&G Imports Ltd (No 1)*.

My advice to Robson Pharmaceutical plc is that they have a genuine difficulty, in the sense that the ECJ has given a very narrow interpretation to **Art 30**, because it has given greater significance to the last sentence of the Article. Robson are seeking to protect their trade mark, whose essential function is to guarantee to consumers or final users the original identity of the marked product, so as to avoid confusion. They could bring an action in the national court seeking to enforce this right by a request for an injunction against PharmaJones Ltd and damages for the infringement of their right. However, as has been shown above, the ECJ has developed a clear principle in these cases in such examples as *Hoffman-La Roche v Centrafarm*. Whether the national court decides or makes a preliminary reference to the ECJ, it is this principle which will be applied. The problem does not indicate the form of the repackaging or what information is printed on it. However, it is clear from the question that PharmaJones Ltd did not communicate with Robson Pharmaceutical about their intention to repackage and import into Germany. This is one of the conditions laid down in *Hoffman-La Roche v Centrafarm* and met successfully in the *Pfizer* case. It is possible that on PharmaJones Ltd failing to meet all the conditions, Robson Pharmaceutical may be able to protect how they currently operate if it is not considered to be a means of arbitrary discrimination or a disguised restriction on trade between Member States. If the repackaging had led to defacing or removal of important information, this form of repackaging would not be considered appropriate, as was decided in the *Zino Davidoff* case.

However, if PharmaJones Ltd give the appropriate notice, assuming the packaging is acceptable, they will then meet all the conditions laid down by the ECJ with regard to exhaustion of trade mark rights within the EC. However, the 'grey or parallel import' market is a very profitable one and is worldwide. Thus with regard to the importation from Malaysia, the rights of the trade mark owner have not been exhausted and Robson Pharmaceutical can take action to enforce their rights, as happened in *Sebago Inc v GB Unie SA* (1998) and *Bristol Myers Squibb v Parnova* (1993).

Question 26

Analyse TWO of the following cases which came before the ECJ, and explain their importance in the development of Community law:

(a) *Cassis de Dijon* – Case 120/78;

(b) *Commission v Ireland* – Case 249/81;

(c) *Centrafarm v Sterling Drug* – Case 15/74.

Answer plan

When approaching a question like this, the temptation is to produce too descriptive an answer. The facts are important, but are only one element of the answer. You should try to deal with the following:

• the facts, the legal points raised and the decision of the Court.

- the kind of case it was – whether a preliminary reference or a direct action and which Article of the Treaty it was based upon.
- the cases chosen for this type of question have usually played their part in developing or reinforcing European Court judgments – what part has this case played?

Answer

(a) Cassis de Dijon – Case 120/78

This action was brought in a German court because of the application of a German law which forbade the marketing of liqueurs with a low alcohol content. The French liqueur called Cassis de Dijon had a maximum strength of 20% alcohol by volume, whereas German law required a minimum content of 25%. The French company claimed that the German law was contrary to **Art 28** (then **Art 30**), as it interfered with the free movement of goods. Although the German authorities were not affecting the free movement of goods by imposing quotas, their actions were still covered by **Art 28** (then **Art 30**). This is because the Article also forbids measures having an equivalent effect to quotas.

The German authorities claimed that the law did not discriminate against the French liqueur, as the same minimum content also applied to German producers. To allow the 'milder' French drink to be treated as a liqueur would lead to a reduction in alcohol content applied to German producers and thus a lowering standard. In order to avoid the application of **Art 28** (then **Art 30**), the German Government had to plead **Art 30** (then **Art 36**). This Article allows a government of a Member State to derogate from its obligations under **Art 28** on such grounds as public policy, public morality, public security or the protection of the health and life of humans, animals and plants. Specifically, the German Government argued that its minimum standard law was inspired by the wish to protect the consumer from alcoholism, that is, public health. However, **Art 30** ends by saying that it shall not be used as a means of disguised restriction of trade.

The ECJ said that, in the absence of common rules to the production and marketing of alcohol, it is for the Member State to regulate, in that they are necessary to satisfy fiscal supervision, the protection of public health, the defence of the consumer and the fairness of commercial transactions. These points were raised by the German Government. They said that public health was protected by fixing a minimum alcohol content, as beverages with a low alcohol content more easily induce a tolerance towards alcohol. There would be a general lowering of standards, as the lowest alcohol content permitted in any Member State would become the Community standard. This was rejected by the Court, as stronger beverages were generally consumed in a diluted form. They also rejected the claim that lower alcohol contents would lead to unfair practices against consumers.

As far as the Court was concerned, the requirements set by the German Government relating to the minimum alcohol content did not serve the general interest and interfered with the fundamental principle of the free movement of goods. It would be a much simpler matter to ensure that suitable information is conveyed to the purchaser by requiring the display of an indication of origin and of the alcohol content on the packaging of products.

(b) Commission v Ireland – Case 249/81

Faced with economic problems, the Irish Government announced in 1978 a programme to create jobs in Ireland's manufacturing and service industries. The main platform for this policy was to persuade individuals to purchase Irish goods. Supported by public funds, a 'Buy Irish' campaign was launched, involving the Irish Goods Council and the use of a 'Guaranteed Irish' symbol. In 1981, the European Commission delivered its Reasoned Opinion that the campaign was equivalent to a quantitative restriction on imports and in breach of **Art 28** (then **Art 30**). This Article prohibits all quantitative restrictions on imports and all measures having equivalent effect. The concept of measures having an equivalent effect has been interpreted very generously by the Court, to include any activity capable of influencing the behaviour of traders.

The Reasoned Opinion is a requirement when the Commission is seeking to exercise its powers under **Art 226** against a Member State which is failing to fulfil its obligations under the Treaty. It is the final step in the administrative stage before the Commission decides whether to take the Member State before the ECJ. The Reasoned Opinion has to provide details of the failure on the part of the Member State, the action required to be taken and the timescale in which this must be done.

The Irish Government argued that the campaign was not contrary to **Art 28** (then **Art 30**). They did so by arguing that the prohibition only applies to measures which are binding. All that the campaign did was to give moral support and some financial aid for advertising the activities pursued by the Irish industries. The aid was compatible with **Art 87** (then **Art 92**), which permits State aid to industry for such purposes as combating unemployment. They also claimed that there had been no restrictive effect on trade, as the campaign had failed. During the campaign, the proportion of Irish goods to all goods sold on the Irish market fell from 49.2% to 43.4%!

The Court rejected these arguments, because they believed that the Irish Government's considered intention was to substitute domestic products for imported products on the Irish market and thereby to check the flow of imports from other Member States. Even though the campaign did not have any significant success, the Court could not overlook the fact that the activities formed part of a government pro-gramme which was designed to achieve this substitution of domestic products for imported products and, as such, was liable to affect the volume of trade between Member States. The 'Buy Irish' campaign was discriminatory and had a potential effect on imports from other Member States as if it were one of a binding nature.

A measure like this cannot escape the prohibition laid down in **Art 28** solely because it is not based on decisions which are binding on businesses. Even measures which are not binding may be capable of influencing the conduct of traders and consumers and thus of frustrating the aims of the Community set out in **Arts 2** and **3**. The action of the Irish Government was a restrictive practice which represented the implementation of a programme defined by the Government and which affected the economy as a whole by encouraging the purchase of domestic products. Given that the Irish Government had provided some financial funding for the campaign, they were in breach of their obligations under the Treaty. The judgment in this case should not have come as a surprise to the Irish Government, as they had already been the subject of an **Art 226** (then **Art 169**) action by the Commission in Case 113/80. In that case, the Court had held that the Irish Government had breached **Art 28** (then **Art 30**) by imposing a legal requirement that imported 'souvenirs of Ireland' should bear either the name of their country of origin or the word 'foreign'.

(c) Centrafarm v Sterling Drug – Case 15/74

Sterling Drug was the parent company holding a number of patents in several countries, including the Netherlands and the UK, for a treatment of infections of the urinary passages. The trade mark Negram is used for this product. In the UK, the trade mark was the property of Sterling-Winthrop Group Ltd and, in the Netherlands, Winthrop BV, a subsidiary of the UK company.

Centrafarm imported into the Netherlands from England and Germany some of the medicinal preparations manufactured according to the patent method and put onto the market by subsidiaries of Sterling Drug, some of which carried the trade mark Negram. They did this without the agreement of Sterling Drug. By importing from the UK, Centrafarm had been able to take advantage of a considerable price differential. This was almost 50% of the price charged in the Netherlands.

In June 1971, Sterling Drug submitted an application to a Dutch judge sitting in chambers requiring Centrafarm to refrain from any further infringement of their patent. The judge refused, on the basis of his interpretation of the patent law. Sterling Drug succeeded on appeal, and the case finally came to the Dutch Supreme Court on appeal by Centrafarm. This Court used the preliminary reference procedure of **Art 234** (then **Art 177**) to ask certain questions on patent rights in relation to the provisions of the Treaty.

The European Court accepted that the main issue was whether the Treaty rules on the free movement of goods prevented the patentee from ensuring that the product protected by the patent is not marketed by others. It referred to **Art 28** (then **Art 30**) and the prohibition on quantitative restrictions on imports and all measures having equivalent effect. However, it recognised that **Art 30** (then **Art 36**) did allow such restrictions or prohibitions on the grounds justified for the protection of commercial or industrial property, which would include patents. This had to be read in conjunction with the last sentence of **Art 30** (then **Art 36**), which states that such restrictions shall not constitute a means of arbitrary discrimination or a disguised restriction on trade between Member States.

Given that the **EC Treaty** does not interfere with property rights, the Court looked at the exercise of those rights. **Article 30** allows for the derogation from one of the fundamental principles of the Community, but only where the derogation is justified for the purposes of safeguarding rights which constitute the specific subject matter of the property. What are these rights in relation to patents? The Court answered that the specific subject matter of a patent was the guaranteed right of the patentee, as a reward for its creative effort, to manufacture and put into circulation its product for the first time. This could be done directly by the company or by the grant of licences to third parties. In relation to this right, the patent holder could seek enforcement of its rights.

What the Court was concerned to do was not to allow the exercise of a patentee's right to interfere with the development of the Community. If the patentee could prevent the importation of protected products marketed by him or with his consent in another Member State, he would be able to partition off national markets and thereby restrict trade between Member States. Therefore, the action of Sterling Drug, given that it was not necessary to protect their exclusive rights flowing from their patent, was incompatible with the Treaty provisions concerning the free movement of goods. This principle has been applied in subsequent cases, especially where drug companies have sought to use their property rights to block parallel imports from other Member States.

CHAPTER 7

COMPETITION POLICY

▌INTRODUCTION

The competition policy of the European Community is seen as a very important safeguard to its development. Many of the questions set on this topic are of the problem type, notably on the application of **Arts 81** and **82**. However, there are possible essay questions on the main principles, as illustrated by some of the questions in this chapter. It is also possible for questions to be set which have a competition element and relate to the free movement of goods, for example, the Robson Pharmaceutical problem in Question 25. In such circumstances, you can either split your answer between the topics or indicate the possible involvement of one but concentrate on the other.

Checklist

You should have a clear knowledge of the differences between **Arts 81** and **82** and the role each plays in the competition policy of the EU. More specifically, you should understand the following points:

- the type of agreements dealt with by **Art 81**;
- the possible exemptions under **Art 81**;
- the meaning of dominant position under **Art 82**;
- the control of mergers within the EU;
- the sanctions for anti-competitive behaviour;
- the control of public anti-competitive behaviour under **Arts 87** and **88**;
- the role and powers of the European Commission; and
- the remedies available, including those provided by the national courts.

Question 27

Dicero plc have been purchasing large quantities of manopull textiles from Smart International, a German company, for five years. They are the only manufacturers of this product and they control world sales by a system of licensing agreements.

Two years ago, they began imposing retail prices on all purchasers, including Dicero, and restricted the distribution areas any company could control. Dicero were allocated the UK market, whereas companies in France and Italy were given their domestic market plus a share of the world market.

For the last 12 months, Dicero have had discussions with Smart International to try to obtain some of the necessary export markets to allow for viable production levels. They have conceded nothing. In fact, they have stated that, unless Dicero sign a new agreement with them, they will give the UK market to the French company.

Advise Dicero.

Answer plan

This traditional problem question requires the application of **Art 81**, and the following specific points:

- the relationship between Community and national competition law;
- a definition of 'dominance' within the meaning of **Art 82**;
- factors associated with dominance in fact;
- abuse of a dominant position; and
- remedies.

Answer

This problem is concerned with one undertaking, Smart International, acting in a way which appears to be anti-competitive. The EU, having as one of its objectives the removal of barriers to trade between Member States, takes a strong policy against any undertaking which seeks to exercise economic power in the market in a way which sets up barriers to such trade. Under **Art 82**, monopolies in themselves are not prohibited, but it does prohibit certain anti-competitive conduct by such organisations. The Article applies to either goods or services and has a scope that is not limited to those businesses which are established in the EU.

It would seem that Dicero plc may have a remedy under this provision of the Treaty. If they can prove that Smart International are acting in breach of **Art 82**, such action is prohibited by the Article. In order to satisfy **Art 82**, three essential ingredients must be proved. The undertaking must have a dominant position in the market, there must be an abuse of that position and that abuse must affect trade between Member States. If this last requirement is not met, the matter is left to be dealt with by the national competition laws of the Member State concerned.

In order to prove that Smart International are in a dominant position, Dicero need to satisfy the definition of dominance laid down by the ECJ in *United Brands Co v Commission* (1976). This case involved United Brands' position in the banana market. The Court said that dominance means a position of economic strength enjoyed by an undertaking which enables it to prevent effective competition in the relevant market because its strength allows it to act independently of its competitors, customers and ultimately its consumers. The Commission added to this, in the *AKZO Chemie BV* case (1986), that it may also involve the ability to eliminate or seriously weaken existing competitors, or to prevent potential competitors from entering the market.

Although this is the principle of dominance, it has to be looked at more closely if the rules of the Court are to be satisfied. It may be possible to say that this is the way that Smart International are acting, but are they in a dominant position?

Specifically, what is the market in which Dicero are claiming that Smart International are dominant? This is not as straightforward as it may appear, as the European Commission has found when seeking to apply **Art 82**. It is necessary to identify the relevant market. As far as the Court and Commission are concerned, this is a matter of product substitution. In the *Continental Can* case (1972), a large Dutch packaging company was being taken over by a subsidiary of the Continental Can company based in the USA.

The Continental Can company was a large organisation in the packaging industry, controlling 86% of a German metal containers company, which it intended to transfer to the Dutch company if it acquired it. This would have meant that Continental Can would have had significant market power in Europe and specifically in Germany. However, although the Court agreed with the Commission that the takeover could be an abuse, the Commission had not looked at the relevant market. It had not taken into account product substitution. In other words, alternative suppliers of cans could adapt their production to produce cylindrical cans suitable for fish or those who purchased the cans could swap to a different shape or design. Such product substitution can be assessed by reference to the characteristics of the product, its price or the use to which it may be put. Are there any substitutes for manopull? What market is it in?

Although the Commission got the market wrong in *Continental Can*, in the bananas case of *United Brands* it satisfied the Court that the banana market was distinctive. In that case, United Brands had argued that the correct market was the fresh fruit market, in which they were not dominant. However, by means of information about buying habits of consumers and the special characteristics of bananas, the Commission was able to defeat this argument. Could Smart International argue that the consumer had alternative textiles to select from and therefore would not be disadvantaged by their actions? In the *Commercial Solvents* case (1974), the Court stated that **Art 82** (then **Art 86**) was concerned not only with abuses which prejudiced consumers directly, but also those abuses which impair the competitive structure of the market and thus affect consumers indirectly. It would appear that Smart International's action falls into this type of category. The Commission, supported by judgments of the Court, takes a hard line in seeking to protect competition in manufacturing and, in particular, to prevent smaller firms suffering at the hands of more powerful competitors. We are not told the size of Smart International or Dicero, but even where the relevant market has been quite small, as in the *Hugin Cash Registers* case, **Art 82** has been applied, provided an undertaking has been dominant in the particular market.

If it is assumed that it is possible to identify the relevant market, are Smart International behaving in a way which does not need to take into account their competitors, purchasers or consumers? In other words, are they dominant in fact? This requires a wide-ranging economic analysis of the market and Smart International. Following previous Commission decisions, four factors are taken into account. The first of these, and the most important, is market share. How big a share of the market do Smart International have? Secondly, how long have Smart International held this position in the market? Obviously, the longer the period of time, the greater the barriers to entry for new competitors or entrants to the market will be. Thirdly, the financial and technological resources of Smart International: can they use their resources to use predatory pricing to undercut potential rivals or to maintain their technological advantage? Lastly, access to raw materials and outlets may give Smart International more power. Do they control not only raw materials and production, but also applications or retail outlets? This form of vertical integration within their business will be evidence of a dominant undertaking.

Finally, in order to come within **Art 82**, it must also be proved that Smart International are dominant within the common market or in a substantial part of it. We are told that Smart International control sales in the world but, more importantly, within the European Community by means of licensing agreements. It is clear, therefore, that this criterion is satisfied.

Having identified that there is a dominant position, this does not mean that **Art 82** has been satisfied. It is not the fact that an undertaking is in a dominant position which is sufficient; Dicero must show that there has been an abuse. **Article 82** itself provides a number of examples of abuse. This list is not to be considered exhaustive, but it does illustrate what Dicero could prove. The problem states that Smart International are restricting the distribution area of each company granted a licence. More importantly, Smart International have threatened to refuse to supply Dicero if they refuse to sign the agreement. The refusal to supply in *United Brands* was found to be an abuse. In *Commercial Solvents*, the anti-competitive refusal to supply also amounted to an abuse. This will not always be the situation if the refusal is based on objective criteria and is non-discriminatory. It does not appear that this would be the case with Smart International.

If an undertaking is found to be abusing its dominant position, there is no possibility of exemption as there is with restrictive practices under **Art 81**. Fines can be imposed by the Commission for breach of **Art 82**, ranging from 1,000 to 1m euros, or 10% of the undertaking's turnover. Substantial fines have been imposed in the past, for example, 60 million euros in the *Polypropylene* case (1986). The threat over Dicero may make them reluctant to wait for action to be taken by the European Commission against Smart International. **Article 82** is directly effective and can be applied in the national courts. There has been some reluctance in national courts to do this, because of the detailed economic analysis indicated above, which is often necessary with **Art 82** cases. However, breach of **Art 82** should lead to the application of the same remedies as are available for similar breaches of national law. Therefore, it would be appropriate for Dicero to seek an injunction or a declaration in interlocutory proceedings. In the case of *Courage Ltd v Crehan* (2002) the ECJ recognised the right of an individual to claim damages before a national court for breaches of **Art 82**, and this could provide another remedy for Dicero.

Question 28

Bakers are a successful chain of supermarkets with 55 stores in the north-west region. They have recently expanded the range of cosmetics and hope to complement this by adding perfumes.

Unfortunately for Bakers, they have been refused supplies of exclusive brands by Ouvert, producers of one of the most popular ranges of French perfumes. This could damage the success of the new venture by Bakers, so they have contacted the marketing director at Ouvert requesting an explanation as to why their orders to various Ouvert distributors have been refused. The explanation given by the French company was that Bakers were not on the list of exclusive outlets used by Ouvert because they cannot provide the personal service required for Ouvert brands, and last Christmas they had sold the Ouvert perfumes obtained from a third party at a cut price, raising complaints from recognised Ouvert outlets in the region.

Bakers have written to Ouvert stating that their legal advice is that the refusal to supply them is a breach of EC competition law and that a complaint will be made to the European Commission and legal action taken if necessary to obtain supplies of the perfumes. In response to this letter Ouvert replied that they received a letter from the European Commission some years ago about their exclusive distribution agreements and this informed them that no action would be taken as there was no breach of **Art 81**, and the Commission considered the matter closed.

What advice can you provide to Bakers with regard to what action, if any, they can now take in this matter?

Answer plan

This question concerns **Art 81** and the kinds of restrictive practices which have been identified under EC competition policy as being anti-competitive. You should cover the following points:

- the relationship between **Arts 81 and 82**;
- types of agreements covered by **Art 81**;
- the effect of **Art 81**;
- possible exemption under **Art 81**;
- comfort letters;
- the role of the national courts;
- remedies.

Answer

The Community is very concerned to safeguard legitimate competition undertaken by businesses such as Bakers. This is achieved by Treaty articles which deal specifically with restrictive trade practices (**Art 81**) and monopoly situations (**Art 82**). For **Art 82** to be involved there has to be 'an undertaking which is in a dominant position' in the market for particular goods and abuses that position. Although Ouvert may have an exclusive range of perfumes, there are alternatives indicating that they do not have a dominant position in the market for perfumes generally so it would seem that **Art 81** dealing with restrictive trade practices is the area of competition policy that could be involved. If Ouvert are in breach of **Art 81**, their action will be considered anti-competitive and therefore contrary to EC law, subject to the possibility of exemption under **Art 81(3)**.

Article 81 covers agreements which have as their object or effect the prevention, restriction or distortion of competition within the common market. A fundamental question is whether there is an agreement between Ouvert and its distributors which is making it difficult for Baker to obtain supplies of the perfumes? The agreement does not have to be a formal written one to fall within **Art 81**, because it also covers concerted practices, which include 'gentlemen's agreements'. In *ICI v EC Commission*

(1972), the ECJ defined such practices as a form of co-ordination between enterprises that has not yet reached the point where there is a contract in the true sense of the word, but which in practice consciously substitutes a practical co-operation for the risk of competition. Therefore, because there are a number of recognised distributors for Ouvert perfumes, there must be an agreement between the parties, even if we are not told what form it takes.

It is clear that such agreements entered into by Ouvert are within the scope of **Art 81**, but are they amongst those which are identified as being incompatible with the common market? **Article 81** lists a number of examples of such agreements which impede the free movement of goods or services throughout the Community and thus distort competition with the market. The list is not exhaustive, but it does include one which seems to apply to the situation facing Bakers. This is where the agreement directly or indirectly fixes purchase or selling prices, or any other trading conditions. It would seem from this that there is one aspect of the problem facing Bakers which is covered, namely, selective distribution agreements. This is the term used by the European Commission for sales conducted through a network of author-ised dealers or outlets. Only certain selected dealers are admitted to the network, and only they may receive supplies. This type of agreement is often very attractive to manufacturers because, quite legitimately, it gives them control over the way in which their product is sold, and can help them maintain an upmarket image and sell their goods at a premium retail price. It is stated in the problem that one of the reasons for Ouvert refusing to supply Bakers is the fact that they had previously sold the products at below the price indicated by Ouvert, generating complaints from other outlets in the region. If an agreement comes within **Art 81** it is automatically void. This means that the agreement can only be implemented at the risk of the parties to it. It can also mean that if action is taken by the European Commission under the procedure of **Regulation 1/2003**, the parties to the agreement, notably Ouvert in this problem, could be heavily fined by the Commission. The fine could amount to 1 million euros, or 10% of the company's worldwide turnover, whichever is the greater.

However, although **Art 81** states that all such agreements are void, it gives the power to the Commission to grant exemptions. What the Commission looks for in the agreement is a contribution to the improvement of production or distribution of goods, or the promotion of technical or economic progress, with the proviso that customers are allowed a fair share of the resulting benefit. It is also necessary that the restrictions in the agreement go no further than is necessary for the objectives to be achieved and it does not provide the possibility of eliminating competition in respect of a substantial part of the products in question. If Ouvert had sought an individual exemption, they would have had to prove that the agreement with the outlets met these conditions, but obtaining an individual exemption is a lengthy process and Ouvert do not indicate that they had entered into such an exemption application with the Commission or tried to conform to any block exemption.

However, Ouvert do indicate that they entered into some correspondence with the Commission about their distribution agreements, but what is the status of the letter they had received? Was the letter what is known as a 'comfort letter', a device used by the Commission following informal discussions based on information provided by an undertaking and indicating that in their view no infringement of **Art 81** was taking place? Such letters do not grant exemption and were a means by which the Commission attempted to reduce its workload, as confirmed by the ECJ in the *Perfume* cases (1980). They were merely an administrative letter and were not binding on the Commission, who could reopen the file at any time, or the national courts who could consider a complaint for breach of **Art 81**. However, a new framework for competition law was established in **Regulation 1/2003**, and the Commission no longer issues such 'comfort letters', although it may issue a 'guidance letter'. The outcome for Bakers is that the letter referred to by Ouvert is not legally binding and does not provide them with any defence to their refusal to supply the perfumes.

It would seem that the refusal by Ouvert to supply Bakers is contrary to **Art 81**. Is there any action open to Bakers? It would be possible to complain to the European Commission on the expectation that they will utilise the machinery under **Regulation 1/2003** to enforce **Art 81**. However, this would be a lengthy business, and a speedier remedy should be considered. Bakers have threatened legal action, so this may be a possibility. As the letter from the Commission mentioned by Ouvert is not legally binding, it is not possible to go to the ECJ to seek its annulment under **Art 230** in an action for judicial review, but national courts are required to apply **Art 81** as it is directly effective (*BRT v SABAM* (1974)), thus providing the best course of action for Bakers. The national court will be able to use the conditions listed in **Art 81(3)** to decide amongst other things whether the agreement affords the undertakings the possibility of eliminating competition in respect of a substantial part of the products in question, namely the Ouvert perfumes (*M6 & Others v Commission* (2001)). If the agreement is found by the court to be incompatible, then it is void, because only the European Commission can grant an exemption, not the court. Thus the remedies available in national courts for breach of **Art 81** are those remedies available for similar breaches of national law (*Rewe-Zentralfinanz* (1976)), although the court will not have the power to order fines. In the case of Bakers the remedy will be an injunction or a declaration in interlocutory proceedings, and possibly damages. In the UK, the possibility of the court awarding damages for breach of **Art 81** remained uncertain following the case of *Garden Cottage Foods Ltd v Milk Marketing Board* (1984), but this has been cleared up by the case of *Courage Ltd v Crehan* (2002). In this case the ECJ recognised the right of an individual to claim damages before a national court for breaches of **Art 81**.

Question 29

Why does the EU need a competition policy? How effective is it?

Answer plan

This straightforward essay-type question requires the following points to be covered:

- the basis of EU competition policy;
- **Arts 81, 82, 87** and **88 EC**;
- procedures under **Regulation 1/2003**;
- power to issue decisions and levy fines by the European Commission and the system of appeals to the CFI; and
- control of the Commission's exercise of powers via actions for annulment (**Art 230 EC**) and damages (**Art 288 EC**).

Answer

The EU is based on the acceptance by the Member States that they will operate free market economies within the territory of the Union. **Article 2 EC** refers to a high degree of competitiveness because competition is the best stimulant of economic activity since it is said to guarantee the widest possible freedom of action. The Treaty does not define the concept of 'competition' but refers to certain measures which interfere with competition and are therefore prohibited, subject to exemptions granted by the Commission. Thus **Art 3(g)** sets as one of the objectives of the Community, the institution of a system ensuring that competition in the common market is not distorted. Competition policy is another instrument which the Community can use to ensure that objectives set out in the Treaty are obtained. For example, that economic integration will take place to produce 'one common market'. In this way the growth in the standard of living and quality of life of the citizens of the Union should be achieved.

The Treaty applies to all competitive activity whether undertaken by individuals, businesses or governments. The chapter of the Treaty dealing with competition contains mainly two sets of rules, reflecting this private and public economic activity which takes place. **Articles 81 and 82** apply to enterprises which might be involved in restrictive practices or which are abusing a dominant position within the market. **Articles 87** and **88** cover aid granted by Member States. However, in addition to the

117

Treaty specifying anti-competitive activity there needs to be a means of policing and enforcing it. Each Member State has its own policies and agencies that deal with competition because there is some 'domestic or national' anti-competitive activity that does not come within the dimension of European law because it is minor or does not have the potential to affect trade between Member States. The competition agencies in Member States work closely with the European Commission but it is the Commission that is charged by the Treaty with enforcing Community competition policy. It has the power to issue decisions which under the definitions in **Art 249** are binding upon those to whom they are addressed.

The Commission's powers relate to four main areas. It has the power to collect information, to grant exemption under **Art 81**, to impose fines and to make interim measures. The powers it has and the procedures it must follow are laid down in **Regulation 1/2003**. These substantial powers are necessary if the Commission is to fulfil its role. However, the procedural requirements are strict under **Regulation 1/2003** and there is a general duty of confidentiality because they are dealing with commercially sensitive information. A breach of these duties or procedures can result in an action being brought under **Art 230 EC** before the Court of Justice, and ultimately the Commission decision can be annulled. It is also possible for an action for damages to be brought against the Commission, as happened in the *Adams* case (1986). Adams brought an action under **Art 288 EC** against the Commission for breach of confidentiality when they allowed to be disclosed to his employers, Hoffman-La Roche that he had assisted them.

Article 81 deals with restrictive practices such as price fixing, refusal to supply or limiting the market. Here the Commission's task is to monitor agreements with a view to granting negative clearance or exemption. To do this the Commission needs information supplied by the applicant and other parties. The Commission has the power to impose fines not exceeding 1 per cent of turnover where applicants intentionally or negligently supply incorrect or misleading information. The power of granting exemption under **Art 81(3)** is only given to the Commission. Before doing so the Commission must publish a summary of the relevant application or notification and all interested parties must be invited to submit their comments. If the final decision is adverse to the applicant, the Commission must give him an opportunity to be heard on the matters to which he objects. Due to the need to speed up the process of considering applications for exemption, the Commission has issued a number of block exemptions which allow undertakings to arrange their business affairs so as not to be in breach of competition policy.

In order to make a decision related to Community competition policy under **Art 82**, the Commission normally needs further information in order to come to an opinion on the legality of the behaviour in question. There are two basic ways to obtain this information, by either investigations or written requests for information. For example, if the Commission is investigating the behaviour of a dominant firm, it may write not only to the company concerned but to the smaller undertakings that have dealings with the company. If the replies from the undertakings are incorrect or incomplete the Commission has the right to impose fines. On some occasions it is necessary to undertake detailed market analysis and to this end the Commission has been given exhaustive powers. The Commission may conduct general enquiries into whole sectors of the economy if economic trends suggest that competition within the common market is being restricted or distorted. Additional information may be requested from governments or competent authorities in Member States. In all these instances the Commission can request any information which it considers 'necessary' to enable it to carry out its tasks. In addition to requesting information, the Commission can seek it by carrying out on-the-spot investigations. These include the power to enter premises, examine books or business records, to copy such records and to conduct oral examinations. These investigations may be 'voluntary' or 'compulsory'. Where they are compulsory, Commission officials are required to produce a decision specifying the subject matter and purpose of the investigation. Normally, the Commission will resort to an unannounced visit where a serious risk exists that the undertakings, if forewarned of the inspection, will destroy any incriminating evidence. In *National* (1980), a 'dawn raid' had taken place at National Panasonic's offices, with a search and seizure operation taking place before the company's lawyers could arrive. National claimed that although the raid was authorised by a decision under **Regulation 1/2003**, some prior warning should have been given. The Court of Justice, hearing an action under **Art 230** to have the decision annulled, disagreed. They held that under the regulation the Commission was entitled to undertake such investigations as are necessary to bring to light any breaches of **Arts 81** and **82** (formerly **85** and **86**). However, it is for the Court to control the investigative powers of the Commission as was stated in another case involving a 'dawn raid' (*Hoechst* (1989)). In some instances the Commission may request the competent authority of the Member State, such as the Office of Fair Trading, to carry out necessary investigations on its behalf. All undertakings are bound to comply with the legitimate demands of the Commission even if the information is self-incriminating. If they fail to co-operate or give false or misleading information they are liable to penalties.

The Commission has the power to impose fines of up to 1 million euros or 10% of the world annual turnover of the undertaking, whichever is the larger, where **Arts 81** or **82** have been infringed. This applies whether the infringement has arisen intentionally or negligently. The amount of the fine will depend upon the seriousness of the behaviour, its duration and the size of the undertaking involved. A deliberate infringement will normally deserve a heavier fine than where an undertaking has been purely negligent. The Commission has not been hesitant in using its power to impose fines. In the *Pioneer Hi-Fi* case (1980), a fine of almost 7 million euros was imposed for breach of **Art 81**, although it was subsequently reduced on appeal to the Court. Any fine levied is paid to the Commission and no amount of it goes to the injured victim of the anti-competitive practice. They must seek a remedy in their national courts. The Court of First Instance, under **Art 229**, has unlimited jurisdiction with regard to fines. Where the amount of the fine is being challenged, this will normally be done by way of proceedings under **Art 230** to annul the decision imposing it.

In relation to the competition policy of the European Community, the Commission does have very wide powers because the policy raises complex issues which may take up to two years before they are resolved. In some instances such a delay may cause irreparable damage to some of the undertakings. To deal with this possibility the Commission is given the power to take immediate action in the form of interim measures to stop objectionable behaviour. These measures are of a temporary nature aimed at safeguarding the status quo, as in the *Camera Care* case (1980). In the exercise of all these powers the Commission is subject to the law of the Community, including the general principles of Community law which have been identified by the Court. The Court of First Instance has the power to confirm, reduce, cancel or increase fines and penalty payments imposed by the Commission. As all legally binding actions by the Commission are required to be made by decisions, these can be challenged before the Court of Justice via an action under **Art 230** (formerly 173). There is, therefore, clear judicial control of the Commission to ensure that it exercises its powers within Community law. Given the identified need in **Art 3(g)** to have a machinery to ensure that competition within the Community is not distorted, the powers given to the Commission are necessary to achieve this. The Commission is only concerned where the competition rules have been abused or infringed. It recognises that European companies have to compete in the global market but the Commission wants to see a balance between the need for profits and the benefits to the consumer. As the competition policy of the EU has extraterritoriality and is imposed on all companies trading within the EU regardless of their country of registration, the policy has been very effective in maintaining that balance.

NOTE

This answer concentrates on the powers associated with **Arts 81** and **82**. It would be possible to concentrate more on **Arts 87** and **88** as there are an increasing number of actions being taken by the Commission against the governments of Member States who are attempting to shield sectors of their economies from competition.

Question 30

What is meant by 'an abuse of a dominant position'?

Answer plan

This is a very popular type of question. It is straightforward, but you should cover the following points:

- **Art 82** and the EU competition policy;
- the role of the Commission;
- definition of 'dominant position' from *Continental Can*; and
- the decision in *United Brands*.

Answer

The term 'dominant position' is associated with **Art 82** and the policy against anti-competitive behaviour by businesses. There is nothing in Community law which does not allow for a dominant position to be established. What **Art 82** is concerned with is the abuse of that dominant position within the common market or a substantial part of it. It is designed to restrain the conduct by a dominant firm that harms those with whom it deals. Such an abuse is prohibited, in so far as it may affect trade between Member States.

In *Continental Can* (1972), the Commission defined its view of a dominant position. It said that undertakings are in a dominant position when they have the power to behave independently without taking into account their competitors, purchasers or suppliers. This arises due to the undertaking's share of the market or because of the availability of technical knowledge, raw materials or capital in addition to market share. It does not mean that there should be an absolute domination, in the sense that the undertaking can eliminate all other competitors. It is enough that its market strength allows it an overall independence of behaviour. The concept of dominance was developed further in *AKZO Chemie BV* (1986), in which the Commission stated that the ability to eliminate or seriously weaken existing competitors or to prevent potential competitors from entering the market may be involved in a dominant position.

In *Continental Can*, the Court insisted that the Commission analyse an undertaking's market power in two steps. First, it needed to define the relevant market and, secondly, it should assess the undertaking's dominance within that market. This is not an easy exercise, because markets are not always easy to identify. If the market is given a narrow definition, perhaps ignoring the possible substitutes available, it may indicate a large market share, which overstates the market power of the undertaking's product. If a wide definition is given to the market, the undertaking's market share is understated. The Court is quite stringent in requiring the Commission to define the relevant market and to give reasons for its definition. In the *Continental Can v Commission* case, the Commission's finding that the Continental Can company was in a dominant position over the supply of cans and closures used for meat and fish products was not accepted by the Court.

The main problem was that the Commission had not paid sufficient attention to substitute products. The meat and fish suppliers could turn to glass or plastic containers, or the manufacturers of cylindrical cans could move towards the production of the flat cans traditionally used for meat and fish products. In the *United Brands* case, the company sought to prove that the Commission had got the market wrong once more. However, the Court accepted that the Commission was right in identifying the relevant market as that of bananas. Although United Brands said that the relevant market was that of fresh fruit, in which they were not dominant, the Commission showed that bananas were consumed particularly by the very young, the old and the sick and were little affected by the pricing and consumption of other fruit.

It is clear that establishing dominance within a particular product market requires detailed economic analysis. From this analysis, a number of factors are used to determine dominance. The market share held by the undertaking is a crucial factor when determining dominance. In the *Continental Can* case, for example, the company had 80% of the German market. *United Brands* had 45% of the banana market, so it is possible to see the wide variation in market share which can be involved. The Commission considers that a share of between 20% and 40% may amount to dominance in certain markets. The period of time in which the undertaking has held its position in the market will be important. What are the financial and technical resources of the 'dominant' undertaking? Can it eliminate competitors by intensive advertising campaigns or by predatory pricing? The access to raw materials and markets can also be important. In the *United Brands* case, the company was vertically integrated, owning plantation, shipping, storage and distribution businesses for bananas. In *Commercial Solvents*, the company, which refused to supply another Italian company with aminobutanol, had a near-monopoly in its production. The refusal to supply in this case is an example of the final factor which may determine dominance, namely, the behaviour of the firm. A firm's behaviour may indicate that it is dominant within the definition given above from the *Continental Can* case, that is, it is able to act independently of its competitors, customers and, ultimately, consumers. Another example would be the discriminatory pricing system used by United Brands.

Article 86 is only infringed where dominance is within the common market or a substantial part of it. It is not entirely clear how large an area, or what proportion of supply, amounts to a 'substantial part of the common market'. In *Sugar* (1975), the Court stated that the pattern and volume of the production and consumption of a particular product as well as the habits and economic opportunities of vendors and purchasers must be considered. The Commission provided some useful guidance on the relevant geographical market in its Notice on Agreements of Minor Importance, where it noted that the cost of transport is particularly important. It is also necessary to consider the temporal aspect when looking at the question of dominance. The time of year can have a large impact on a particular market, especially when looking at fresh produce.

As indicated earlier, it is not the dominance in fact which **Art 82** is designed to deal with, but the abuse of that dominant position. What amounts to an abuse under **Art 82**? The Article itself does give some examples of anti-competitive behaviour, but the list is not intended to be exhaustive. There are two main categories of abuse: exploitative and anti-competitive. Exploitative abuses arise where the dominant undertaking takes advantage of its position by imposing harsh or unfair trading conditions. The most common examples of these are unfair prices, unfair trading conditions, discriminatory treatment and refusal to supply. Unfair price was defined in *United Brands* as a price which bears no reasonable relation to the economic value of the product. Although the Court did not state its opinion on the point, the Commission argued that United Brands were charging excessively high prices for their Chiquita brand of bananas. When United Brands refused to allow importers to sell the bananas when they were still green, they were found to be imposing unfair trading conditions. This was despite United Brands' argument that they imposed this requirement to ensure that the consumer obtained a better product. Some of the prices charged by United Brands differed by up to 100% in different Member States, such was their power to impose discriminatory pricing. Finally, United Brands refused to supply one of its main customers who had invested heavily in the appropriate plant and buildings, because it had taken part in an advertising campaign for a competitor. Such is the power of the undertaking in a dominant position.

Anti-competitive abuses are less easy to prove than exploitative abuses. They are not usually so harsh, but they have the same effect, in that they reduce or eliminate competition, for example, the tying-in agreement which came before the Court in *Hoffman-La Roche* (1977). This undertaking had a dominant position in seven separate vitamin markets. Customers undertook to buy all or most of their requirements from La Roche as part of tying-in agreements. As a 'reward', such companies received fidelity rebates in the form of discounts. The agreements also included 'English' clauses, which allowed a customer who found suppliers offering similar products elsewhere to ask La Roche to match these prices. If La Roche failed to do so, the company was free to purchase the products elsewhere. Although not oppressive for the companies concerned, the Commission found that these tying-in agreements limited their customers' freedom to buy from alternative suppliers. Once the alternative suppliers had been identified, La Roche was of a size to be able to take pre-emptive action to remove its competitor. Both the Commission and the Court found these practices to be abusive.

The kind of predatory pricing used by La Roche is another example of anti-competitive abuse. In *AKZO Chemie BV* (1986), a firm in a dominant position in the production of organic peroxides used this strategy where prices are reduced below cost in order to drive potential competitors out of the market. Other examples of anti-competitive abuse include refusal to supply, exclusive reservation of activities and import and export bans. In *Continental Can*, the Commission applied **Art 82** (then **Art 86**) in the context of a proposed merger or takeover. The Commission's decision said that the proposed takeover constituted an abuse of their dominant position within the common market, that is, in Germany. Such a case is unlikely to happen now under **Art 82**, as there is now **Regulation 4064/89** and **Regulation 139/2004**, a special measure to deal with mergers and acquisitions.

Question 31

Analyse TWO of the following cases which came before the ECJ, and explain their importance in the development of Community law:

(a) *Consten and Grundig v Commission* – Cases 56 and 58/64;

(b) *ICI (Dyestuff)* – Case 48/69;

(c) *United Brands* – Case 27/76.

Answer plan

When approaching a question like this, the temptation is to produce too descriptive an answer. The facts are important, but are only one element of the answer. You should deal with the following:

- the facts, the legal points raised and the decision of the Court.
- the kind of case it was – whether a preliminary reference or a direct action and which Article of the Treaty it was based upon.
- the cases chosen for this type of question have usually played their part in developing or reinforcing European Court judgments – what part has this case played?

Answer

(a) Consten and Grundig v Commission – Cases 56 and 58/64

This case concerned attempts by private traders to carve up the internal market in the face of one of the fundamental objectives of the Community: the removal of national barriers to trade. Consten was a French firm of wholesalers for electrical products. Grundig was a German firm which manufactured radios, television sets and similar products in Germany. The reason the two cases are joined is because they both arose from the exclusive distribution contract made between the two businesses in 1957. Under this contract, Grundig promised not to deliver to any other French distributor and to include in any contract they entered into with other firms elsewhere a clause preventing their goods from being transferred to France. Consten promised in return to buy Grundig's products, and not from any other competitors, and not to deliver outside France. One final fact was that the products subject to the contract all carried the trade mark GINT, that is, Grundig International. Consten registered this mark in France with Grundig's consent.

Two important events happened subsequent to this contract in 1957. First, in 1958, the **Treaty of Rome**, setting up the European Community, came into force and with it the Articles dealing with anti-competitive activity. In 1962, **Regulation 17** was adopted, which provided the machinery for the Commission to deal with any anti-competitive behaviour. Under this regulation, agreements like the one between Grundig and Consten had to be registered. This was done by Grundig. Secondly, also at this time, French competitors were getting Grundig products into France and selling them at lower prices. Consten had sued a number of these businesses in the French courts for unfair competition and infringement of their trade mark.

Acting under **Regulation 17**, the Commission, in 1964, took a decision addressed to Grundig and Consten stating that their contract was in breach of **Art 81** (then **Art 85(1)**). They were forbidden to hinder the acquisition by competitors of the goods covered by the contract for resale in France. The firms wished to challenge these decisions, which they did under **Art 230** (then **Art 173**) in an action for annulment. **Article 81** prohibits agreements which may affect trade between Member States and which have as their object or effect the prevention, restriction or distortion of competition within the common market. Grundig and Consten claimed that they were not competitors and so there was never any question of them promising not to compete with each other. Supported by the Italian Government, they argued that the word 'agreement' in **Art 81** (then **Art 85**) only applied to contracts between competitors at the same level – horizontal agreements. However, the Court held that **Art 81** (then **Art 85**) refers in a general way to all agreements which distort competition within the common market. Therefore, as the Treaty does not make a distinction between the level at which the firms operate or whether they are competitors or not, such a distinction cannot be implied into the Treaty.

Competition can be distorted within the meaning of **Art 81** by agreements which prevent or restrict competition between one of them and third parties. The contract created an unjustified advantage at the expense of the consumer, contrary to the aims of **Art 81**.

The firms also argued that the **Art 81** reference to 'affect' meant affect in a detrimental way, ie, for the worse. The contract, they argued, strengthened Grundig and allowed for greater competition between them and their rival manufacturers. The Court held that what is important is whether the agreement is capable of constituting a threat, either direct or indirect, actual or potential, to freedom of trade between Member States in a manner which might harm the attainment of the objectives of a single market between States. Thus, the fact that the agreement encouraged an increase in the volume of trade between States is not sufficient to exclude the possibility that the agreement may 'affect' such trade, especially as Consten was prohibited from re-exporting to other Member States.

The final argument put forward against the Commission's decision was that Consten owned the trade mark in France. Under **Art 295** (then **Art 222**), it is stated that the Treaty does not prejudice the rules in Member States governing the system of property ownership. Yet, the Commission's decision had stopped Consten's use of its trade mark protection to prevent parallel imports of Grundig products. The Court's view was that the GINT trade mark was intended to place an obstacle in the way of parallel imports. As the agreement was void under **Art 81** (then **Art 85(2)**), this would be ineffective if the trade mark could still be used by Consten to achieve the same objective. There is a distinction between the rights inherent in a trade mark, which are recognised by **Art 295**, and the exercise of those rights. The rights of the owner of a trade mark are limited, to the extent that the exercise of those rights may infringe **Art 81**.

(b) ICI Ltd v EC Commission – Case 48/69

This case, which is often called the *Dyestuff* case, involves the competition policy of the European Community and, in particular, **Art 81**. This Article is concerned with restrictive practices arising from agreements and concerted practices which affect trade between Member States. However, what amounts to a concerted practice was one of the key questions in this case.

ICI was among the undertakings producing aniline dyestuffs which together accounted for 85% of the market. There had been three uniform price increases introduced almost simultaneously in 1964, 1965 and 1967. The increases covered the same product. In January 1964, there was a 10% increase, followed in autumn 1964 by a 10–15% increase which was to come into effect in January 1965. At a meeting in Basle in August 1967, one of the producers announced an 8% increase and two other producers subsequently announced a similar increase. The Commission concluded that there had been a concerted practice between the undertakings, and using its powers to enforce the Community's competition policy it imposed fines on all the undertakings involved. The undertakings challenged the Commission's decision by a direct action before the European Court under **Art 230** (then **Art 173**). They claimed that the price increases merely reflected parallel behaviour associated with an oligopolistic market, where each producer followed the price leader.

The Court upheld the Commission's decision. In its judgment, the Court stated that the inclusion of concerted practices in addition to agreements between undertakings in **Art 81** (then **Art 85**) was for a specific purpose. The object is to bring within the prohibition of the Article a form of co-ordination between undertakings which, without having reached the stage where an agreement properly so called has been concluded, knowingly substitutes practical co-operation between them for the risks of competition. The behaviour of the participants is therefore important, because it is that which is identified as the concerted practice. However, the Court recognised that this behaviour could not be conclusive, but it was strong evidence to suggest that the market was not 'operating normally', having regard to the nature of the products, the size and number of undertakings involved and the market volume they controlled. This idea of the 'normal conditions' of the market has been criticised, as it does not take into account the type of activity which occurs in oligopolistic markets, although on the facts of the case it is very difficult to find any support for the dyestuff producers.

The identification of a concerted practice requires the evidence provided by the Commission to be considered as a whole, taking into account the parties involved and the specific features of the market for the product in question, that is, the freedom of the consumers to choose their supplier. In this instance, the general and uniform increase in prices can only be explained by a common intention on the part of the undertakings. This intention was to adjust the price level and to avoid the risk which could accompany such price increases of changing the conditions of competition.

(c) United Brands – Case 27/76

United Brands Co is a conglomerate owned by a company based in the USA. It is the world's largest seller of bananas. In the opinion of the European Commission, United Brands holds a dominant position in the banana market in a substantial part of the European Community. This is based upon the fact that it handles 40% of the trade in bananas in the EC and has overwhelming economic power based upon the vertical integration of its banana business. United Brands owns numerous plantations in tropical banana-growing countries and a fleet of refrigerated banana boats. In addition, it controls banana ripening in consumer countries and takes direct charge of the advertising campaigns and sales promotion activities related to its brand, Chiquita. It is the only firm to have all these advantages in the banana market, and is thus in a position to use them to place major obstacles in the way of effective competition in the banana market.

The European Commission reached the decision that United Brands was abusing its dominant position, contrary to **Art 82** (then **Art 86**). This was based upon a number of points, including:

(a) United Brands prohibited its distributors and ripeners from selling green bananas, which meant there was market fragmentation;

(b) it charged its customers prices which differed according to the Member State in which they were located. Such differences could amount to 100%, although there were no objective reasons for this discrimination;

(c) it charged unfair prices for sales to its customers in Germany, Denmark and the Benelux countries; and

(d) finally, for no objectively valid reason, it refused, for nearly two years, to supply one of its main Danish customers.

The Commission considered these to be serious violations of **Art 82** (then **Art 86**) and imposed a heavy fine of 1m euros and ordered United Brands to put an end to its infringements. The importance of this case lies in the fact that the Commission investigated United Brands' entire marketing policy in the light of **Art 82**, perhaps because of the problems it had experienced in the *Continental Can* case (1972). They were not attacking the commercial dynamism of United Brands, which is not contrary to **Art 82**, but because a dominant firm has an obligation not to indulge in business practices which are at variance with the goals of the Community's competition policy. It is not being in a dominant position which is contrary to **Art 82**, but the abuse of that position.

United Brands appealed to the European Court against the decision of the Commission, seeking its annulment under **Art 230** (then **Art 173**). They claimed that the 'relevant market' identified by the Commission was too narrow and should have been the fresh fruit, rather than the banana market. The Court upheld the Commission's choice of bananas as the relevant market. However, it quashed the Commission's decision that United Brands' prices were excessive, because the Commission should at least have asked United Brands about its costs. Overall, the Court upheld the Commission's decision, including its condemnation of United Brands' refusal to supply, although the fine was reduced to 850,000 euros. The definition of a dominant position given in the Court's judgment has been followed very closely in subsequent cases involving infringements of **Art 82**. The definition is that a dominant position involves economic strength which enables an undertaking to prevent effective competition and to act independently of its competitors, customers and ultimately of consumers.

Question 32

Critically review the Commission's application of the Merger Directive.

Answer plan

It is quite rare to have a problem question set on mergers, although this may change as the case law on the Merger Regulation develops. Where questions are set they are generally this type of essay. The main points which should be covered in your answer are:

- the role of **Arts 81** and **82** (formerly **Arts 85** and **86 EC**) in merger policy;
- the need for a specific merger policy;
- the **Merger Regulation 4064/89** as amended by **Regulation 1310/97** and now **Regulation 139/2004**;
- the requirements of the regulation;
- the benefits of the regulation;
- the case law of the Court of First Instance with regard to the **Merger Regulation**.

Answer

Although the competition policy of the EC has a strong emphasis against restrictive practices or the abuse of a dominant position, these are not the only activities that EC law seeks to control. There are also activities of Member States or mergers of public companies that can be seen to be anti-competitive. EC law seeks to control or limit these in so far as they impact on the Community. The competence to deal with mergers is given to the Commission under **Regulation 4064/89**. This regulation has been amended by **Regulation 1310/97** to facilitate greater procedural harmony in the assessment of different types of concentrations. If a proposed merger qualifies as a concentration, the next question is whether it has a 'Community dimension'. The test for this is one of sales or turnover. Initially the worldwide turnover specified was 5 million euros, but **Regulation 1310/97** has reduced this and in so doing has increased the supervision role of the Commission over mergers. The new **Art 1(3)** provides that those mergers involving a worldwide turnover of 2,500 million euros where the aggregate Community turnover is more than 100 million euros will be subject to examination by the European Commission. Such mergers must be notified to the Commission.

Mergers can be categorised into horizontal, vertical and conglomerate mergers. Horizontal mergers arise where companies make the same products and operate in the same level of the market. Vertical mergers are those where the undertakings operate at different levels but in the same product market. Lastly, conglomerate mergers are where there is no connection between the businesses in any product market. With regard to the impact on competition, it is horizontal mergers that have the most damaging potential.

It is the European Commission that has the responsibility to police the competition policy of the European Community, including that relating to mergers. Within the Competition Directorate DG IV, there is the Merger Task Force (MTF), which oversees merger control within the EC. For the policy to be effective there has to be notification by the companies concerned. **Article 4(1) of Regulation 4064/89** as amended requires such notification to the MTF and failure to do so can lead to fines being imposed under **Art 14(1)(a)**. Where the MTF considers that the notification falls within the ambit of the **Merger Regulation**, it must publish that notification. The MTF can instigate an investigation into the proposed merger or concentration, during which time the merger should be suspended. Failure to do so can lead to a heavy fine being imposed by the Commission (**Art 14(2)**).

The investigation by the MTF is conducted in two stages. In the first stage the MTF can decide under **Art 6(1)** whether the concentration is outside the regulation. The second stage arises where the Commission has serious doubts about the compatibility of the merger or concentration with the common market. **Article 8** of the regulation provides a number of options for the Commission, including finding that the merger or concentration does not in fact breach the criteria by which such matters are judged. The regulation states that the Commission has four months from the initiation of the proceedings to make its decision. If it fails to do so, the merger will be deemed to be compatible with the common market. However, if the Commission determines within the time limit that it is incompatible with the common market because competition will be significantly impeded, the Commission can issue a decision to that effect. This may stop the merger going ahead or demand the reversal of a merger that has already taken place.

The Commission has made it clear that the determination of whether or not a concentration exists will be based on issues of law and fact. However, the Commission has been criticised for some of its decisions, such as where it blocked the merger between Aerospatiale-Alenia and de Havilland. The criticism of the decision centred on the Commission's definition of the relevant product market. Those who supported the merger claimed that the Commission had taken too narrow a definition of the market as 20- to 70-seater aircraft. However, the Commission has resisted all attempts to re-open the case. This case can be seen as an exception in that the majority of notifications do not lead to the Commission blocking the merger. This is helped by the fact that the Commission can, where it has some concerns, impose conditions before clearing a merger, such as in the merger between Nestlé SA and Perrier SA in 1993.

However, the most recent difficulty that has arisen for the Commission relates to collective dominance. The Commission has taken the view that the **Merger Regulation** applies to collective dominance, where a merger creates or strengthens a dominant position between the parties and others in the market for particular goods or services. In *Gencor Ltd v Commission* there was a proposed concentration between two firms in the platinum market, which the Commission thought could lead to a dominant position between these two undertakings and another business. On appeal to the Court of First Instance, the Court confirmed that this type of collective dominance was covered by the **Merger Regulation** and issued guidance for its application. Following on from the tests established by the ECJ in the *Woodpulp* case, the Court of First Instance said that the extra-territoriality of the regulation was satisfied because the platinum was to be sold in the EC although it was produced in South Africa. The Court thought that under public international law it was foreseeable that the proposed concentration would have an immediate and substantial effect in the EC.

The wide interpretation given by the CFI to the regulation with regard to collective dominance has caused some problems for the Commission when it comes to proving the *existence* of collective dominance. In *Airtours plc v Commission*, the CFI held that the Commission had made errors of assessment in its analysis of competition in the 'relevant market'. In the UK the tour operator market is dominated by a small number of large operators. The operators were Thomson's with 27% of sales, Airtours with 21%, Thomas Cook with 20% and First Choice with 11%. If Airtours combined with First Choice they would have a larger share of the market, but more importantly there was the opportunity for the remaining three large operators to have a dominant position on the market as no other operator had more than 5% of sales. The Commission had not supported its assessment of the foreseeable reaction to the purchase by Airtours of First Choice plc, one of its main competitors. Therefore, the Commission's decision blocking the concentration was annulled. The outcome of this case has emphasised the role of the transparency test in deciding whether there is collective dominance. But, as with the tests for dominance under **Art 82**, this is difficult to prove. In the case of *Schneider Electric SA v Commission*, a merger by Schneider with another French producer of low-voltage electrical equipment blocked by the Commission was annulled. The economic analysis by the Commission, in the view of the CFI, was flawed. This was followed soon after by the case of *Tetra Laval BV v Commission*, where the CFI was very critical of the Commission's analysis. The Commission overestimated the anti-competitive effects of the merger and the evidence produced by the Commission was insufficient to support its conclusion.

The Commission's powers with regard to mergers are no longer dependent on trying to use **Art 82** as it did in the *Continental Can* case (1973) or **Art 81** in the

Philip Morris case (1987). The demands of business and the EC have led to the present amended **Regulation 4064/89** to provide a 'one-stop procedure'. This provided businesses with a clear reporting requirement showing the distinctive involvement of the Commission as against the various merger bodies within the Member States. The Commission has strong powers of investigation and the ability to impose fines. However, one large problem has been the tight time limits within which it has to act. Although it can be understood in the modern global economy that decisions have to be made swiftly, it does impose burdens and constraints on the Commission. The cases above of *Tetra Laval* and *Schneider* illustrate that to investigate the market and the likely impact of the proposed merger or concentration within the time scale of the regulation creates problems. It is likely that the Commission will be seeking the views of the Member States and the business community on reforming the application of the **Merger Regulation**. Following that review by the Commission a new **Regulation 139/2004** was introduced, coming into effect in May 2004. This new regulation simplifies the notification proceedings to speed up the decision making on 'compatibility with the common market' for any proposed 'concentration'.

CHAPTER 8

THE FREE MOVEMENT OF WORKERS

INTRODUCTION

This is perhaps the most developed area of mobility within the Community, apart from the free movement of goods. Very often, there are problem questions associated with the rights of workers and their dependants to move around the Community in order to search for work or take up offers of employment. The starting point on this topic should be **Art 39**, the directives and regulations adopted to provide the detail for this Community freedom and the judgments of the ECJ which have developed the principles of interpretation and application of Community law.

Checklist

You need to put this free movement policy for workers within the context of the development of a 'common market for labour' as a necessary factor of production. In particular, you should understand:

- the right given to workers under **Art 39** to enter and remain in a Member State;
- the possible derogation by Member States under **Art 39** and **Directive 64/221**;
- the possible reservation of 'public service' jobs under **Art 39**;
- **Directive 68/360** and **Regulation 1612/68** on the rights of entry and the right to remain; and
- **Regulation 1251/70** and the right to remain after employment.

Question 33

Maria is a Spanish single parent living in Madrid with her young daughter and mother. She has recently lost her job due to redundancy. While she was a student,

Maria had spent some time in England on an exchange programme. Remembering the vacancies she had seen advertised in the newspapers, she decides to travel to London to seek employment.

Unfortunately, she finds it hard to find employment and is considering seeking help from social security. She is informed at the social security office that her child and mother must return to Spain immediately if she cannot support them. If she cannot find a job within three months, she will have to return to Spain herself.

Advise Maria.

Answer plan

This question requires you to apply the principles of free movement of workers to a problem involving Maria. What are we going to do about Maria? It is necessary to state the laws affecting her, her daughter and her mother and then apply them to the specific information in the problem. Obviously, the bulk of the answer will centre on Maria, because generally the rights of the daughter and mother are derived from hers. You should cover the following points:

- **Art 39** and the right to accept offers of work;
- **Directive 68/360** and the case of *Procureur du Roi v Royer* on searching for work;
- time limitation on searching for work and the factor of social security; and
- **Regulation 1612/68** on dependants.

Answer

Maria only needed a valid passport or identity card to enter the UK. No visa or equivalent documentation could have been demanded from her or her family. However, if she wishes to remain in the UK to look for work, she will have to meet certain requirements. As there is no indication in the problem that Maria is contemplating setting up her own business or wishes to practise a profession, it is assumed that she comes within the category of 'worker' as far as the European Community is concerned. **Article 43** or **49** will not be considered, as they refer to the right of establishment and the right to provide services on a temporary basis.

Article 39 gives an individual who is a worker in one Member State the freedom to move to another Member State to accept offers of employment actually made. There is no definition of worker in the Treaty, but subsequent secondary legislation and case law have provided such a definition. In the *Lawrie-Blum* case (1987), the ECJ suggested that the essential characteristics of a worker are of someone who performs services for another during a certain period of time and under the direction of another in return for remuneration. Unfortunately, Maria has not received such an offer of employment before coming to the UK and, therefore, does not come within the definition of either **Art 39** or of a worker. However, does she have any rights as an individual who is seeking employment as a worker?

In 1968, the Council adopted **Directive 68/360**, which deals with the abolition of restrictions on the movement and residence of workers and their families. Although this Directive does not specifically cover those who enter another Member State in search of employment, it has been generously interpreted by the ECJ to facilitate such a search. In the case of *Procureur du Roi v Royer* (1976), the Court held that **Art 3** of the Directive included the right to enter a Member State to search for work. When the Directive was being adopted, it had been minuted that individuals who moved to another Member State without a specific job offer should be allowed to enter that Member State in order to look for work. This had been pointed out in the *Levin* case (1982). However, this right was to be for a limited period of three months on the proviso that the individual could support him or herself without recourse to public assistance. Although this minute had no legal effect, the Court held, in *Antonissen* (1991), that Community law gives immigrants seeking employment the right to enter another Member State and stay there for a sufficient period of time to find out about the job market opportunities and, if appropriate, to find employment.

Thus, from the case law of the Court, Maria does have the right to enter the UK for the purpose of seeking work, but what time period does she have? In the cases above, the period of three months was indicated. This was perhaps due to the reference, in the EC legislation on social security in **Regulation 1408/71**, to the fact that payment of unemployment benefit for up to three months could be made in another Member State while the claimant is looking for work. In fact, under UK law, the period is stated to be six months. However, in the *Antonissen* case mentioned above, the Court went on to say that if, after this period, the immigrant provides evidence that he or she has a genuine chance of obtaining employment, he or she should not be subject to immediate deportation. The corollary of this is that if he or she has not found employment and cannot satisfy the authorities he or she has any genuine job opportunity, he or she can be deported.

It would appear that Maria does have a period in which she can seek employment in the UK, but what of her mother and daughter? Obviously, the daughter does not come within the category of someone seeking to exercise her rights as a worker within the Community. The mother may be of such an age that she too could claim the same right as Maria, that is, to remain for six months whilst she is seeking employment. However, if we assume that she is dependent on Maria, what are her rights? The situation seems to be a little complicated, in that the rights of members of a worker's family and dependants are dependent upon the status of worker being granted to an individual, such as Maria. Those who may be identified as having the right to install themselves with the worker are defined in **Art 10(1)** of **Regulation**

1612/68. They include the worker's spouse, descendants who are under the age of 21 and dependent relatives. There is no difficulty in concluding that the mother and daughter come within this definition in relation to Maria. However, as indicated above, Maria is not yet a worker within the Community definition. The concern that those who are seeking employment and their dependants should not become a burden on another Member State would indicate that the rights of people seeking employment could be terminated if they become such a burden. Therefore, if this is what is happening, the case of Maria and her family's rights are terminated and they could be deported.

The only way that Maria and her family can remain in the UK is if she can find employment. It is worth it for Maria or even her mother to consider part-time employment if full-time employment is not available; however, if her mother obtained employment, it may not be so easy to prove that Maria and her daughter are dependent upon her. This is because it was held in the *Levin* case, mentioned above, that the term worker and its associated rights applied to those who only worked part-time provided the work was 'real' work and not nominal or minimal. In *Kempf* (1986), a part-time music teacher from Germany was working in the Netherlands and receiving supplementary benefits from the Dutch Government due to her low income from teaching. When she claimed a residence permit as a worker it was refused, even though such a permit is a recognition of the worker's rights under the Treaty and not a prerequisite for finding employment.

However, the Court held that a person who pursued a genuine and effective activity as an employed person, even on a part-time basis, could have the status of a worker. In *Raulin* (1989), the ECJ said that the national court should take account of all the services actually performed, and the duration of the activities, when considering whether the work is genuine and effective. If Maria can gain this status, she will be granted a residence permit for at least five years and this will be automatically renewable. The rights and benefits associated with such a status, such as not to be discriminated against on the grounds of nationality with regard to education, social advantage, access to employment and training and housing, will also apply to her mother and daughter as long as she remains as a 'worker'. This is because their rights depend upon the national of one Member State pursuing an activity as an employed or self-employed person in the territory of another Member State. In *Ninni-Orasche* (2003) the ECJ stated that ultimately whether a person is a 'worker' was a question for the national court to decide.

Question 34

Critically review the development of the European law affecting the free movement of workers, the right of establishment and the freedom to provide services.

Answer plan

This essay type question allows you to demonstrate your knowledge and understanding of the wider perspective of the free movement of workers and the right of establishment and the right to provide services discussed in the following chapter. However, this question is in this chapter because, as you will see, the free movement of workers forms the bulk of the answer. Depending upon your preparation you could expand on the right of establishment etc, and still provide a good answer to the question.

The main points you should cover are:

- **Art 39 EC** – free movement of workers;
- **Art 43 EC** – freedom of establishment;
- **Art 49 EC** – freedom to provide services;
- restrictions on mobility – not a general mobility right;
- power of derogation under the Treaty; and
- policy of the EU to remove barriers and widen the scope of free movement.

Answer

The treaty establishing the main pillar of the EU, the European Community, is the European Economic Treaty, which as its title suggests is predominantly concerned with economic activity. The Treaty deals specifically with the economic activity of individuals with regard to the free movement of workers, the right of establishment and the right to provide services. The philosophy of a common market requires the removal of all obstacles to the free movement of the factors of production in the form of labour and enterprise. Thus, rather than provide an absolute freedom of migration, the Treaty confines itself to specific economic situations, although as the Community has matured as an organisation, this has been relaxed to a certain extent, as recent directives illustrate, with the proviso that the individuals concerned will not become a burden on the Member State they move to. This applies mainly to students and retired persons.

One of the objects of the Community is to establish a 'common market in manpower', which would serve the purpose of moving labour or workers around the Community. Formalities at borders and points of entry have disappeared, especially in those countries within the **Schengen Agreement**. No visas are required from EC nationals, only an identity card or passport. Under **Art 39 EC** workers who are nationals of a Member State are free to move to another Member State to accept offers of employment actually made and to remain in that Member State for the purpose of carrying on employment. The rights under **Art 39 EC** will be applied even where a Member State considers that the EU has been used to circumvent immigration law, as in *Secretary of State for the Home Department v Akrich* (2003). There is no definition of 'worker' in the Treaty but subsequent secondary legislation and case law has provided a number of characteristics to support a wide meaning of the term. A worker is someone who performs services for another during a certain period of time and under the direction of another in return for remuneration (*Lawrie-Blum* (1987)). In parallel with the development of the law on discrimination, the Court included those workers who are 'part-time' within the definition, as long as the work was 'real' work and not nominal or minimal (*Levin* (1982)). In addition, it was held in *Antonissen* (1991) that those individuals who move to another Member State to seek employment have a temporary right to remain in that Member State to search for work. This should be for a minimum of three months.

Once employment has been obtained the worker has a right to a residence permit in that Member State, valid for five years and automatically renewable. The freedom of movement of workers is mainly based on the principle of non-discrimination on the grounds of nationality, although it is possible for a Member State to derogate from this obligation under **Art 39(4)** where the work is in a public service and the individual would be exercising discretion and authority affecting the State. However, it can be seen from the main provision of **Art 39** and its extension by the case law indicated above, that it is confined to those who are seeking to take part in economic activity. If the worker loses his job voluntarily and is unable to find another, his residence permit may not be renewed and he may be deported if he is no longer involved in economic activity. This occurred in *Williams v Dutch Secretary of State* (1977) where a British subject was continuously unemployed in the Netherlands.

In addition to the worker, under **Directive 68/360**, members of the family, and other dependants, also obtain rights of entry and residence in the Member State as the principle of non-discrimination must be extended to them. This is an essential requirement as it would otherwise make the practical implementation of mobility of labour meaningless. Those who can join the worker are defined by **Art 10(1)** of **Regulation 1612/68**. In *Baumbast v Secretary of State for the Home Department* (2002), the ECJ said that the worker's step-daughter also came within the category of **Art 10(1)**. Family rights terminate with the primary rights of the worker and also when a dependant ceases to be a member of the family. The death of the worker will not deprive members of his family of their right to remain in the Member State. If they have not acquired their own right to remain, they are given preferential treatment if the death of the worker is associated with his employment, such as an occupational disease or an industrial accident. However, in the case of *Givane v Secretary of State for the Home Department* (2003) the ECJ upheld the view of the UK Government to require the residence to be immediately preceding the death. Freedom of movement could prove illusory if by moving from one Member State to another the worker loses the rights acquired under social security regulations, notably those associated with the pension entitlement of the worker and his dependants. Overall, therefore, the freedom of movement for the worker means applying the same treatment to the migrant worker and his dependants as the nationals of the Member State of residence.

Although a worker is an individual, the right of establishment necessary to exercise a profession or to render a service is not confined to individuals but also includes companies. In *Segers* (1986), the ECJ held that to allow a Member State in which a company carried on its business to treat that company in a different manner solely because its registered office was in another Member State was contrary to the Treaty. This was confirmed in the *Centros Ltd* case where a company registered in England was refused recognition by the Danish Trade and Companies Board. The Danish authorities objected because Centros Ltd did not have the minimum paid-up capital required under Danish company law but the ECJ said that they had to recognise a bona fide company registered in another Member State. There is no definition of the group of persons entitled to the right of establishment. The rules of entry and residence are broadly the same as for workers mentioned above. **Article 43** contemplates a group of people who, in principle, pursue activities as self-employed persons or set up and manage undertakings within the meaning of **Art 48**. Such persons belong, as a rule, to recognised professions whose status and membership is regulated by law. Therefore the full enjoyment of the right of establishment depends upon the recognition of professional qualifications. Without this recognition the mobility of this part of the 'common market in labour' would be severely restricted.

Thus the European Commission has concentrated on this recognition of professions as the main barrier to such mobility. Initially, the Commission attempted to compare various professional qualifications and training in the Member States and aimed at harmonisation through directives. However, this was a very slow process with limited success. For example, the directive on recognition of qualified architects took over 13 years to reach agreement. There has been some success with a number of sectoral directives being adopted including directives on doctors, nurses, dentists and veterinary surgeons. The change in policy was reflected in the **Mutual Recognition Professional Qualification Directive 89/48** that came into force in April 1991. Basically, this Directive requires that someone who has qualified to practise a profession in one Member State be able to practise in another Member State. This right is subject to the power of the host Member State to require some additional training but within specific limits of time and assessment. The underlying philosophy of the Directive is that professional education and training may vary in detail between Member States, but that any fully trained professional in a given field is likely to have the same knowledge as that required of his counterpart in a different Member State. The ECJ has also extended this policy in some of its judgements, such as the recent case of *Morganbesser* (2004) where it stated that Member States must take into account any period of practice for admission to the legal profession undertaken in another Member State.

Finally, to complement the right of establishment there is also the freedom to provide services under **Arts 49–55**. The provision of services for remuneration or payment is often connected with the exercise of a profession and in this respect is inseparable from the right of establishment. The main difference is that the individual who is providing the service remains resident in another Member State and temporarily pursues his activity where the service is provided. In these circumstances the individual must be allowed to do this without discrimination and on the same conditions as the State imposes on its own nationals. In *Carpenter v Secretary of State for the Home Department* (2003), the ECJ held that Mrs Carpenter could rely on EU law to remain in the UK because her husband was providing services under **Art 49**. The recognition to provide services under the Treaty cannot be used to try to circumvent national law as was attempted in the *Omega* case (2005). The company was based in Bonn where it operated a 'laserdrome' where laser guns were used. The German police objected, but Omega claimed that as the guns were supplied by an English company, they were protected by **Art 49**. The ECJ agreed that the provisions in the Treaty on freedom to provide services did apply, but **Art 46** allowed the justification of the ban.

It can be seen from this discussion of the rights of workers, the self-employed and companies that the Treaty and secondary legislation do give priority to the mobility of 'labour' and 'enterprise' for economic purposes. Although the European Court has held that **Arts 39, 43 and 49 EC** are based on the same principles as far as entry and residence and non-discrimination on the grounds of nationality are concerned, reference is often made in the judgments of the Court to 'economic activity'. The ECJ has recently taken this further by using the concept of citizen of the European Union under **Art 18 EC** to allow such citizens to rely on that fact to claim rights of residence in other Member States. In the *Baumbast* case (2002) mentioned above, the ECJ held that **Art 18 EC** was directly effective and could be used by a 'carer' of an EU national. The same outcome was achieved in the case of *Chen v Secretary of State for the Home Department* (2004), where the Court referred to a 'primary carer'.

Question 35

Alfonse is a German national who qualified as an accountant and who has been working in Germany, where he was trained. He recently applied for a job with the Wessex local authority in England, which had advertised for accountants. Although it had already filled the post, Wessex offered him an associate contract which amounted to two-thirds of a full-time post. Alfonse wishes to accept this offer of employment, but he has been informed by the British immigration authorities that he cannot take up this post because:

(a) UK legislation requires that posts with local authorities must be filled by UK nationals only; and

(b) as the post is not full-time, it does not come within EC legislation and has to be based on UK law alone.

Advise Alfonse.

Answer plan

As Alfonse is an accountant, this question could have been worded differently so that it came within the context of the right of establishment dealt with in Chapter 9. This illustrates the need to read any question, especially a problem question like this one, very carefully. The main points to cover in this question are:

* **Art 39** and **Regulation 1612/68** on the rights of workers;
* what is a worker? – *Levin* and *Lawrie-Blum*; and
* restrictions under **Art 39** and the *Belgium* case (1981).

Answer

Under EC law, there is a freedom of movement for workers to move around the Community to take up offers of employment. This is based upon **Art 39** and the associated secondary legislation which has been issued to provide the detail necessary to identify the specific rights of the Community worker. The main question in this problem is whether Alfonse comes within this category of worker, and whether there are any specific characteristics of the post which could deprive him of the ability to exercise his rights.

Article 39 is quite clear in providing the right for workers who are EC nationals to accept offers of employment actually made. This is confirmed by **Art 1** of **Regulation 1612/68** on freedom of movement of workers within the Community, which refers to the right to 'take up an activity as an employed person'. Unfortunately, neither gives a definition of worker, but the ECJ has decided that the words should be given their ordinary meaning and should not be interpreted restrictively. However, the concept only covers pursuit of effective and genuine activities. In *Levin* (1982), the Court held that the concept of 'worker' is a Community concept and is not dependent for its meaning on the laws of the Member State. How does the Court decide if someone comes within the Community concept of worker? In *Lawrie-Blum* (1987), the Court suggested that the essential characteristics which should be identified in a 'worker' are that he performs services in a particular time period for and under the direction of another in return for remuneration. Obviously, Alfonse satisfies the basic requirement under Community law in that he is a national of a

Member State, but does he come within the definition in *Lawrie-Blum*? From the facts given in the problem, it would seem that he is going to perform the service of an accountant for Wessex local authority, in return for which it is going to pay him a salary as remuneration. Does the fact that he is only employed on a two-thirds contract affect his position? In the *Levin* case mentioned above, the Court held that the term 'worker' applied even to those who worked to a limited extent, that is, part-time, provided that the work was real. There has to be some economic activity on the part of the person who claims to be a worker. This was confirmed in *Kempf* (1986), where a music teacher was working part-time in the Netherlands and applied for a residence permit. In normal circumstances all those who are workers exercising their rights under **Art 39** have a right to such a residence permit, which must be valid for at least five years and automatically renewable. This permit is proof of the right granted by the Treaty itself and which exists independently of the document.

The definition of 'worker' in the Community sense rarely causes difficulty in practice, because if an economically active claimant under **Art 39**, like Alfonse, is not a worker he is probably self-employed, in which case **Art 43** or **49** come into play. **Article 43** deals with the right of establishment, including the right to take up and pursue activities as a self-employed person or to set up a business. **Article 49** deals with the freedom to provide services. The European Court has held that **Arts 39, 43** and **49** are based on the same principles as far as entry and residence and non-discrimination on the grounds of nationality are concerned. Therefore, categorisation under **Art 49**, as opposed to **Art 43** or **39**, will rarely be crucial.

However, even if Alfonse does have a right to enter the UK to take up his post, albeit part-time, does the second point mentioned by the immigration authorities raise any obstacles for him? Under **Art 39**, it is specifically recognised that **Art 39** will not apply to employment in the public sector. In other words, it is possible for a Member State to discriminate in favour of its own nationals on the grounds of nationality for certain jobs. This appears to provide a wide discretion to Member States, but it has been given a very narrow interpretation by the ECJ. In *Sotgui v Deutsche Bundespost* (1974), Sotgui was employed as a postman. His employers, the German post office, paid an extra allowance to workers living apart from their families in Germany, but refused it to Sotgui, an Italian national working in Germany. The Court held that the exemption provided by **Art 39** (then **Art 48(4)**) did not apply to all employment in the public service, as this was too wide a definition. Rather, it applied to those activities in the public service which were connected with the exercise of discretion or official authority involving the national interest. On the specific point of discrimination raised by *Sotgui*, the Court went on to say that **Art 39** (then **Art 48(4)**) only applied to access to employment and did not permit discrimination once a person had been employed in that occupation.

In another case, *Commission v Belgium* (1981), which is similar to that facing Alfonse, the Court held that a Belgian law which stated that posts in the public service could be limited to Belgian nationals was declared to be contrary to **Art 39** (then **Art 48**). As with the term 'worker', the concept of 'public service' is a Community concept and is not to be interpreted only on national terms. It should apply only to those exercising official authority, as it was intended to apply only to employees safeguarding the general interests of the State. Does this mean that Alfonse can take up his post? It would appear that he will not be in a position to exercise official authority. He will not have the status of a civil servant, although this was held by the Court, in *Lawrie-Blum*, not to mean that **Art 39** (then **Art 48(4)**) applies.

To enter the UK to take up this offer of employment, all Alfonse needs is a valid passport or identity card and a letter from Wessex local authority offering him the job. If, as indicated in the problem, he is refused entry by the immigration officer, he is entitled to have access to the normal rights of appeal available under national law. If he is successful, as he should be, in obtaining entry to take up his post he is entitled to a residence permit, renewable automatically at the end of five years, and not to be discriminated against on the grounds of nationality with regard to conditions of employment, housing, social security, etc.

Question 36

Analyse TWO of the following cases which came before the ECJ, and explain their importance in the development of Community law:

(a) *Lawrie-Blum* – Case 66/85;

(b) *Rutili* – Case 36/75;

(c) *Bonsignore* – Case 67/74.

Answer plan

When approaching a question like this, the temptation is to produce too descriptive an answer. The facts are important, but are only one element of the answer. You should try to deal with the following:

- the facts, the legal points raised and the decision of the Court.
- the kind of case it was – whether a preliminary reference or a direct action and which Article of the Treaty it was based upon.
- the cases chosen for this type of question have usually played their part in developing or reinforcing European Court judgments – what part has this case played?

Answer

(a) Lawrie-Blum – Case 66/85

Deborah Lawrie-Blum was a British national who passed the first examination at the University of Freiburg to become a teacher at a *Gymnasium*. She was refused admission to the probationary service leading to the second examination, which qualifies successful candidates for appointment as teachers. The law of the *Land* Baden-Württemberg required the possession of German nationality for admission to the probationary service. Mrs Lawrie-Blum contended that this refusal on the grounds of nationality had infringed her rights under **Art 39** (then **Art 48**), whereas the *Land* argued that a probationary teacher is not a 'worker' within the meaning of **Art 48**. During the proceedings which followed in the German court, a preliminary reference was made to the European Court under **Art 234** (then **Art 177**).

The *Land* claimed that since a trainee teacher's activity falls under education policy, it is not an economic activity within **Art 2** of the Treaty. The term 'worker' within the meaning of **Art 39** (then **Art 48**) and **Regulation 1612/68**, they argued, covers only those persons whose relationship to their employer is governed by a contract subject to private law and not persons whose employment relationship is subject to public law. The period of preparatory service should be regarded as the last stage of the professional training of future teachers.

The European Commission took the view that the criterion for the application of **Art 39** (then **Art 48**) is the existence of an employment relationship, regardless of the legal nature of that relationship and its purpose. The fact that the period of preparatory service is a compulsory stage in the professional development of a teacher, and that it is spent in the public service, is not relevant if the objective criteria for defining a 'worker' are satisfied. These criteria would include such things as the existence of a relationship of subordination *vis à vis* the employer, the actual provision of services by the employee and the payment of remuneration.

The ECJ said that the freedom of movement for workers was one of the fundamental principles of the Community. Therefore, the term 'worker' should not be left to be defined by the individual Member States, but should have a Community meaning. Given its fundamental importance, the Community concept of 'worker' must be given a broad interpretation. The essential feature of an employment relationship is that for a certain period of time a person performs services for and under the direction of another person, in return for which he receives remuneration.

Applying this concept to the facts of Mrs Lawrie-Blum's case, for the entire period of preparatory service she is under the direction and supervision of the school to which she is assigned. It is the school that determines the services to be performed by her and her working hours and it is the school's instructions that she must carry out and its rules which she must observe. The amounts she receives may be considered as remuneration for the services provided and for the duties involved in completing the period of preparatory service. Consequently, the three criteria for the existence of an employment relationship are fulfilled in this case.

The argument put forward by the *Land*, that services performed in education do not fall within the scope of the Treaty because they are not of an economic nature, was rejected. The Court said that all that is required for the application of **Art 39** (then **Art 48**) is that the activity should be in the nature of work performed for remuneration, irrespective of the sphere in which it is carried out. The economic nature of someone's activities cannot be denied merely because their activities are governed by public law. The Court had already stated, in *Sotgui* (1974), that the nature of the legal relationship between employee and employer is immaterial as regards the application of **Art 39** (then **Art 48**).

(b) Rutili – Case 36/75

Roland Rutili was an Italian national, although he had lived in France since birth. He had married a French woman and, until 1968, had held a privileged resident's permit. He was resident in the département of Meurthe-et-Moselle, where he worked and engaged in trade union activities. As a result of Rutili's alleged political actions during the parliamentary elections in March 1967 and the events of May and June 1968, and of his participation in a demonstration during the celebrations of 14 July 1968, the Ministry for the Interior made a deportation order against him. On 10 September 1968, an order was issued requiring Rutili to reside in the départment of Puy-de-Dôme. In November 1968, the Minister for the Interior revoked the deportation and residence orders affecting Rutili, but decided to prohibit him from residing in particular départments. In January 1970, Rutili applied for a residence permit for a national of a Member State of the EC. In October 1970, following an appeal by Rutili, he was issued with a residence permit by the Prefect of Police valid for five years, but restricting his residence in line with the views of the Minister for the Interior. In December 1970, Rutili brought proceedings seeking the annulment of the decision limiting the territorial validity of his residence permit.

The *Tribunal Administratif* in Paris decided to stay the proceedings under **Art 234** (then **Art 177**), so that questions could be put to the ECJ. The first question concerned the interpretation of 'subject to limitations justified on grounds of public policy' in **Art 39** (then **Art 48**). The Court said that this concerned both those legislative provisions adopted by each Member State to limit the freedom of movement and residence within its territory, and the individual decisions taken in application of such provisions. The object of the provisions of the Treaty and secondary legislation is to regulate the situation of individuals and to ensure their protection, thus the national courts must examine whether individual decisions are compatible with Community law. The second question asked for the precise meaning of the word 'justified'. The freedom of movement of workers is one of the fundamental principles of the Treaty, and therefore any derogation must be strictly interpreted so that its scope cannot be determined unilaterally by each Member State. Therefore, the word 'justified' seeks to limit the discretionary powers of Member States and to protect the rights of those who are seeking to exercise their rights under **Art 39**.

The duty imposed upon Member States is to base the measure adopted exclusively on the personal conduct of the individuals concerned, as required by **Art 3** of **Directive 64/221**, and to refrain from adopting any measures which are not related to the requirements of public policy, or which adversely affect the exercise of trade union rights. They should immediately inform anyone against whom a restrictive measure has been adopted of the reasons on which the decision is based, so that these people can consider an appeal.

In particular, measures restricting the rights of residence which are limited to only part of the national territory may not be imposed by a Member State on nationals of another Member State who are subject to **Art 39**, except in the case and circumstances in which such measures may be applied to nationals of the State concerned. Therefore, the judgment in *Rutili* reinforces the non-discrimination approach of the Treaty. A Member State does not have the power to restrict the movement of nationals of other Member States within its territory unless it has the power in similar circumstances to restrict its own nationals.

(c) Bonsignore – Case 67/74

Carmelo Angelo Bonsignore was an Italian national residing in Germany. He was convicted of a firearms offence, in that he was in unlawful possession of a firearm which accidentally caused the death of his brother by his careless handling of the firearm. The local German criminal court found him guilty of possession of the firearm and imposed a fine for breach of the firearms legislation. The court also found him guilty of causing death by negligence, but imposed no penalty on this count, considering that no purpose would be served in the circumstances, notably the mental suffering caused by the death of his brother. Following this criminal conviction, the Aliens Authority ordered that he be deported. Bonsignore appealed against this decision, during which a reference was made to the European Court under **Art 234** (then **Art 177**).

The reference was required because the German court wished to know the interpretation of **Art 3(1)** and **(2)** of **Directive 64/221**, which dealt with the co-ordination of special measures concerning the movement and residence of foreign nationals which are justified on the grounds of public policy, public security or public health. These are the grounds available under **Art 39** which allow a government of a Member State to derogate from its obligations under the Treaty.

The German court hearing the appeal was of the view that deportation was not justified because of the special circumstances of the case. There was no special preventive characteristic of Bonsignore in the case. The only reason could be to deport Bonsignore as a general preventive measure, as an example to others who may also be in illegal possession of firearms. The Directive had been introduced into German law by a special Law on the Entry and Residence of Nationals of Member States of the European Community, passed in 1969. The German court wanted to ensure that the German legislation was applied in accordance with the requirements of Community law, hence its request for interpretation.

The first question refers to whether **Art 3(1)** and (2) of the Directive are to be interpreted as excluding the deportation of a national of another Member State as a deterrent to other foreign nationals from committing criminal offences of the type committed by the person to be deported. The second question posed the alternative meaning of these Articles in the Directive, namely, that the EC national to be deported will commit further offences if he remains in the Member State.

The ECJ said that according to **Art 3(1)** and (2) of **Directive 64/221**, measures taken on grounds of public policy or of public security shall be based exclusively on the personal conduct of the individual concerned and that previous criminal convictions shall not in themselves constitute grounds for the taking of such measures. These Articles have to be interpreted in the light of the objectives of the Directive and the need to ensure the uniform application of **Art 39**, without discrimination between nationals and non-nationals of a Member State.

Article 3 of the Directive provides that measures adopted on grounds of public policy and for the maintenance of public security against nationals of Member States cannot be justified on grounds outside the personal conduct of the individual involved. This has to be the situation where a government is seeking to depart from one of the fundamental principles of the Community, that is, the free movement of persons. Thus, we have the requirement that a deportation order may only be made for breaches of the peace and public security which might be committed by the individual concerned. Therefore, the outcome for Bonsignore was that the European Court said, in answer to the **Art 234** (then **Art 177**) reference, that **Directive 64/221** prevents the deportation of a national of another Member State if the purpose is solely to deter other aliens, that is, of a preventive nature. In the recent 2005 cases of *Orfanopoulos* and *Oliveri*, the ECJ stated that the Member State should take into consideration a number of factors before making an expulsion on grounds of public policy. These included how long the individual had been in residence, his age, stated health, family and economic situation, and integration into the host Member State.

CHAPTER 9

THE FREEDOM OF ESTABLISHMENT AND THE FREEDOM TO PROVIDE SERVICES

▌INTRODUCTION

Very often, these topics are joined with the free movement of workers, and therefore a good understanding of all three aspects should be obtained. This is especially true as the Court has held that the principles of non-discrimination, etc, are the same whether it is **Art 39** (the free movement of workers), **Art 43** (the freedom or right of establishment for the self-employed and companies) or **Art 49** (the freedom to provide services). Problem questions are very popular in this area of Community law although, on law degrees, it is not uncommon to have an essay question on the freedom of establishment for lawyers.

Checklist

You should be familiar with the following areas:

- **Art 43** and the freedom of establishment;
- **Art 49** and the freedom to provide services;
- **Art 50** and what constitutes a service;
- the right to receive services;
- derogation under **Art 46** and **Directive 64/221**;
- **Directive 73/148** on rights of entry and residence;
- **Directive 75/34** on the right to remain after employment for the self-employed and their families;
- the special problems of 'professionals' and the **Mutual Recognition Directive**; and
- special measures to deal with companies operating within the Community.

Question 37

Pierre is a fully qualified engineer in France. As a result of attending the 'Engineering 2000 Fair' in Paris, he applied for a two-year postgraduate course at a British university. He was accepted onto the course and arrived at Dover with Anne-Marie, his Canadian cohabitee. His luggage was searched and found to contain pornographic videos, which were confiscated. The immigration officer checked the Home Office computer, which indicated that the French police had reported that Pierre was a member of an anarchist organisation. On the basis of this information, the immigration officer refused them permission to enter the UK, on the grounds that their exclusion would be conducive to the public good.

Advise Pierre on his rights, if any, under EU law.

Answer plan

This question deals with the mobility of students within the Community. It concentrates on the right of individuals to move to another Member State to receive services as against the provision in the Treaty which deals with the right to provide services. This provision should be discussed and applied, along with the following points:

- Arts 39, 43 and 49 to identify if Pierre is covered by any of these provisions;
- the case of *Luisi*, which identified rights of recipients of services;
- the meaning of vocational courses – *Gravier v City of Liège*;
- **Directive 64/221** on derogation; and
- **Directive 93/96** for students.

Answer

The **EC Treaty** has, as one of its basic freedoms, that of the ability of individuals to move between Member States in order to carry out certain activities. The Treaty specifies three situations, namely, the free movement of workers, the right of establishment and the freedom to provide services. As Pierre does not seek to establish a business in the UK, the Treaty provisions associated with establishment have no application to the problem. Is he a worker? The concept of worker is a Community concept and is not dependent for its meaning on the laws of any particular Member State. The essential characteristic of a worker, according to *Lawrie-Blum* (1986), is that he performs services during a particular time period for and under the direction of another in return for remuneration. This concept has been generously interpreted by the ECJ, in *Procureur du Roi v Royer* (1976), to include the right to enter another Member State in order to search for work. However, although he is a qualified engineer, Pierre is not seeking to enter the UK as a 'worker', but to take up his place on a two-year postgraduate course. **Article 39**, specifying the rights of workers, does not provide any assistance to him. It is the last category associated with services which needs to be considered if the EC law is to provide any assistance to Pierre and Anne-Marie.

Articles **49** and **50** provide for the removal of restrictions on the freedom to provide services. More importantly for Pierre, they have been interpreted by the ECJ to embrace the freedom to receive services. This would include the postgraduate course which he wishes to take. It was stated by the Court, in *Luisi v Ministero del Tesoro* (1983), following the Commission's view in *Watson and Belman* (1976), that there was a freedom for the recipient of services to go to another Member State, without restriction, in order to receive a service there. Although the case involved the transfer of money out of Italy in breach of Italian currency law for the purpose of tourism and medical treatment, the principle in the judgment included persons travelling for the purpose of education. The right of residence exists during the period for which the service is provided, which, in Pierre's case, would be the two years' duration of the course. Any breach of this freedom would be *prima facie* a breach of **Arts 49** and **50**.

Would Pierre's course qualify under this right to receive services? As an economic-orientated Treaty, the main concern would seem to be education or training of a vocational kind. However, the Court has given a wide definition to the meaning of vocational education. In *Gravier v City of Liège* (1984), it was held to include all forms of teaching which prepares for and leads directly to a particular profession, or which provides the necessary skills for such a profession. Although Pierre is already a qualified engineer, the postgraduate course he has applied for would seem to satisfy this definition, in that it deals with a specialist area of engineering skills. Thus, he may claim equal access, and on the same basis as nationals of the Member State, that is, UK nationals. This was confirmed in *Blaizot v University of Liège* (1987), which involved a university veterinary studies course. However, as with all the freedoms arising from the Treaty, there are exceptions where the Member State may derogate from their obligation under the Treaty. These are specifically those in **Arts 46** and **55**, which allow for derogation on the grounds of public policy, public security and public health. As there is no indication that Pierre offers any threat with regard to public health, it is public policy or public security which may be used by the UK Government to justify its actions. The public policy provision has been interpreted strictly by the European Court to ensure, as it stated in *Van Duyn v Home Office* (1975), that its scope is not unilaterally determined by the Member State without control by the European Community institutions. In *Rutili v Ministre de l'Intérieur* (1976), the Court held that restrictions on the movement of an EC national on the grounds of public policy could only be accepted where the behaviour of the individual constitutes a genuine and sufficiently serious threat to public policy.

Article 3(1) of Directive 64/221 states that any exclusion on the grounds of public policy or public security must be based exclusively on the personal conduct of the individual. Is Pierre's membership of an anarchist association sufficient personal conduct to exclude him? In *Van Duyn*, a Dutch national was refused entry to the UK to take up employment with the Church of Scientology because the UK regarded the activities of the Church as objectionable and socially harmful. The Court held that, although past association with an organisation does not count as personal conduct, present association does, and the activities in question must constitute a genuine and sufficiently serious threat to public policy affecting one of the fundamental interests of society. Do French anarchists pose such a threat, given that there are probably British anarchists? In *Van Duyn*, mentioned above, the Court allowed the UK to apply a stricter standard on an EC national than the one it applied to its own nationals, because the UK deemed that it was necessary. It would appear that, if Pierre is a member of such an organisation and the UK Government does believe that he constitutes a genuine and sufficiently serious threat to society, it can exclude him. If they do, it must be on the membership of the anarchist association, because the pornographic videos would not, in themselves, amount to a reason to exclude him. In the *Bonsignore* case (1975), it was accepted that the concept of personal conduct expresses the requirement that a deportation order may only be made for breaches of the peace and public security which might be committed by the individual concerned.

Under Art 6 of Directive 64/221, Pierre is entitled to know on which ground, that is, public policy or public security, the decision is based, unless this information contravenes State security. This allows the individual to prepare his defence. If the UK fails to comply with Art 6, it may lead to the quashing of a deportation order, as happened in *R v Secretary of State for the Home Office ex p Dannenberg* (1984). Under Art 8, Pierre is entitled to the same legal remedies in relation to a decision on entry. In the UK, an immigrant normally has a right of appeal against immigration decisions to a person called an adjudicator and then to the Immigration Appeal Tribunal. Such appeals cover issues of fact, law and the exercise of discretion, so the merits of the decision would be fully reviewed.

In June 1992, a directive specifically issued to cover the situation of students came into force. It was challenged by the European Parliament before the ECJ on the grounds that the co-operation procedure should have been used, rather than the Parliament just being consulted. As a result, Directive 90/366 was replaced by Directive 93/96, which only applies if the person concerned does not come within one of the categories in the free movement provisions of the Treaty. The Directive is purely supplementary and the case law indicated above still applies to Pierre. What about Anne-Marie? She is a Canadian national and, as such, does not receive the benefits associated with the European Community, which are for EC nationals only. However, does her relationship with Pierre provide her with any rights of entry? If

Pierre was allowed entry to take up his place on the postgraduate course, would she be able to enter with him? Perhaps because of the limited duration of a course, under **Directive 90/366** there is a narrow definition which only includes the student's spouse and dependent children and not family members. If Anne-Marie was married to Pierre, there would be no problem, in that the nationality of the spouse does not need to be that of one of the Member States. However, she is his cohabitee, and is not included in the Directive. In *Netherlands State v Reed* (1986), the Court held that the term 'spouse' included cohabitee. Although this case was concerned with the mobility of workers, it will not help Anne-Marie even if the Court applied its principles of interpretation across the mobility categories. The decision was on the basis of non-discrimination, in that the Dutch authorities were required to give Reed the right of residence, as they recognised the rights of cohabitees under Dutch law. Therefore, the judgment will not assist migrants in a similar situation unless the State they wish to enter has the same rule as the Dutch. The UK does not have such a rule.

It would seem that if the Court is satisfied that there are grounds for the UK Government to derogate from the Treaty, they will uphold the refusal to allow Pierre to enter the UK to take up his postgraduate course. If they are not satisfied, and Pierre is allowed to enter the UK as a student, he must be given a residence permit for the duration of the course. However, whatever happens to Pierre, it can be seen from the Reed case, above, that Anne-Marie will not be allowed to benefit from the rights given to him. She must seek a visa in her own right as a Canadian national. However, the definition of 'family member' in the **Citizens' Free Movement Rights Directive 2004/38** refers to 'durable relationship' and is not limited to a 'spouse'.

Question 38

Critically discuss the development of EU law with regard to the right of a lawyer to practise in another Member State.

Answer plan

This essay question requires a discussion of the development of Community law on the right of establishment and the provision of services as they apply to lawyers. In particular, the following points should be raised:

- freedom of establishment under **Arts 43–48**;
- **Directive 77/249** and the right to provide services;
- problems of lawyers and other professionals;
- the impact of the **Mutual Recognition Directive**.

Answer

A lawyer could be a 'worker', in the sense that he or she is employed within an organisation to manage its legal affairs, in which case, the normal rules associated with the free movement of workers would apply. However, generally speaking, the ability to practise as a lawyer, as a professional, is more complicated and involves issues about the right to provide services and the right of establishment. The Community principle of equal treatment is not always sufficient to ensure that the immigrant is able to practise a profession in another Member State. In the case of lawyers, it is obvious that recognition of their professional qualifications and admission to the appropriate professional organisation is also required and can cause problems. Generally, each Member State has remained free to regulate the exercise of the legal profession in its territory. The ECJ said that Member States are required to recognise a legal diploma obtained in another Member State to register the holder for pre-qualifying practical training, although in the *Morgenbesser* case (2004) the ECJ said that this was not automatic. There was the possibility that some Member States may review the individuals' qualifications with regard to the possible exceptions to mutual recognition provided by the Directive.

There is no directly applicable provision in the **EC Treaty** requiring Member States to recognise qualifications acquired in another Member State or obliging them to allow immigrants to practise a profession without the appropriate qualifications (*Auer (No 1)* (1979)). This seems reasonable, given that the services on such professionals have a big impact on those who seek their advice and services. However, **Art 47** requires the Council to adopt directives on the mutual recognition of diplomas, certificates and other evidence of formal qualifications. Without a relevant directive, the migrant is likely to find that Community law is of limited assistance. The Commission had attempted to remedy the situation by promoting separate directives for each profession, such as medicine, dentistry, veterinary medicine and midwifery. The objective of these directives has been to make it easier for a person practising a profession in one Member State to practise that profession in another Member State. However, the important difference between these professions and lawyers is that, although the principles of medicine or dentistry are much the same in every Member State, those of law differ. It is therefore hardly surprising that the progress on facilitating the free movement of lawyers has been very slow. **Directive 77/249** was specifically aimed at lawyers, but it is only concerned with the provision of services and not the right of establishment. It makes provision for lawyers to carry out their profession in another Member State on a temporary basis. 'Lawyer' under this Directive is defined by a list of terms to reflect the diversity in the European Community. The function of the list is to indicate those practitioners who are able to benefit from the rights conferred by the Directive and the activities to which it applies. Thus, anyone who is recognised as a 'lawyer' for the purpose of the Directive can perform the work of a lawyer in another Member State, but only on a temporary basis. While performing this work, he or she must use the title of the home country, as it would appear in that country. Thus, a French lawyer must call himself 'avocat', even when he is working in the UK or Germany. This avoids any misunderstanding and indicates the specialism of the lawyer in the law of the appropriate Member State. In this capacity, the foreign lawyer can do all the work of a local lawyer, unless the national law of the Member State reserves certain activities for its national lawyers and on the proviso that he represents a client in court work in conjunction with a local lawyer. This has meant in the UK that such foreign lawyers cannot undertake probate or conveyancing work, which is reserved for UK lawyers.

It could be expected that, in time, the European Commission would issue a directive which would widen the scope of recognition for lawyers of one Member State to establish themselves and practise in another. However, recognising the time involved in such a process as producing specific directives, the Commission changed its strategy and concentrated on producing a general directive that would apply to all professions. This Directive applies to the legal profession and is the **Mutual Recognition Directive 89/48**. Like all directives on establishment, **Directive 89/48** benefits Community citizens with regard to qualifications awarded in a Member State. Under this Directive, recognition is to be given to diplomas as defined by **Art 1(a)**. There must be three essential characteristics for such 'diplomas'; it must be awarded by a competent authority in a Member State following the successful completion of a course lasting at least three years at a university or equivalent institution, plus professional training. Finally, such a 'diploma' must qualify the holder for the pursuit of a regulated profession in a Member State. The profession of a lawyer is in the list of regulated professions. **Article 3** of the Directive provides the basic rule that if a Member State requires a 'diploma' as a condition for exercising a regulated profession, it must accept a 'diploma' obtained in another Member State. In contrast to the situation where a lawyer is providing a 'service' of a temporary nature, when he or she is exercising the right of establishment, the lawyer is entitled to use the professional designation of the Member State in which he or she practises. Thus, a French *avocat* who establishes himself and practises in the UK can call himself a solicitor. Negotiations began within the EU legal organisations with regard to the **Rights of Establishment Directive** or the **'Lawyers Directive' 98/5**, which is designed to facilitate the practice of a lawyer on a permanent basis in a Member State other than the one he or she obtained his or her qualification in. Having proved that he or she is already registered as a lawyer in another Member State, after three years as a lawyer in that Member State, he or she will have the right to gain admission to the legal profession of the host country and use the appropriate professional title. Thus, if he or she was an *avocat*, he or she could become a solicitor after that period elapsed.

This would seem to make it straightforward for a lawyer qualified in one Member State to practise in another. However, the Directive does recognise that professional training varies between Member States and allows the Member State where the individual wishes to practise to set certain conditions. This may involve an adaptation period during which supervision by a qualified practitioner is required of the foreign national or an aptitude test of professional knowledge. In England, the test for foreign lawyers wishing to practise as solicitors is called the Qualified Lawyers Transfer Test. Having successfully completed this test, the normal rules concerning registration and admission to the appropriate professional body will apply. However, such registration or admission cannot be refused on any grounds contrary to Community law. As with any member of the legal profession, once registered or admitted, migrant lawyers must obey the rules of professional conduct laid down by the Member State in which they practise. Should these rules be incompatible with the Treaty's freedom of movement principles, they will not be applied. For example, a French rule requiring migrant doctors to give up their registration in their country of origin before being allowed to register in France was contrary to the Treaty. Although it happened before this general directive came into effect, the case of *Ordre des Avocats v Klopp* (1984) illustrates this point with regard to the legal profession. This case involved a French rule that an *avocat* cannot establish chambers in more than one place. Klopp was a German who qualified as a lawyer in Germany and opened an office there. He then re-qualified in France and applied for admission as an *avocat*, but his application was refused because he was not prepared to give up his office in Germany. The Court held that such a requirement was contrary to the Treaty.

Question 39

'Company law is one of the most important and active areas in the harmonisation of the national laws of the Member States. The European Community's objective is to create a uniform system of company law.'

Discuss.

Answer plan

Although it is not very common to get examination questions on European Community policy towards company law, it does form part of the syllabus of most European law courses as part of the freedom of establishment. Where questions do arise, they are generally in the form of an essay question like this one. The best way to approach these questions is on the basis of freedom of establishment and the right to provide services, and the implications these have for the recognition of companies in the various Member States. The answer will use authority based on the Treaty, as there are very few cases on these aspects of company law. The main points to cover are:

- **Art 43** and the right of establishment;
- **Art 48** and the meaning of company;
- **Art 44** and the need for safeguards;
- **Arts 49** and **50** and the provision of services by companies;
- **Art 293** and negotiations of conventions;
- directives adopted for harmonisation, with examples;
- European Economic Interest Groupings; and
- the European Company.

Answer

Although there are many developments associated with the rights of workers and the self-employed within the European Community, it must be remembered that companies play the predominant part in any modern economy. It is to be expected, therefore, that provision should be made for companies to move around the Community to take part in economic activities. The main provisions of the **EC Treaty** concerned with the right of establishment and the freedom to provide services apply to companies. However, one of the main problems encountered is that whereas individuals, whether as workers or self-employed, are uniform in their identity across the Community, this does not apply to companies. Member States have different requirements with regard to such matters as incorporation, registration and liability. If there is to be true mobility for companies, action has to be taken to make sure that these differences are not used to create barriers to the mobility of companies. This was reinforced in the build-up to the completion of the single market policy in 1992, when the European Commission said that such an internal market cannot exist unless companies incorporated in one Member State are permitted to do business in another. The case of *Centros Ltd* (1999) confirmed this principle by requiring the Danish Trade and Companies Board to register a company set up, but not trading, in England.

The **EC Treaty** identifies two rights for companies, namely, establishment and provision of services. Under **Art 43**, companies have the right to establish themselves in another Member State by setting up agencies, branches or subsidiaries. Having so established themselves, the companies have the right not to be discriminated against and must be treated under the same conditions as those laid down by the Member State for its own nationals. What companies can benefit from this freedom? The same rule applies to companies as it does to individuals, who must be nationals of a Member State if they are to benefit from the freedom specified in the Treaty. **Article 48** specifies that, as far as companies are concerned, they must be formed in accordance with the law of a Member State and have their registered office, central administration or principal place of business within the Community. The ECJ held, in the *Segers* case (1986), that to allow a Member State in which a company carried on its business to treat that company in a different manner solely because its registered office was in another Member State would render **Art 48** valueless. Just as there is a requirement that workers and the self-employed should receive remuneration in order to satisfy the Treaty, so companies which are non-profit making do not come within the definition of **Art 48**. The remuneration requirement is repeated in **Art 49**, dealing with the right to provide services. This provision deals with a company established in one Member State providing services of an industrial, commercial or professional nature in another Member State. The main difference with services is that, in contrast to establishment, the company is entering another Member State only temporarily to pursue this activity.

As indicated above, companies should be able to establish themselves or provide services on the basis of non-discrimination on the grounds of nationality. They should also not be subject to any more burdensome rules in the host Member State than are absolutely necessary. The European Community has attempted to deal with this last point by seeking uniformity in the whole Community, or at least on the basis of 'equivalents'. **Article 293** requires the Member States to negotiate conventions with each other in order to secure uniformity of recognition of business practices across the Community. The Article specifically mentions the mutual recognition of companies within the meaning of **Art 48**. As a result of this requirement, a **Convention on the Mutual Recognition of Companies and Bodies Corporate** was signed in 1968 by the six founder members of the EC. However, it is not in force as it was not ratified by the Member States. Given this failure, but recognising the importance of company law, the policy of the EC has been to move forward on the basis of directives dealing with specific matters.

The company law of each Member State has developed through its own legal and political traditions, and hence there are wide variations, not only in terms, but also in concepts. It was thought necessary, if the freedom of establishment was to be a reality, that there should be a minimum safeguard to protect the shareholders or members of companies and others who enter into transactions with the company. This is specifically mentioned in **Art 44**. If companies in the EC are to deal across national boundaries, it is important that investors, customers and creditors are able to deal with confidence with enterprises from other Member States, whether directly or through their subsidiaries or agencies. The fact that over 13 directives have been proposed reflects the extensive programme of harmonisation of company law embarked upon by the European Community. Although not all of these directives have been adopted, those which have cover such technical matters as company capital, company accounts, appointment of auditors and disclosure of information. These are important because companies established or providing services in different Member States facing the need to adjust to different regulatory regimes may lead to duplication of accounting, licensing and other requirements. This would act as a disincentive to penetrating other national markets. It may also reduce the opportunities for benefiting from economies of scale.

Another way of seeking to reduce the problems for companies operating in more than one Member State is to establish EC corporate structures. The first step was taken in this development with the establishment of European Economic Interest Groupings (EEIGs) by **Regulation 2173/85**. These EEIGs permit companies and others to co-operate within the Community on a cross-border basis, and thus provide a vehicle for joint ventures. EEIGs have the mixed characteristics of companies and partnership. They are not separate, in the sense that the companies are still liable for the debts of the EEIG, but they do have a separate legal capacity. Such groupings have to be registered, which in the UK is a requirement to register with the Registrar of Companies. An EEIG cannot have more than 500 employees, or offer any share participation to the public. Obviously, there are certain limitations with EEIGs, but they do provide a flexible vehicle for economic activity.

The ultimate aim of the Community is to have a new company formation which will have legal capacity throughout the Community. This is to be the European Company, or *Societas Europaea* (SE), which will be established by registration with the European Court in Luxembourg under a distinctive European Community company statute. Even though registration would be with the Court, the SE would be domiciled in a particular Member State. The intended role of the SE is to facilitate cross-border co-operation by means of large-scale mergers and associations. It can be seen that this is perhaps the natural extension from the EEIG, which facilitates such ventures but on a smaller scale. There have been some criticisms of the establishment of the SE, which has led to delay in the adoption of the necessary Community legislation. However, the Nice IGC in December 2000 reached a political agreement on the social aspects of the SE and in October 2001 the Council finally adopted the regulation and directive on the SE, which will enter into force in October 2004.

It can be seen from the points discussed above that the Treaty clearly identified the need to harmonise areas of company law if companies were to exercise the rights of establishment and provision of services. However, Community legislation has progressed slowly as the national requirements of the Member States varied widely. The directives which have already been adopted have helped companies involved in cross-border activities, but the ultimate establishment of the European Company has not been achieved. The regulation allowing for EEIGs was a major advance, but is aimed at smaller joint ventures. The objective of the Community is to ensure that company law across the Community does not act as a barrier to economic activity by companies and provides safeguards for those who are doing business with them. To this end, the Community seeks to provide a minimum standard of uniformity in company law across the Member States.

Question 40

Analyse TWO of the following cases which came before the ECJ, and explain their importance in the development of Community law:

(a) *Reyners* – Case 2/74;

(b) *Van Binsbergen* – Case 33/74;

(c) *Walgrave and Koch* – Case 36/74.

Answer plan

When approaching a question like this, the temptation is to produce too descriptive an answer. The facts are important, but are only one element of the answer. You should deal with the following points:

- the facts, the legal points raised and the decision of the Court.
- the kind of case it was – whether a preliminary reference or a direct action and which Article of the Treaty it was based upon.
- the cases chosen for this type of question have usually played their part in developing or reinforcing European Court judgments – what part has this case played?

Answer

(a) Reyners – Case 2/74

Although born in Belgium, Jean Reyners was of Dutch nationality. Although resident in Belgium, where he had been educated and been made *docteur en droit belge*, it had not been possible for him to be admitted to the practice of the profession of *avocat* in Belgium. The reason for this is that the Belgian *Code Judiciaire* provides that no one may hold the title of *avocat* or practise that profession unless he is a Belgian and holds the *docteur en droit*. Having previously obtained this qualification, it was the nationality requirement which was impeding Reyners. It was possible to obtain dispensation from the condition of nationality in cases determined by the King, on the advice of the General Council of the *Ordre des Avocats*. This was provided for in a decree of 1970, but was limited to the nationals of countries which themselves admitted Belgians to the profession. Unfortunately, the Netherlands Bar was only open to the Dutch.

Reyners had made a number of applications for dispensation from the nationality requirement, but they had all been refused. He finally applied to the Conseil d'Etat of Belgium, the highest public law court, to have this provision of the decree quashed on the grounds of its incompatibility with the **EC Treaty**. To enable it to decide the case, the court stayed the proceedings and a reference was made for a preliminary ruling under **Art 234** (then **Art 177**). The main questions under the **Art 177** procedure were whether **Art 43** (then **Art 52**) on the right of establishment became directly applicable at the end of the transitional period and whether the 'official authority' exception in **Art 45** (then **Art 55**) applied to *avocats*.

The governments of Member States were divided on the direct effect of **Art 43** (then **Art 52**). Although the German Government supported the possibility of direct effect in its intervention, the governments of Belgium, Ireland, Luxembourg and the UK disagreed. They based their views on the fact that **Art 43** (then **Art 52**) was wider and vaguer than the prohibition of non-discrimination on the grounds of nationality and the fact that it was to be enforced by directives left discretion to Member States. The view of the German Government was that the provisions which impose on Member States an obligation which they have to fulfil within a particular period become directly applicable when, on the expiration of this period, the obligation has not been fulfilled.

The Court held that the rule on equal treatment with nationals is one of the fundamental legal provisions of the Community. Therefore, if there is a set of legislative provisions effectively applied by the country of establishment to its own nationals, these are capable of being directly invoked by nationals of all the other Member States. The fact that the freedom of establishment should have been attained at the end of the transitional period is made easier by, but is not dependent on, the implementation of a programme of measures. The fact that the progression has not been made leaves the obligation itself intact beyond the end of the period provided for its fulfilment. After the expiry of the transitional period, the right of establishment is sanctioned by the Treaty itself with direct effect.

Art 45 provides for a derogation from the right of establishment when the activities which are involved in that State are connected, even occasionally, with the exercise of official authority. Given that the freedom of establishment and the rule on equal treatment are fundamental to the Community, the Court stated that **Art 45** (then **Art 55**) cannot be interpreted so as to defeat the objective of the Treaty. It wanted to avoid the effectiveness of the Treaty being defeated by unilateral provisions of Member States. Although each Member State must be looked at individually, the professional activities of *avocats* do not constitute, as such, the exercise of official authority. For **Art 45** to apply, there has to be a direct and specific connection with the exercise of official authority.

This decision does not mean that any citizen can simply move to another Member State and set up in business or a profession. Each Member State has its own rules which apply to its own nationals covering such matters as qualifications. However, if the professional or other qualification is already recognised in the host country as being equivalent, **Art 43** forbids the refusal of permission on the grounds of nationality (*Patrick* (1978)) or a requirement that the arrival obtain the national qualification (*Thieffry* (1977)).

(b) Van Binsbergen – Case 33/74

Van Binsbergen was a Dutch national who wished to challenge a social security decision against him. He had authorised Kortman, a Dutch national established in the Netherlands, to act on his behalf and bring an appeal against the decision. Kortman was an experienced legal adviser and representative in social security matters. However, during the case, Kortman moved his home to Belgium, and it was from there that he corresponded with the Dutch court. The court concluded that Kortman was now practising from Belgium. Under a Dutch statute on procedure in social security cases, legal representation could only be provided by persons established in the Netherlands. They therefore said that he could no longer act for Van Binsbergen.

Kortman invoked **Arts 49** and **50** (then **Arts 59** and **60**) providing for the progressive abolition, during the transitional period, of restrictions on freedom to provide services within the Community. The Dutch court made a preliminary reference to the European Court under **Art 234** (then **Art 177**). There are some similarities with the *Reyners* case (1974), only here it is a question of services rather than establishment. In fact, after *Reyners*, it should be quite straightforward to hold **Arts 49** and **50** (then **Arts 59** and **60**) to have become directly effective at the end of the transitional period, at least as regards discrimination on the grounds of nationality.

The problem was to identify the discrimination involved in the case. Kortman, Van Binsbergen, the social security court and the domestic law in question were all Dutch. However, the fact that the Dutch law did disqualify any legal adviser of any country who was not established in the Netherlands was relevant. The establishment requirement is a restriction within **Art 49**, but does the Article have direct effect in the sense of providing a right which the national courts must enforce?

The European Court said that the restrictions to be abolished under **Arts 49** and **50** (then **Arts 59** and **60**) included any requirements imposed upon the person providing the service on the basis of nationality or residence which do not apply to persons established within the Member State. This latter requirement of habitual residence could have the result of depriving **Art 49** of all useful effect, as its object is to abolish such restrictions.

However, this has to be balanced against the possibility of the person providing the service taking advantage of his right to avoid professional rules of conduct which would be applied if he was established in that State. Therefore, a residence requirement could be imposed if the desired ends could not be achieved by less restrictive means. Such rules must be considered objectively and would be permissible provided they satisfied certain criteria.

These are that they are non-discriminatory, objectively justified and not disproportionate.

Following the principles in *Reyners*, the Court held that **Arts** 49 and 50 (then **Arts** 59 and 60) did have direct effect. However, the importance of *Van Binsbergen* is that it shows that the ECJ were careful to limit the area in which **Art** 49 (then **Art** 59) works directly, namely, with restrictions based on nationality and residence.

(c) *Walgrave and Koch – Case 36/74*

Bruno Walgrave and Norbert Koch were both Dutch nationals who offered their services for remuneration to act as pacemakers on motorcycles in medium distance cycle races. They provided these services under agreement with the 'stayers', who cycle in the lee of the motorcycle, or the cycling associations or with sponsors. Competitions in which their services were requested included the world championships. The rules for the world championships to apply after 1973 stipulated that the pacemaker must be of the same nationality as the stayer. Walgrave and Koch considered that this rule was incompatible with the **EC Treaty**, as it prevented a pacemaker of one Member State from selling his services to a stayer of another Member State. They therefore brought an action against the Union Cycliste Internationale, which was the body that made the rule.

The national court made a reference to the European Court under **Art** 234 (then **Art** 177) relating to the interpretation of **Arts** 39, 49 (then **Arts** 48, 59) and 7 (now repealed). **Article** 39 (then **Art** 48) provides for the free movement of workers, whereas **Art** 49 (then **Art** 59) deals with the freedom to provide services. **Article** 7 is one of the fundamental principles of the Community, in that it prohibits any discrimination on the grounds of nationality. However, the rules in question were not made by a government of a Member State, but by an international sporting federation, which is not subject to public law. Could the prohibition be applied to them? That was the important question raised by this case.

The practice of sport is subject to Community law only in so far as it constitutes an economic activity within **Art** 2. The Court stated that the activities referred to in **Art** 49 (then **Art** 59) are not to be distinguished in their nature from those in **Art** 39 (then **Art** 48) merely because of the form of the regulation covering employment. The prohibition of discrimination found in these Articles does not only apply to public authorities, but extends to rules of any other nature aimed at regulating gainful employment and the provision of services.

The abolition by Member States of obstacles to the freedom of movement for persons and the freedom to provide services are fundamental objectives of the Community contained in **Art** 3(c). This abolition would be compromised if barriers of national origin could be neutralised by obstacles resulting from autonomous associations or organisations which do not come under public law. Therefore, these Articles may be taken into account by the national court in judging the validity or the effects of a provision inserted in the rules of a sporting organisation. The *Bosman* case (1996) would be another example where the activities of professional sportsmen had been affected.

The national court had anticipated this possible answer, so it asked whether the fact that this was an international organisation made any difference. The key point for the Court was where the relationship governed by the rules was entered into or the place where they took effect. If these were within the territory of the Community, then the Community view on non-discrimination would apply. Thus, any races, for example, which took place in a Member State could not do so under rules prohibited by the Treaty.

CHAPTER 10

FREEDOM FROM DISCRIMINATION

INTRODUCTION

The main focus of freedom from discrimination is based on the economic aspect of employment and sex discrimination. However, you should look at Chapter 2, where the protection of fundamental rights was identified as one of the general principles of Community law. The general principle has a wider meaning than merely discrimination based upon sex. This chapter concentrates on the general principle of equal pay for equal work for men and women, laid down in **Art 141**, and the directives issued to provide the detail required for the full implementation of this principle. Generally, the questions asked on this topic are of an essay type, because of the wider knowledge of national employment law normally required for problem questions. Such questions are more likely to arise in employment or industrial law papers. However, it is possible for questions to be constructed in a way that deals specifically with Community law.

Checklist

Following on from the general principle of non-discrimination, you should understand the following points and the appropriate cases:

- **Art 141** on the principle of equal pay for equal work for men and women;
- the meaning of 'pay' within **Art 141**;
- the extent of the direct effect of **Art 141**;
- **Directive 75/117** on equal pay for work of equal value;
- **Directive 76/207** (the **Equal Treatment Directive**) for men and women in employment;
- **Directive 79/7** with regard to equal treatment in matters of social security;
- **Directive 86/378** regarding equal treatment for occupational pension schemes;
- **Directive 86/613** regarding equal treatment in self-employment;

- **Art 13 EC**; and
- **Directives 2000/43, 2000/78** and **2002/73**.

Question 41

'The European Union has extended the scope of sex equality to other areas of discrimination.'

Discuss.

Answer plan

This discussion question provides an opportunity to review the case law and recent changes in the Treaty with regard to sex equality. However, that discussion must go beyond the recital of cases such as *Defrenne* or *Marshall*. This may be the starting point but the essay should then be developed to include the following points:

- *Defrenne* judgment in 1976;
- scope of **Art 141** (then **Art 119**) through the meaning of pay and worker;
- **Equal Pay Directive 75/117** and **Equal Treatment Directive 76/207**;
- general principle of non-discrimination;
- **Art 13** of the **EC Treaty**;
- **Directives 2000/43, 2000/78** and **2002/73**.

Answer

In **Art 3** of the **EC Treaty**, the European Community lists the main activities which it will achieve at the same time as eliminating inequalities and promoting equality between men and women. This indicates the special status given by Community law to the principle of equality. This principle has been repeated in secondary legislation, mainly directives, and the case law of the European Court. In fact, it has mainly been the judgments of the Court that have elevated the principle to its special status.

The main example given of this special status accorded to the principle of equality can be seen through the case law relating to equal treatment of men and women in terms and conditions of employment within the European Community. It is the cases associated with **Art 141** which show this development clearly. **Article 141** requires each Member State to ensure that men and women should receive equal pay for equal work. Equal pay, under this Article, refers not only to wage levels but also to any payment in kind in respect of remuneration for employment.

In its judgment in *Defrenne (No 2)* (1976), the Court held that **Art 141** (then **Art 119**) has a double aim which covers both economic and social aspects of employment. It seeks to ensure that States which have implemented the equality principle do not suffer a competitive disadvantage, and to achieve social progress. In 1978, whilst delivering its third judgment associated with Madame Defrenne's case, the Court expanded the principle of equal pay into a general fundamental right of equality which required the elimination of discrimination based on sex. With regard to the application of the principle of equality in employment, it is not only **Art 141** which is important, as a number of important directives have been adopted which have expanded the application of the principle. **Article 141** itself refers expressly to pay but the ECJ has adopted a liberal interpretation to the question of what constitutes pay. In *Garland v BREL* (1982), the Court held that the grant of special travel facilities to former employees after retirement constituted pay, even in the absence of any contractual entitlement to such facilities.

In *Bilka-Kaufhaus v Weber von Harz* (1986), Weber was a female part-time worker who was seeking to challenge her employer's occupational pension scheme. Although the scheme was non-contributory for full-time employees, with the employer paying all the contributions, this was not the case with part-timers. The Court held that the benefit constituted consideration paid by the employer to the employee in respect of her employment and thus came within **Art 141** (then **Art 119**). In this case, the Court seemed to draw a distinction between contractual and statutory pension schemes. However, **Art 141** was held to be applicable to a statutory social security benefit in *Rinner-Kuhn v FWW Spezial Gebäudereinigung GmbH* (1989). This case also involved a part-time employee who was employed as a cleaner. She challenged the German legislation which permitted employers to exclude workers who worked less than 10 hours per week from entitlement to sick pay. Despite statements in *Defrenne and Newstead v Dept of Transport* (1986) that social security schemes were outside the scope of **Art 141**, the Court held that sick pay fell within the Article. Therefore the German legislation was contrary to **Art 141** (then **Art 119**).

It is not only the case law associated with **Art 141** to which the principle of equality in employment has been applied. As indicated above, a number of directives have been adopted to implement or supplement **Art 141**. The **Equal Pay Directive 75/117**, for example, requires the elimination of all discrimination on the grounds of sex with regard to all aspects and conditions of remuneration. In *Jenkins v Kingsgate (Clothing Productions) Ltd* (1981), the Court held that this Directive restates the equal pay principle of **Art 141** (then **Art 119**) without altering its scope. Guidelines were provided in the later case of *Bilka-Kaufhaus*, mentioned above, to assist in identifying what might constitute objective justification for such differences in pay. The onus is on the employer to prove that the difference in treatment corresponded to a genuine need of the enterprise, that it was a suitable way to obtain the objective pursued by the business, and that it was necessary for that purpose. This could perhaps be described as the application of a principle similar to proportionality.

Another important Directive was the **Equal Treatment Directive (76/207)**. This Directive dealt with access to employment, vocational training, working conditions and social security. In the UK, this Directive has been used in the context of different retirement ages for men and women. The most important case in this respect was *Marshall v South West Hampshire Area Health Authority* (1986), where Marshall successfully challenged her employer's decision to force her to retire at an earlier age than male employees. The important factor in the case was acceptance by the Court that this Directive had direct effect. **Article 2** of the Directive allows derogation from the equal treatment principle on specific grounds. This was raised in *Johnston v Chief Constable of the RUC* (1986) by the police employers as a defence to their refusal to renew Johnston's contract of employment due to the special requirements of policing in Northern Ireland and the need for the police to carry firearms. The Court held that there was no general public safety exception to the equal treatment principle available under the **EC Treaty**, and that it was for national courts to decide whether the conditions specified in **Art 2** are satisfied. The Directive has also been used by pregnant employees who have been discriminated against (*Dekker* (1991) and *Webb v EMO Air Cargo (UK) Ltd* (1994)), even where this is due to the fault of a Member State rather than the employer (*Alabaster v Woolwich plc* (2004)).

Article 141(4) allows Member States to pursue a policy of positive or affirmative action in favour of the 'under-represented sex'. In *Kalanke v Bremen* (1995), the ECJ considered **Art 2(4)** of the **Equal Treatment Directive**. This Article concerns measures taken to promote equal opportunity for men and women, including removing existing inequalities which affect women's opportunities. However, the judgment in Bremen was greeted with dismay in several Member States, as it construed the provision very narrowly. The Commission issued a communication suggesting that the judgment in Bremen did not affect quota systems. The ECJ clarified the situation in *Marschall* (1997), which allows women to be given priority for promotion in the event of equal suitability, competence and professional performance. The potential weakness in the area of positive or affirmative action was recognised by the insertion in the **Amsterdam Treaty** of Art 141(4).

The case of *P v S* (1996) appeared to suggest a more general prohibition on discrimination embracing transsexuality; the ECJ judgment in *Grant v South-West Trains* (1998) quashed this suggestion. In the *Grant* case, the ECJ said that EC law did not currently cover discrimination on the basis of sexual orientation. The ECJ felt that it was not its function to bring about a positive change which was properly to be enacted by legislation (*D v Council* (2001)). In *KB v NHS Pensions Agency* (2004), the ECJ held that British legislation preventing post-operative transsexuals from marrying in their acquired gender could be regarded as a breach of EU sex discrimination law because it was against the jurisprudence of the ECHR. There have been occasions when the ECJ has extended individual rights not to be discriminated against as a general principle of EC law. In *Sabbatini* (1971), the plaintiff used the general principle of non-discrimination against her employer, the European Parliament. Following this, the case of *Prais v Council* (1975) extended protection to discrimination based on religion. Both cases were brought against EC institutions and the principle needed wider application.

This perhaps led to the most important recent development when **Art 13** (previously **Art 6(a)**) was introduced into the **EC Treaty** by the **Amsterdam Treaty**. Article 13 provides that the Community may take appropriate action to combat discrimination based on sex, racial or ethnic origin, religion or belief, disability, age or sexual orientation. There has been much activity in this field since then. In 2000, two directives were adopted. **Directive 2000/43** implements the principles of equal treatment between persons irrespective of racial or ethnic origin, and **Directive 2000/78** establishes a general framework for equal treatment in employment and occupation. The latter Directive covers religion or belief, disability, age and sexual orientation. The Council now has the authority to take appropriate action to combat discrimination based on sex, racial or ethnic origin, religion or belief, disability, age or sexual orientation. The new **Equal Treatment Directive 2002/73** amends **Directive 76/207** to bring discrimination on the gounds of sex into line with other forms of discrimination. Since the 1960s, the institutions of the EU have taken a wide view of categories of discrimination and this new Directive reflects that range. When these Directives become operative they will have a strong impact in some Member States.

Question 42

To what extent does **Art 141** give workers in the Member States directly effective rights to equality, irrespective of sex?

Answer plan

This question covers the narrow area of **Art 141**, but it must be remembered that this Article is very important in the development of equal pay and non-discrimination on the grounds of sex. Particular reference should be made to the following cases:

- *Defrenne* (1976);
- *Macarthys v Smith* (1980);

- *Bilka-Kaufhaus v Weber von Harz* (1986);
- *Rinner-Kuhn* (1989); and
- *Enderby v Frenchay HA* (1994).

Answer

Article 141 requires each Member State to ensure the application of the principle that men and women should receive equal pay for equal work. Although this is an instruction to the Member States, by stating in the *Defrenne* case (1976) that the Article has direct effect, the Court has identified a right which can be enforced by the individual employee in the courts of the Member State. Under the principle of direct effect, three conditions have to be satisfied; namely, that the provision must be clear and unambiguous, it must be unconditional and it must take effect without further action by the EU or Member States. Once these conditions are met, the individual is not dependent upon the Member State or the institutions of the Community for the right granted by the Treaty or other source of Community law.

The principle of equal pay was said by the Court in *Defrenne* (1976) to form one of the foundations of the Community. Its role was seen as a way of achieving one of the social objectives of the Community, namely, the improvement of living and working conditions for men and women. This requires a levelling up of pay for women, rather than a levelling down of that for men. As was restated in *Enderby* (1994), the purpose is to remove obstacles which disadvantage women in employment. If this was to be achieved, the Community was conscious of the need to ensure that those States which had incorporated such equality principles were not disadvantaged in a competitive sense as against those States whose undertakings were not obliged to meet such an objective.

In *Defrenne v Sabena* (1976), the ECJ had upheld the direct effect of **Art 141** (then **Art 119**). Madame Defrenne had been employed by the Belgian airline Sabena as an air hostess. She complained of being paid a lower salary than her male colleagues, although the work they did was the same. In an **Art 234** (then **Art 177**) reference, the Belgian court asked if **Art 141** could be relied upon before national courts. In its judgment, the Court said that discrimination on the grounds of sex could be indirect and disguised discrimination or direct and overt discrimination. The latter type of discrimination was more easily identified and could be based solely upon the criteria of equal work and equal pay referred to in **Art 141**. In such cases, **Art 141** was directly effective and gave use to individual rights which national courts must protect. It was necessary for additional measures to be taken with regard to indirect discrimination. This was achieved by the **Equal Pay Directive 75/117**, which supplements **Art 141**. **Article 1** of this Directive provides for the elimination of all discrimination on the grounds of sex with regard to all aspects and conditions of remuneration. It must be remembered that **Art 141** on its own is not sufficient to cover all aspects of equal pay, although this has not stopped the Court extending the scope of the Article through a number of very important judgments.

In the course of the **Art 234** (then **Art 177**) reference in *Defrenne*, the UK Government and the European Commission submitted that **Art 141** (then **Art 119**) would only have direct effect as between individuals employed by the State and not those employed by a private employer. In other words, they were claiming that it should only have vertical and not horizontal direct effect. The Court rejected this argument, claiming that **Art 141** (then **Art 119**) is mandatory in nature and must extend not only to the action of public authorities, but to all contracts between individuals. This judgment cleared the way for individuals to challenge their employers directly on the basis of the **EC Treaty** in national courts, where they believed themselves to be victims of sex discrimination in matters of pay.

Article 141 states that men and women should receive equal pay for equal work. In *Macarthys Ltd v Wendy Smith* (1980), the Court held that a requirement of contemporaneity of employment is not to be read into the Article. Smith was paid £50 per week, whereas her male predecessor had received £60. Under UK legislation, the requirement was for the male and female workers to be doing the same job at the same time if a comparison was to be made. However, the ECJ held that the only issue was whether or not the work was 'equal' and it did not matter whether or not the man and woman whose work and pay were to be compared were employed at the same time in the undertaking or not.

Although it was initially thought that 'pay' in **Art 141** was limited to the wages or salary received by the employee, it has been given a much wider interpretation by the European Court. For example, in *Garland v BREL* (1982), the special travel facilities granted to former employees on retirement were held to constitute pay, even if there was no contractual obligation to make such facilities available for those who had retired. Mrs Garland therefore had a right not to be discriminated against on the grounds of sex in comparison with a retired male employee.

There have been a number of cases involving pension schemes, including those where the claimant has been a part-time employee. In *Bilka-Kaufhaus v Weber von Harz* (1986), Weber claimed that the pension scheme of her employer infringed **Art 141** (then **Art 119**). Under the scheme, part-timers had to be employed by the business for at least 15 out of the last 20 years, whereas full-time employees benefited from the non-contributory scheme without any time requirement. As the contributions paid by the employer were to supplement existing social security schemes, they amounted to consideration paid by the employer to the employee within the meaning of **Art 141** (then **Art 119**). Perhaps the most important case in pensions is the case of *Barber v Guardian Royal Exchange* (1990). Under the employer's scheme, the normal pensionable age for women was 57, and for men, 62. The Court held that, since the worker received these benefits from his employer as a result of his employment, they constituted 'pay' within **Art** 141 (then **Art** 119). The immediate impact of the *Barber* case has been that employers have been required to harmonise pension ages for men and women in contracted-out schemes. The limitation to contracted-out schemes reflects the judgment of the Court that State pensions are not 'pay' within **Art** 141 (then **Art** 119). This was applied in *Roberts v Birds Eye Walls Ltd* (1992).

Sick pay has also been held by the Court to come within the meaning of **Art** 141. In the *Rinner-Kuhn* case, a part-time office cleaner challenged the German legislation which permitted employers to exclude part-time workers from entitlement to such pay. This discretion given to employers brought the payment of sick pay to part-timers within **Art** 141 (then **Art** 119). Lastly, redundancy payments were held in the *Barber* case, mentioned above, to be pay within **Art** 141 (then **Art** 119), irrespective of whether payment is made under a contract of employment, on an *ex gratia* basis or under statute.

It can be seen from the cases above that **Art** 141 has been interpreted by the Court to give workers in the Member States directly effective rights to equality, irrespective of sex. Cases have been brought mainly by female workers, but males in the *Barber* case successfully used the Article to obtain equality with regard to redundancy and occupational pension payments. The direct effect of the Article has been limited by the Court, restricting it to direct discrimination, but with the support of the directives adopted on equality, notably the Equal Pay Directive, the Court has not limited the extensive application of the Article as a basic principle. This is illustrated by the way that the Court has given a wide interpretation to the meaning of 'pay' within **Art** 141.

Question 43

Critically review how the EU has dealt with the issue of sex discrimination in employment.

Answer plan

This question deals with the general topic of discrimination but offers the opportunity to display knowledge of recent cases and new directives. In this area of law the cases are very important because they demonstrate the support given by the ECJ to the discrimination law of the EU. The following are important points:

- Art 141 EC;

- **Equal Treatment Directive 76/207** as amended by the **Equal Treatment Directive 2002/37**;
- *Defrenne* (1976);
- *Bilka-Kaufhaus v Weber von Harz* (1986);
- *Enderby v Frenchay Health Authority* (1994);
- *Grant v South-West Trains Ltd* (1998); and
- *KB v NHS Pensions Agency* (2004).

Answer

The Treaty requires Member States not to discriminate on the basis of nationality when dealing with citizens of the EU. This is important because the recent judgments of the ECJ have stated that whether an individual is a 'worker' is a matter of fact for the national court (*Ninni-Orasche* (2003)). When deciding a case of discrimination, the law developed by the EU has two categories: direct and indirect discrimination. Direct discrimination is the more obvious category where a worker, normally a woman, is paid less than her male colleagues without any justification. Indirect discrimination deals with more subtle forms of discrimination between workers.

The first main area of discrimination in employment that came before the ECJ was the principle of 'equal pay for work of equal value'. This was based on the then **Art 119 EC**, now numbered **141 EC**. In the case of *Defrenne v Sabena* (1976), the ECJ decided that there was sufficient in **Art 141** to allow Madame Defrenne to claim equal pay with male stewards working for the national Belgium airline. This was a form of direct discrimination where a worker suffers from less favourable pay or treatment and there is a causal connection between the sex of the worker and the lower pay. It is sufficient for the worker to prove an example of the equivalent work by a man being better paid than a women doing similar work. It is for the employer to then prove that the difference in pay is based on some objective criteria, not based on the sex of the worker who is claiming that he or she has been discriminated against. Direct discrimination of this type can only rarely be justified. To widen the scope of this form of direct discrimination the ECJ has given a wide definition of pay to include sick pay, contributory pension rights, bonuses and other payments such as concessionary fares.

Although the law on direct discrimination was tackled first, the European law was concerned that other forms of discrimination should be dealt with. The **Equal Treatment Directive 76/207** lays down a general principle for equal treatment in conditions of employment, other than pay. **Article 2 (1)** of the Directive states that the application of the principle of equal treatment 'shall mean that there shall be no discrimination whatsoever on grounds of sex either directly or indirectly by reference in particular to marital or family status'. The ECJ saw a link between the narrow wording of **Art 141 EC** and the wider application of the Directive to indirect discrimination. Indirect discrimination is a legal concept which enables cases of unequal treatment, for which there is an objective justification but which in fact results in the woman being disadvantaged, to be included as an instance of unlawful sex discrimination. The case of *Enderby v Frenchay Health Authority* (1994) illustrates this wider context. Here Dr Enderby, a speech therapist, brought proceedings against her employer before an industrial tribunal, claiming that she was involved in work of equal value to that of a principal clinical psychologist and a grade three principal pharmacist, but her pay was substantially lower. In the *Enderby* case, her professional group was characterised as a 'purely female profession' and her counsel put forward the argument that in a purely female profession, the membership of that profession can have effects which are similar to a link with part-time work. The fact that speech therapists are almost exclusively women is also at least partly due to the connection between the social role of women and work. The opportunities of working part-time and of flexible arrangements of working are particularly attractive to women.

The Advocate General in the *Enderby* case stated that the purpose of the law was to deal with situations where women are placed at a disadvantage in their working lives. Therefore, in accordance with the teleological method of interpretation, a pragmatic approach ought to be pursued. This is a method that does not easily come to the UK judiciary. The ECJ held in the *Enderby* case that differences in pay between two different jobs assumed to be of equal value, one of which was performed almost entirely by women and the other predominantly by men, constituted *prima facie*, sex discrimination. However, the Court also accepted that the differentials could be justified by objective criteria. Thus with both direct and indirect discrimination the claimant can raise a rebuttable presumption of discrimination. In the first case with a specific comparison and in the other by a comparison of groups, which places the onus on the employer to adduce evidence in rebuttal of that presumption or to produce a justification. **Article 141** (formerly 119) **EC** requires the employer to justify objectively the difference in pay between job A and job B.

What reasons can be put forward by an employer to justify objectively the difference in pay? In some circumstances the employer may be compelled by the labour market to offer higher remuneration for members of a particular professional group in order to attract suitable applicants. The only question then is the extent to which the objective reason can serve to justify the difference in pay. In *Nimz* (1992), the Court held that collective agreement which allows employers to maintain a distinction as regards overall pay between two categories of workers who are both performing the same type of work but on part-time and full-time bases, does constitute discrimination against female workers *vis à vis* male workers, if in fact a much lower percentage of men work on a part-time basis than women. Such an agreement must therefore in principle be regarded as contrary to **Art 141 EC**, unless the difference in treatment between the two categories of workers can be shown to be based on objectively justified factors unrelated to any discrimination on grounds of sex. In *Bilka-Kaufhaus* (1986), the employer argued that full-time employees gained experience and thus skills and abilities more quickly than part-timers working less than three-fourths of normal hours. However, the Court held that this was not sufficient to justify objectively the difference in treatment. In the *Danfoss* case (1989), the employees' union produced statistics relating to the wages paid to 157 workers between 1982 and 1986, which showed that the average wage paid to men was 6.85% higher than that paid to women. The employers claimed that these differences were due to the application of criteria for additional payments based upon mobility, training and length of service, but the Court said that they had to be justified. If the claimant is successful, they should not be deprived of appropriate levels of damages by any national law (*Levez v Jennings* (1999)).

Clearly, EU law on discrimination in employment deals with those situations where it is based on sex or gender but the ECJ has taken the law further. The ECJ has interpreted discrimination based on sex to include transsexuals. In the case of *P v S* (1996), a male worker told his employer that he intended to undergo 'gender reassignment', which would be preceded by a period when he would dress and behave as a woman. P started his treatment to change his gender but was dismissed and he then claimed unlawful sexual discrimination. The ECJ held that discrimination arising from gender reassignment was based on the sex of the person, and therefore the EU law on discrimination applied. However, in *Grant v South-West Trains Ltd* (1998), the ECJ decided that the EU law did not cover sexual orientation discrimination, presumably on the basis that as a female homosexual, Grant was being treated the same as a male homosexual, that is, there was no discrimination on the grounds of sex. The matter was resolved when in May 1999 the new **Art 13 EC**, inserted by the **Treaty of Amsterdam**, dealing with sexual orientation, came into effect. Recently, in the case of *KB v NHS Pensions Agency* (2004), the ECJ held that British legislation preventing post-operative transsexuals from marrying in their acquired gender could be regarded as a breach of EU discrimination law. This judgment relied heavily on the case law of the European Court on Human Rights, which had held that such individuals should be allowed to marry. If they could not marry they were being treated less favourably than other relationships.

The requirements of **Art 141 EC** and the associated directives are mandatory in nature so the prohibition of discrimination on the grounds of gender between male and female workers applies to public and private organisations. The anti-discrimination law has been extended by other directives. Perhaps the most important was the **Framework Directive 2000/78** which covers religion or belief, disability, age and sexual orientation. A new **Equal Treatment Directive 2002/73** came into effect in October 2005. It did not repeal the **Directive 76/207** but substantially amended it. It provides greater protection for workers who suffer discrimination or harassment at work and therefore brings the area of sex discrimination law into line with other discrimination law affecting employment.

Question 44

Analyse TWO of the following cases which came before the ECJ, and explain their importance in the development of Community law:

(a) *Defrenne (No 2)* – Case 43/75;

(b) *Marshall* – Case 152/84;

(c) *Barber* – Case 262/88.

Answer plan

When approaching a question like this, the temptation is to produce too descriptive an answer. The facts are important, but are only one element of the answer. You should deal with the following:

- the facts, the legal points raised and the decision of the Court.
- the kind of case it was – whether a preliminary reference or a direct action and which Article of the Treaty it was based upon.
- the cases chosen for this type of question have usually played their part in developing or reinforcing European Court judgments – what part has this case played?

Answer

(a) Defrenne (No 2) – Case 43/75

Madame Defrenne was employed as an air hostess by Sabena, a Belgian airline company. She claimed that, in paying their male stewards more than their air hostesses, even though they were performing identical tasks, Sabena was in breach of **Art 141** (then **Art 119**). It was conceded by the employer that Defrenne did the same job as that done by male stewards, but, until 1966, she was paid less than them under the terms of a collective agreement negotiated between Sabena and the unions. She began her action in 1968, claiming the difference between her remuneration and that of men from 1963 to 1966. Under Belgian law, there is a five-year limitation rule, so she was taking her claim as far back as she possibly could. She began her action in a Belgian labour court, which made a reference to the European Court under **Art 234** (then **Art 177**), seeking the interpretation of **Art 141** (then **Art 119**).

Article 141 provides that equal pay for work of equal value will be ensured during the first stage of the Community (ie, five years). This period expired at the end of 1961 without any action being taken by the Member States to implement **Art 141** and the Commission had made a recommendation on the issue. As a result of this, the Member States adopted a Resolution which purported to give themselves more time, that is, extending this first stage. When this period, too, expired, the European Commission failed to use the procedure under **Art 226** (then **Art 169**) against defaulting States, something it was criticised for by the Court. However, Madame Defrenne claimed that this failure on the part of the Member States did not affect her rights under **Art 141** (then **Art 119**), because it had direct effect. The Member States and the Commission did not consider that the Article had, in fact, become directly effective at the end of the first stage, when the Member States had failed to fulfil their obligations under the Treaty.

The ECJ had found Articles of the Treaty to have direct effect before this case, as in *Van Gend en Loos* (1963), but, generally, this was in cases where the Articles involved a cross-border or transnational element. In the case of *Van Duyn* (1975), **Art 39** (then **Art 48**), which deals with discrimination on the grounds of nationality, was found to have direct effect. But, that concept of discrimination is straightforward when compared with **Art 141** (then **Art 119**) which requires 'equal pay for equal work'. However, the Court identified that discrimination could be direct or indirect. With direct or overt discrimination it was possible for an individual to make a challenge without the need for further supplementary measures to identify what the term means. With regard to such actions, the Court held that **Art 141** (then **Art 119**) was directly effective, because the criteria set for the principle of direct effect to apply were present.

It was necessary for directives to be issued to deal with the more disguised indirect discrimination, but Madame Defrenne was successful in her action for equal pay. As part of the social policy of the Community, the Court believed that the principle of **Art 141** (then **Art 119**) was a fundamental right of Community citizens. This 'social' right was supported by the economic fear on the part of some Member States that the failure to have equal pay would lead to variations in business overheads, and thus competition between the Member States. However, the Court recognised the financial impact of its judgment that **Art 141** (then **Art 119**) would have direct effect in both the public and the private sector. The Court limited its ruling by stating that anyone who had not already initiated an action in their Member State would not be able to claim 'back pay' in the way that Madame Defrenne had. All future cases would not be able to claim for a period dating back to before the judgment in this case.

(b) Marshall – Case 152/84

Miss Marshall was employed by Southampton Area Health Authority as a senior dietician until she reached the age of 62. When she reached this age, she was dismissed, even though she had expressed the wish to continue in employment until she was 65 years of age. The sole reason for her dismissal was that she was a woman who had passed the retirement age applied by the health authority to women. The authority's general policy was that its employees should retire when they reached the age at which State retirement pensions became payable. This was 60 for women and 65 for men. The authority was willing to waive its general policy for particular individuals in particular circumstances. This it had done for Miss Marshall by employing her for two more years after she reached 60. Marshall complained to an industrial tribunal against her dismissal, which she claimed was contrary to the **Sex Discrimination Act 1975** and **Directive 76/207**, in that it unlawfully discriminated against her on the grounds of her sex.

The health authority claimed that, in laying down the retirement ages for its employees, it was merely reflecting the different retirement ages for State pensions. These differences in age were permitted by **Art 1(2)** of **Directive 76/207**. In addition, they argued that an EC directive could never impose obligations on individuals and could only have direct effect against a Member State in its capacity as a public authority, and not as an employer. The case reached the Court of Appeal, where a reference was made under **Art 234** (then **Art 177**) to the ECJ. The Court of Appeal asked two questions on the interpretation of **Directive 76/207**. The European Court's answer was that the principle of equality of treatment was one of fundamental importance, and therefore **Directive 76/207** was to be strictly interpreted. Thus, the exception to the prohibition of discrimination on the grounds of sex in relation to the granting of old age pension and retirement ages was in this category. **Article 5(1)** of **Directive 76/207** was to be interpreted as meaning that a general policy dismissing women when they reached the State pension retirement age constituted discrimination on the grounds of sex, contrary to the Directive.

Although the ECJ accepted the principle that a directive could not impose obligations on an individual, that is, horizontal direct effect, this was not true where the State was involved. It did not matter in what capacity the State was involved, in that it could be as an employer or as a public authority. In this case, Miss Marshall was able to invoke **Directive 76/207** against her employer, the health authority, since this authority was an 'emanation of the State'. The main point was to stop a Member State taking advantage of its own failure to comply with Community law.

(c) Barber v Guardian Royal Exchange – Case 262/88

Barber was an employee of Guardian Royal Exchange (GRE). He was a member of a contracted-out pension scheme established and wholly financed by his employer. Under this scheme, the normal pensionable age was 62 for men and 57 for women. In the event of redundancy, the scheme provided for immediate payment of a pension to men aged 55 or women aged 50. Barber was made redundant at the age of 52, so he did not qualify immediately for a pension, but would receive a deferred pension payable when he reached the age of 62. He complained to an industrial tribunal, claiming unlawful discrimination on the grounds of sex. The tribunal dismissed his application, as did the Employment Appeal Tribunal. Barber appealed to the Court of Appeal, which made a reference to the European Court under **Art 234** (then **Art 177**). The reference asked whether benefits paid to a redundant employee by his employer were subject to either **Art 141** (then **Art 119**), dealing with equal pay, or the **Equal Pay Directive 75/117** and the **Equal Treatment Directive 76/207**. The Court answered that **Art 141** (then **Art 119**) did apply.

The previous case law of the European Court had been uncertain. In *Garland v BREL* (1982), the Court had held that certain benefits paid after retirement constituted pay. In *Worrington v Lloyds Bank Ltd* (1982), the Court rejected adjustments in gross pay designed to compensate for differential pension contributions as being incompatible with **Art 141** (then **Art 119**). In *Bilka-Kaufhaus GmbH v Weber von Harz* (1986), it had held that a purely contractual pension paid by an employer came within **Art 141** (then **Art 119**), whereas in *Burton v British Railways Board* (1982), the Court had held that a man denied access to a voluntary redundancy scheme on account of his age had not been a victim of a breach of **Art 141** (then **Art 119**). In addition to this, the Community has always made it clear that State pensions are excluded from the scope of **Art 141**.

The reasoning of the *Barber* judgment was that the private, contracted-out occupational pension constituted consideration paid indirectly by the employer, and therefore fell within the scope of 'pay' within **Art 141** (then **Art 119**). This also applied to any benefit paid on redundancy. Putting these two together, it meant that the pension and redundancy payments payable to Barber came within **Art 141** (then **Art 119**). As there were different age qualifications for men and women under the pension scheme payable on redundancy, this offended against the principle of equal pay for men and women stated in **Art 141** (then **Art 119**).

This was a very important judgment with far-reaching implications for individual workers and the administration of occupational pension schemes. Both the Commission and the UK Government had mentioned to the Court in their interventions that this case would have financial consequences for these pension schemes. They asked the Court to limit the impact of its judgment, as the Court had done earlier in *Defrenne* (1976). This is what the Court actually did. The Court ruled that the direct effect of **Art 141** (then **Art 119**) to such occupational pension schemes would generally only apply to cases arising after the date of the judgment in this case, with one exception. This was that cases already initiated, or where claims had already been raised under national law, could proceed on the basis of direct effect of **Art 141** (then **Art 119**).

The reason given by the Court for this limitation of the impact of its judgment in *Barber* was that **Directive 79/7** had authorised Member States to defer from the principle of equal treatment for men and women in certain matters, including contracted-out occupational pension schemes. Thus the administrators of such schemes had been entitled to believe that they were not acting contrary to **Art 141**. In the interests of legal certainty, the retroactivity of this judgment would have severe effects on the financial balance of such schemes. **Protocol 2 of the Maastricht Treaty** reinforces this point by stating that, although there is full and immediate acceptance of the implications of the *Barber* judgment, problems have been created for employers, pension funds, insurance companies, etc. Therefore, the Protocol confirms that equal treatment in occupational schemes must be applied in respect of employment after 17 May 1990.

CHAPTER 11

EXTERNAL RELATIONS

INTRODUCTION

The external relations of the European Community include its ability to enter into agreements with third countries and international organisations. Therefore, the key point of this topic relates to the competence of the Community to enter such agreements. Generally speaking, the questions which occur on this topic are essay type, although on very rare occasions the direct effect of a treaty provision may appear in a problem question.

Checklist

Students should ensure that they understand the general point on the legal personality of the Community (**Art 281**) and the following points:

- the express external competence of the Community, including the common commercial policy (**Arts 131–134**), association agreements (**Art 310**) and agreements with international organisations (**Arts 302–304**);
- the procedure laid down in the Treaty for negotiating international agreements (**Art 300**), including the roles of the Council, Commission and the European Court;
- the implied external powers of the Community associated with the doctrine of parallelism;
- mixed agreements; and
- the direct effect of Treaty provisions.

Question 45

What are the express treaty-making powers of the EU? Do individuals derive any rights from such treaties?

Answer plan

This essay question, the most common form of question on external relations, requires an answer which covers the following points:

- express treaty-making powers, including the common commercial policy and association agreements;
- *Opinion 1/75;*
- *Opinion 1/78;*
- direct effect of Articles of treaties;
- *International Fruit Co;*
- *Bresciani;* and
- *Haegeman v Belgian State.*

Answer

This question raises two issues for consideration: community competence and the ability of individuals to enforce any rights arising from these treaties. Express treaty-making power is granted by the **EC Treaty** in two cases: commercial agreements (**Art 133**) and association agreements (**Art 310**). **Article 300** lays down the general rules regarding the procedure to be followed where the treaty-making power is exercised, but does not itself confer such powers on the Community. In addition, **Arts 302–304** require the Community to co-operate with international organisations, and this is generally achieved by international agreements. The general rule is that all such international agreements are negotiated by the Commission and concluded by the Council.

The common commercial policy of the EC is a very important area of Community activity. Although it does not come within **Pt 2** of the **EC Treaty**, which deals with the foundations of the Community, its appearance in **Pt 3**, dealing with the economic policy, reflects its importance. As the Community is based upon a customs union, it is necessary for not only a removal of internal barriers to trade, but also a common policy towards goods coming from outside the Community. This is where the common external tariff is required, as well as other measures related to the regulation of external influences of a commercial character on the internal market and its producers.

The common commercial policy is covered by **Arts 131–134**. It is **Art 133** which gives an indication of the scope of the policy. It relates to tariff rates, trade agreements, export policy and measures to protect trade such as are necessary to deal with dumping or subsidies. The ECJ has stated that this list is not exhaustive, but merely examples of its scope. In *Opinion 1/75 (Understanding on a Local Costs Standard)*, the Court stated that the commercial policy is made up of a combination and interaction of internal and external measures. It reflects a progressive development of a body of rules which come together to apply to the field of common commercial policy. In this Opinion, it was explicitly stated by the Court that the Community had exclusive power in this field of the common commercial policy. If this was not accepted, it would allow individual Member States to adopt positions on export credits which may differ from those of the Community and distort the institutional framework in which the common commercial policy should operate. Under **Art 133**, the Commission submits proposals to the Council for implementing the common commercial policy. If negotiations are required with third countries, these are authorised by the Council but undertaken by the Commission. Any agreement is concluded by the Council on behalf of the Community.

However, in its *Opinion 1/78 on the International Agreement on Natural Rubber*, the Court did recognise that in certain circumstances the participation of the Member States in an international agreement was necessary. This Opinion concerned an international agreement designed to achieve a balanced growth between the supply and demand for natural rubber. This required a guaranteed stable export earning for exporting countries, whilst ensuring supplies for importing countries at a fair price. In order to achieve this, it was decided to establish a buffer stock to even out fluctuations in the market for natural rubber. Although the subject matter of this agreement fell within the common commercial policy of **Art 133**, the financing of the buffer stock was to be provided by the Member State. If the financing had been provided by the Community, the Community would have exclusive power. Thus, as finance was to be provided directly by the Member States, they could participate in the agreement together with the Community.

Association agreements are governed by **Art 310**, which provides for such agreements with a non-Member State or an international organisation. Such agreements often act as preliminary to, or substitutes for, membership of the Community.

If the Community enters into agreements with third countries or international organisations, can these be invoked by individuals before their national courts? The effect of treaties on individuals within the European Community varies from one Member State to another, depending upon whether it is a monist or dualist State. For example, in Belgium, France, Greece, Luxembourg and the Netherlands, treaties can usually be invoked in national courts and are normally given priority over national laws, whereas in other Member States, such as the UK and Ireland, treaties cannot be invoked at all, but are considered to be purely a matter for the executive. In such countries, the content of such treaties can only be made binding as to individuals through separate legislation.

In the second *Haegeman* case (1974), the ECJ referred to the fact that treaties with third countries are concluded by an act of the Council and that their provisions form an integral part of Community law. The main principle which has to be considered in this respect is the direct effect of these agreements. In dealing with this question, there is no indication in the Treaty itself that such agreements may be directly effective, and the ECJ has not been wholly consistent in its approach. When deciding questions of direct effect, the Court is seeking to satisfy three requirements. These are that a measure must be clear and unambiguous; it must be unconditional; and it must take effect without further action by the EC Member State. These apply to any measure which an applicant claims is directly effective.

In the *International Fruit Co* case (1972), the company claimed that certain EC regulations violated **Art XI** of the **General Agreement on Tariffs and Trade (GATT)**. The Court had to decide whether the international agreement was capable of conferring rights on citizens of the Community which they can invoke before national courts. It was clear that the **GATT** agreement was binding upon the Community and thus its Member States. However, the general scheme and terms of the **General Agreement** were such that only the Contracting Parties or States could act if one of the other Contracting Parties acted contrary to the agreement. Therefore, the **GATT** agreement was not capable of conferring on citizens of the Community rights which they could invoke before national courts.

However, in the *Bresciani* case (1976), the Court accepted that an association agreement did confer rights on Community citizens which the national courts of the Community must protect. In this case, Bresciani was importing raw cowhides from Senegal, a State which came within an association agreement under the **Yaounde Convention**. Under Italian law, an inspection fee was charged, covering the cost of examinations and laboratory tests. This fee amounted to a charge having an equivalent effect to a customs duty and was prohibited under the Treaty. Also, in *Haegeman v Belgian State* (1974), the ECJ accepted that the association agreement with Greece was an act of the institutions of the Community and therefore within an **Art 234** (then **Art 177**) preliminary reference for interpretation.

Therefore, there are a number of specific subject matters where the Treaty grants express treaty-making powers to the Community, notably under the common commercial policy, the association policy and relationship agreements. This was confirmed in the 'open skies' cases concerning agreements made by some Member States and the USA (*Commission v UK* (2002)). In addition, following the *ERTA* case (1971), the external competence of the Community has been extended by the doctrine of parallelism, whereby an internal power may give rise to an external competence. Whatever the origins of the external power, the approach of the Court has not been consistent. The result has made the individual very dependent, on occasions, on the approach taken by the courts of the Member State towards the recognition of treaties with third countries.

Question 46

What is meant by the doctrine of parallelism? What has been its impact on the external competency of the EC?

Answer plan

The doctrine of parallelism is derived from the judgment in the *ERTA* case and, therefore, the answer requires this case to be dealt with and also the following points:

- legal personality of the Community under **Art 281**;
- express treaty-making powers;
- *Cornelis Kramer* case;
- *Opinion 1/75*;
- *Opinion 1/76*;
- *Opinion 1/78*; and
- *Opinion 1/92*.

Answer

The doctrine of parallelism is associated with the external relations of the European Community. The Community was given its own legal personality, separate from its Member States, by **Art 281**. This meant that it had the power to enter into agreements with third countries or international organisations like the **GATT**. Having been given this authority by the Treaty, there are specific Articles of the Treaty which give express powers to enter into agreements on specific matters. For example, the Community may conclude agreements with third countries under **Arts 131–134** on those matters which come within the common commercial policy enumerated in **Art 133**.

As far as the Member States were concerned, the Community only had those external powers which were expressly conferred by the Treaty. If there were no such express powers, they felt that none were to be implied. The Member States were rudely awakened when the ECJ gave its judgment in the *ERTA* case (1971). This case was brought before the Court because of a dispute between the Council and the Commission over the division of powers and responsibilities in exercising the external powers of the EU. This agreement provided the power to regulate the maximum driving hours for lorry drivers. The governments of the Member States

185

claimed that, as treaty-making power had not been expressly granted to the Community, the competence for such agreements remained with them. The Commission had started proceedings under **Art 230** (then **Art 173**) for the annulment of the Council's discussions resulting in a common position.

The Commission failed on the merits of the case because the negotiations for the European Road Transport Agreement were well advanced before the adoption of a Council Regulation on road transport. However, the ECJ laid down the general principle that the existence of Community common rules precludes Member States from undertaking obligations with third countries which affect those rules. The Member States objected to this idea, because they said that it ignored the political element of such international treaties. However, the Court had reached this conclusion based upon **Art 281** (then **Art 210**) relating to all the objectives defined in **Pt 1** of the Treaty. This means that each time the Community adopts provisions laying down common rules to implement a common policy envisaged by the Treaty, the Member States no longer have the right to undertake obligations with third countries which affect those rules. This applies regardless of whether a Member State is acting individually or collectively with other Member States. They all have to operate within the framework of the Community. The result is that the Community has exclusive power in all external matters affecting the application of the Community legal system, as the internal measures are inseparable from the external aspect.

The adoption of internal rules is frequently referred to as conferring Community competence in external relations. In the *Cornelis Kramer* case (1976), proceedings had been instituted in the Dutch courts against fishermen accused of contravening laws limiting catches of certain fish. These laws had been adopted in accordance with a recommendation of the North East Atlantic Fisheries Commission, a body established by an international convention ratified by all EC States except for Italy and Luxembourg. The Dutch court asked, by way of an **Art 234** (then **Art 177**) reference, whether the Community alone has authority to enter into commitments of the kind contained in the international convention. The Court held that the Community must enjoy the capacity to enter into international agreements over the whole field of **Pt 1** of the Treaty. However, the Court did concede that transitional interim concurrent rights might be exercised by Member States until such time as the Community itself exercised its own functions. When this happened, the power came within the exclusive power of the Community. This case seems to apply to the *ERTA* decision.

This was discussed in the **Art 300** (then **Art 228**) *Opinion 1/75 on Export Credits*, where the Commission argued that the conclusion of the OECD Local Costs Understanding was a matter of exclusive Community competence. However, the Member States cited *ERTA*, and argued that this could only be true if there were corresponding internal rules. In its judgment, the Court did not deal with this point, but held that the Understanding came within the Community's commercial policy under **Art 133** (then **Arts 113** and **114**) and was thus within an exclusive

Community competence. The Court spoke of the impossibility of concurrent powers being exercised at the same time in regard to the subject matter.

In *Opinion 1/76 (Laying Up Fund)*, the Court made it clear that the existence of rules was not necessarily the prerequisite for the existence of Community competence. The power to bind the Community with third countries flows from the implications of the provision of the treaties creating the internal power. Also, in *Opinion 1/76*, the Court held that the Community is entitled to co-operate with another country in setting up a public international organisation and in granting powers of decision to that organisation. However, the Court stated that the structural elements of the Community cannot be sacrificed by the competence of a new international organisation. This view was repeated in the ECJ's Opinion regarding the European Economic Area (EEA) in 1992. The Opinion of the Court (*Opinion 1/92*) was that the establishment of a joint EEA Court was incompatible with the **Treaty of Rome** 'and would lead to serious legal complications'.

Therefore, Community competence in external relations exists where there is an internal power to act, whether or not it has been exercised, and participation in an agreement is necessary. This is illustrated by the case brought by the Commission against some Member States that had entered into 'open skies' bilateral agreements with the USA (*Commission v UK* (2002)). An internal power is therefore paralleled or mirrored by an external competence. This is the basis of the doctrine of parallelism, which has greatly extended the external competence of the European Community. There have been complications on occasions where the agreement with third countries have been 'mixed' agreements. This is where there is some competence with the Community and some within the powers and responsibilities of the Member States. In *Opinion 1/78 (National Rubber)*, the ECJ accepted participation by the Community and Member States in an agreement which was clearly within the Community's commercial policy. This reflected the pragmatic view often taken by the Court. Under the 'economic' clauses of the agreement, finance was to be provided by the Member States, hence their participation. However, if the finance was provided by the Community, it would have exclusive competence and the participation by the Member States would not be accepted.

Question 47

Analyse TWO of the following cases which came before the ECJ, and explain their importance in the development of Community law:

(a) *ERTA* – Case 22/70;

(b) *Cornelis Kramer* – Cases 3, 4 and 6/76;

(c) *Opinion 1/75*.

Answer plan

When approaching a question like this, the temptation is to produce too descriptive an answer. The facts are important, but are only one element of the answer. You should deal with the following points:

- the facts, the legal points raised and the decision of the Court.
- the kind of case it was – whether a preliminary reference or a direct action and which Article of the Treaty it was based upon.
- the cases chosen for this type of question have usually played their part in developing or reinforcing European Court judgments – what part has this case played?

Answer

(a) ERTA – Case 22/70

In January 1962, under the auspices of the United Nations Economic Commission for Europe, the European Agreement concerning the work of drivers of vehicles engaged in cross-border journeys (ERTA) was signed by five of the then six Member States of the Community. The Agreement never came into effect, owing to a lack of sufficient ratification. Subsequently, negotiations began again in 1967 to revise the Agreement. Meanwhile, work had been going on within the EU with regard to harmonisation of driving and rest periods for drivers of road transport vehicles, resulting in a 1969 regulation. At its meeting in 1970, the Council of Ministers discussed the attitude to be adopted towards the forthcoming ERTA negotiations. They agreed on a common position, as required by the **EC Treaty**. However, the Commission disagreed with this procedure, because it felt that this was now a matter for the Community and not the individual Member States. The Commission brought this case before the European Court under **Art 230** (then **Art 173**), seeking judicial review of the Council's common position and negotiation of the ERTA.

The main point of the case concerned the issue of who had competence with regard to external agreements on this policy area. If it was still with the Member States, then the Council of Ministers' actions would be within the Treaty. However, if it was now a Community competence, the Treaty specified how the negotiations should take place. The Council claimed that as the Community only had such powers as had been conferred on it, authority to enter into agreements with third countries cannot be assumed in the absence of an express provision of the Treaty. More specifically, **Art 71** (then **Art 75**), which conferred upon the Community powers defined in wide terms, implementing the common transport policy, relates only to internal measures.

The ECJ, however, said that, in the absence of specific provisions of the Treaty relating to the negotiation and conclusion of international agreements in the sphere of transport policy, it is necessary to look to the general system of Community law in the sphere of relations with third countries. **Article 281** (then **Art 210**) provides the Community with legal personality to establish links with third countries over the whole field of objectives defined in **Pt 1** of the Treaty. Each time the Community, with a view to implementing a common policy envisaged by the Treaty, adopts provisions laying down common rules, the Member States no longer have the right, whether acting individually or collectively, to undertake obligations with third countries which affect these rules. This applies whatever form the internal rules may take. Once this happens, the Community alone is in a position to assume and carry out contractual obligations toward third countries affecting the whole sphere of application of the Community legal system. The Member States must operate within the institutional framework of the Community, by which the Commission negotiates and the Council concludes such international agreements.

Although, on the facts, the Court found that the Council had not exceeded its powers, the judgment was to have long-term implications for the external competence of the Community. The case developed the idea of parallel internal and external Community competence.

(b) Cornelis Kramer – Cases 3, 4 and 6/76

Criminal proceedings had been brought against certain Dutch fishermen who were accused of having infringed the Dutch rules limiting the catches of sole and plaice. These rules had been adopted on the basis of the provisions of the **North East Atlantic Fisheries Convention**. The Dutch court made a preliminary reference to the European Court under **Art 234** (then **Art 177**) on the external competence of the Community. In essence, the questions asked were on whether Member States retained the power to adopt measures such as those under the Convention, whether such measures are compatible with Community law and whether the Community had exclusive competence in this policy area.

As there was an absence of a specific provision in the Treaty authorising the Community to enter into international commitments in the sphere of conservation of fish, the Court looked to the general system of Community law in the sphere of external relations of the Community. The Court recited the traditional view that **Art 281** (then **Art 210**) gave the Community legal personality, and therefore the capacity to enter into international commitments over the whole range of Community objectives. The Court said that, in this specific case, it must be recognised that authority to enter into particular international agreements may be express or implied from the provisions of the Treaty. The only way to ensure the conservation of fish, both effectively and equitably, was through a system of rules binding on all the States concerned, irrespective of whether they were members of the European Community. In these circumstances, it follows from the duties and powers which

Community law has established internally that the Community has authority to enter into international commitments on fish conservation. However, having established that the Community has authority, the Court needed to look at whether the Community had assumed external responsibility.

The Community had not yet fully exercised its functions in fish conservation and therefore, when the Convention arose, the Member States had the power to assume commitments, such as the Convention. Having had the power to enter the Convention, the Member State now had the power to enforce it within the area of its jurisdiction. However, the Court pointed out quite clearly that the authority of the Member State was of only a transitional nature, until the Community had acted so as to assume exclusive competence in this policy area. This had to happen at the latest six years after accession as, by that time, the Council was required under **Art 102** of the **Act of Accession 1972** to introduce measures for fish conservation. Once this had happened, the Member States were under a duty to use all the political and legal means available to ensure the participation of the Community in the Convention and similar agreements.

(c) Opinion 1/75

Under **Art 300** (then **Art 228**), the ECJ can be asked to give its opinion on the compatibility of proposed international agreements with the **EC Treaty**. This opinion by the Court was on a draft Understanding on a Local Cost Standard, drawn up under the auspices of the OECD. The key question was whether the Community had the power to conclude such an agreement and whether that power was exclusive.

The Treaty does include, in **Arts 132** and **133**, a commercial policy which covers both internal rules and the power to conclude agreements with third countries. The field of the common commercial policy necessarily covers systems of aid for exports, and more particularly, measures concerning credits for the financing of local costs linked to export operations. These were the main provisions of this draft Treaty. The Council had already adopted directives on credit insurance in 1970 and 1971. Therefore, the Court concluded that the subject matter of the Understanding on a Local Costs Standard was within the sphere of the common commercial policy, and thus within the ambit of the Community's powers.

The Court said that a commercial policy is, in fact, made up by the combination and interaction of internal and external measures, without priority being taken by one over the others. Sometimes, agreements are concluded in execution of a policy fixed in advance, while sometimes that policy is defined by the agreements themselves. Such agreements may be outline agreements, the purpose of which is to lay down uniform principles. This was the case with the Understanding on Local Costs.

On the question of exclusive competency, the Court said that, given the Community's commercial policy, it would not be acceptable for Member States to exercise a concurrent power in either the internal or the international sphere.

Article 133 (then **Arts 113** and **114**) shows clearly that the exercise of concurrent powers by Member States and the Community is impossible. To accept the contrary view would be to recognise that in relations with third countries, Member States may adopt positions which differ from those agreed upon by the Community through its institutions. The Court said that it was of little importance that the obligations and financial burdens inherent in the execution of the agreement envisaged by the Understanding are borne directly by the Member States.

The Member States argued before the Court that the conclusion of the Understanding was not a matter of exclusive Community competence based upon the decision in the *ERTA* case. They said that there were no corresponding internal rules, so there could not be any parallel external competence. However, the Court did not deal with this point in its judgment, but held that the Understanding fell within the Community's commercial policy. Following on from the *ERTA* case, this judgment added to the exclusive external powers of the Community.

CHAPTER 12

THE INTERNAL MARKET AND BEYOND

█ INTRODUCTION

The internal market will always be topical, as the EU is based upon a customs union; therefore, the problems encountered with the reality of such an organisation will go in and out of fashion. At the moment, the main questions are on the legal implications leading up to the completion of the internal market, the important cases on the freedoms associated with the Community and the **Maastricht Treaty**. The **Treaty of Amsterdam** and the introduction of a single currency outline the next stage in the development of the Community.

Generally, questions on this topic are essay type questions, simply because problems would usually have to be very complicated to encompass the topic. As this topic changes so rapidly, it is very important to read newspapers to follow the changing political and legal environment in which the Community operates.

Checklist

You should be familiar with the following:

- the background to the **Single European Act 1986**, notably the Commission's White Paper on the completion of the internal market;
- the **Single European Act – Arts** 18 and 95 on the internal market, the changes to the voting procedures in the Council of Ministers and the powers of the European Parliament;
- the **Maastricht Treaty on Economic and Monetary Union**, but more importantly on European Union; and
- the proposed changes to the institutional balance.

Question 48

Discuss the importance of the **Treaty of Nice** in the development of an enlarged European Union.

Answer plan

The work of the Convention on the Future of Europe received a great deal of publicity during the early 2000s as the impending enlargement of the EU approached, and it did produce discussion documents on a large number of important topics that are still part of the current debate. This type of discussion question is increasingly used to get students to discuss these current issues in the context of what the Convention recommended, the failure of the **Constitutional Treaty** and subsequent problems with the compromise **Lisbon Treaty**. You need to include the following points:

- the events leading up the Inter-Governmental Conference (IGC) at Nice in December 2000;
- the background to the enlargement to 27 Member States;
- the impact on the main institutions of the EU, namely the European Parliament, Council and Commission;
- the **Laeken Declaration** and the work of the Convention;
- the Convention recommendations and the **Constitutional Treaty**; and
- the **Lisbon Treaty**.

Answer

As the IGC in 1996 failed to address the issues of institutional reform and enlargement of the EU, the resulting **Treaty of Amsterdam** in 1997 neglected these issues. The result was that these matters became more pressing for the next IGC that culminated in the **Treaty of Nice**, concluded in December 2000. The EU of 15 Member States realised that with the enlargement to 25 or more States in the near future, it was imperative that the institutions were reformed, not only in their membership, but also in the way they operated. Also, if the present policies were continued in the Common Agricultural Policy or the Regional Development Funds, there would be serious financial implications following enlargement. This essay will concentrate on the institutional issues that form an important part of the **Treaty of Nice** and which are the bases of current EU institutional practices.

It was recognised that with the expansion of the EU from 15 to 25 Member States in 2004 and 27 in 2007, the institutions needed to be reformed. Suggestions had been made by the 'Three Wise Men' in their report in the 1970s but there had never been the political will to take the initiatives needed to deal with the Commission and the Council of Ministers. Although the European Parliament had changed – especially since 1979, when direct elections were introduced – the European Commission had been ignored. There had also been suggestions that had raised doubts as to whether the Commission in its 1990s form could work effectively to fulfil its responsibilities under **Art 211**.

The then Commission had 20 members; each Member State nominating one Commissioner but France, Germany, Italy, Spain and the UK nominating two. This was very convenient for the UK, as it was allowed to nominate one person from the government, Neil Kinnock, and one from the main opposition party, Chris Patten. However, if that system were to continue, we would have over 30 Commissioners following enlargement, and this at a time when some argued that it was difficult to find meaningful roles for 20. There would also be the difficulty of managing a Commission of that size, despite the power given to the President of the Commission by the **Treaty of Nice**, and the maintenance of the principle of collective responsibility. The agreement reached in Nice was for each Member State to be limited to one Commissioner from 2005 onwards. This postponed the difficult decision with regard to the size of the Commission because it is inclusive, in that all Member States have at least one Commissioner. This still raises the problem as to the roles or portfolios they may be given. However, from the next stage of enlargement, when there were to be 25 members, the size of the Commission was to be smaller than the number of Member States. This reduction was to be achieved by a selection process based on a rotation system with the principle of equality being paramount. This is likely to lead to challenges by disappointed Member States before the ECJ and in fact did have an impact on the referendum held in Ireland on the Lisbon Treaty in 2008. There is still one Commissioner for each Member State in a European Union of 27!

The European Parliament, as the main democratic institution of the Union, had to be able to accommodate elected representatives from the new Member States. The number of MEPs was increased with the unification of Germany and this amounted in total to 626 members of the European Parliament. There was also the factor that the Parliament's building had been newly refurbished at great expense and could not be increased in size without even more expense. The solution was to put a cap on the number of MEPs, irrespective of any further enlargement. The IGC wanted to ensure appropriate representation of the peoples of the Member States and stated that the number of MEPs may not exceed 732 in the 2009 elections. Therefore, as new Member States joined, the number of MEPs for existing members was to be decreased proportionately. However, importantly for the European Parliament, the **Treaty of Nice** extended the co-decision procedure to seven more areas of policy.

This gave more authority to the European Parliament in these areas, although it does not extend to taxation or social security policies.

The Council generally takes decisions by a qualified majority, which requires a mixture of large and small Member States to agree on a particular issue. Article 205 lists the weighted votes for all Member States, with the larger countries having 29 votes and the smallest only three. Many of the new Member States had small or average size populations, and this was thought by some Member States such as Germany to act to the detriment of the larger existing Member States. Therefore, it was agreed in the **Treaty of Nice** to change the system of qualified majority voting. The new system is often referred to as the 'triple majority', as there are three aspects to it. Any decision must command the agreement of the majority of the overall number of Member States, it must have 255 out of the 342 weighted votes, or 73.9% and, lastly, the votes in favour must represent 62% of the total population of the EU. This last requirement only arises where a Member State so requests. There was also the issue of whether the existing rotation arrangement for the presidency of the Council every six months was workable within an enlarged Community.

With enlargement came an increase in the number of cases coming to the Community Courts, generally from the new Member States. Given the workload that the ECJ annually faces and the demands for a reduction in the time taken for preliminary rulings to be dealt with, reform was necessary. The Court of First Instance was therefore given an increase in powers so that it could hear direct actions and answer questions from the national courts using the **Art 234** preliminary reference procedure. The time-consuming staff cases were delegated to a specialised chamber, the European Union Civil Service Tribunal.

Although the **Nice Treaty** was concluded in December 2000, some linguistic problems had to be resolved, so the final version is dated February 2001. The next stage was the ratification by the various Member States, which proved a problem in one country. In Ireland, a referendum required by the Irish Constitution resulted in a 'No' vote in June 2001. This was finally reversed in another referendum in October 2002, and thus removed the last barrier to the implementation of the **Treaty of Nice**, which came into force on 1 February 2003. However, some matters were not settled at Nice. These included the delimitation of powers between the EU and the Member States, the simplification of the treaties, the roles of the national parliaments and the legal status of the Charter of Fundamental Rights. Following the **Treaty of Nice**, there was the **Laeken Declaration** in December 2001, which clarified these issues but which established the Convention on the Future of Europe to take the discussion further by including representatives drawn from all the stakeholders in the debate. As a discussion forum, the Convention brought together a wide range of views on a 'Constitution for Europe' and other issues, such as a 'United States of Europe with an elected President'.

However, the proposals of the Convention were not put into law because of the rejection in referenda of both the **Constitutional Treaty** in 2005 and, following 'a period of reflection', the subsequent **Lisbon Treaty** in 2008. Originally the **Treaty of Nice** was seen as the first step in the preparation for an enlarged EU, but there have been no follow-up treaties so far. The importance of the **Treaty of Nice** is that currently it is the only reforming treaty recognised by law that was introduced for the expansion of the EU.

Question 49

Why was it thought necessary to have a **Constitutional Treaty**? What were the consequences of its rejection?

Answer plan

This question deals with a very specific topic which has raised a lot of debate since the **Treaty of Nice** was agreed and the European Council set the task for simplifying EU law and making it more accessible to the citizens of the Union. It is a contemporary issue that will require knowledge of EU law and the current political reality in the Union. The www.europa.eu.int website still contains the drafts of the Convention and is a good source for the latest information on the **Constitutional Treaty** and subsequent proposals. The following are important points:

- the **Treaty of Nice** and the **Laeken Declaration**;
- the role and composition of the Convention on the Future of Europe;
- the recommendations of the Convention and the draft it presented to the IGC;
- the **Treaty Establishing a Constitution for Europe** or the **Constitutional Treaty 2004**;
- the **Lisbon Treaty 2005**; and
- ratification requirements to bring the **Constitutional Treaty** into law.

Answer

In the 1990s Europe was undergoing many changes as the former Soviet Union was breaking up and many eastern and central European countries were looking to the European Union as a means of protecting their democratic systems of government and raising the standard of living for their citizens. The European Union had

15 Member States at that time, and needed to undertake some reforms in preparation for the enlargement that was imminent. When the **Treaty of Nice** was ratified and came into force in February 2003 it meant that there were eight treaties and many protocols that together built up the primary sources of EU law. The original treaties signed in the 1950s had been amended, extended and revised over the intervening period as the policy areas of the EU had been enlarged and as the institutions had been affected by increased membership. The documentation as far as the treaties were concerned had become very complex. At the IGC in 2000 the European Council agreed that following the **Treaty of Nice**, with the emphasis on the enlargement of the EU to take place in 2004, priority should be given to reforming the treaties so that there would be one document, one 'constitution', which would simplify the task of identifying the primary source of European law. At the meeting at Laeken in December 2001, the European Council made a declaration establishing the European Convention which was charged with responsibility of agreeing on a 'constitutional treaty' that would be put before the Council for approval. The Declaration identified key issues that the Council wanted to see addressed, including the limitation of competences between the EU and the Member States reflecting the principle of subsidiarity, the status of the Charter of Fundamental Rights and the role of national parliaments in the context of European legislation.

Given that the idea of the **Treaty Establishing a Constitution for Europe** or **Constitutional Treaty** was to replace all other treaties apart from EURATOM, it was considered important that the membership of the Convention should be inclusive and transparent. It was important that the European institutions were brought closer to the EU citizen because the decline in voting in European Parliamentary elections was worrying to the Council. The main parties in the debate about the future of Europe were brought together under the chairmanship of Giscard d'Estaing, a former President of France. The Convention included representatives of the existing Member States and those states who were to join the EU in 2004, the European Parliament and the Commission plus representatives of national Parliaments. Other bodies such as the Economic and Social Committee had observer rights. It can be seen that this was quite a large group, too large to discuss the detail of a treaty. Therefore, a number of working groups were established to look at particular issues like subsidiarity and the **Charter of Fundamental Rights**. These groups produced reports and recommendations which were considered by the Convention as a whole. There was also a Praesidium established which was made up of the chairman, vice-chairmen and nine other members of the Convention. This body was considered to be very powerful in the production of the draft **Constitutional Treaty** and heavily influenced by its chairman!

The Convention had its first meeting in March 2002 and reported to the IGC in 2004 as requested when it was established. The European Council, now representing the 25 Member States plus the candidate countries of Romania and Bulgaria, signed the **Treaty Establishing a Constitution for Europe** on 29 October 2004. The Treaty abolishes the three-pillar structure introduced by the **Treaty on European Union** in 1993, where the dominating pillar was the European Community. The other pillars introduced in 1993, namely the area of Common and Foreign Security Policy and some of the areas of Justice and Home Affairs, remain embedded in the **Constitutional Treaty**. The Treaty also takes the opportunity of stating what has been reflected in the jurisprudence of the European Court of Justice for many years. The main example of this is the statement that 'the Constitution shall have primacy over the law of the Member States'. This question of supremacy of Community law was settled in the *Van Gend en Loos and Costa v ENEL* cases in the mid-1960s. The Treaty recognises that the EU has received powers from the Member States and any powers or competences not transferred remain with the Member States. There is also a list of competences which are shared between the EU and the Member States and where the EU can only take a co-ordinating or supporting role. This would seem to have met the challenge set for the Convention in the **Laeken Declaration**.

There are important new developments in the **Constitutional Treaty** with regard to the EU institutions. Some argue that these changes reflect a shift in power towards the European Council, the main forum for the Member States. **Article I-19** of the **Constitutional Treaty** stated that 'the institutional framework comprises: the European Parliament, the European Council, the Council of Ministers or Council, the European Commission and the Court of Justice of the European Union'. The Court of Auditors is no longer included in this list but is mentioned in the category of 'other institutions and advisory bodies'. Instead of the current six-monthly rotating presidency system of the Council of Ministers, which has been heavily criticised for providing no continuity, there is to be a system of 'Team Presidency'. Under this system the Council was to be chaired by a team of three Member States holding the Presidency for 18 months. This is a little vague at the moment because it merely adds together the traditional six-monthly period for three Member States into one period, but it is intended to provide greater coherence and consistency in the various Council meetings. The system of qualified majority voting or QMV within the Council was also to be changed to reflect the need for a 'dual majority'. This required a qualified majority to reflect not only the voting strength of the Member States but also a minimum percentage of the EU's population. This would allow Member States representing 35% of the EU's population to block any legislative proposal.

Perhaps of greater significance is that there was to be an elected President of the European Council. The President will chair the European Council and 'drive forward' the European agenda. He or she will be elected for two and a half years by the European Council, that is, the Member States, and this term of office will be renewable once. The role of the President of the European Council is to facilitate cohesion and consensus within the Council, which will report to the European Parliament after each of its meetings. It is understandable that the President of the Commission was not enthusiastic about this development, as there could be two individuals with the title of president, and this may confuse the citizens of the EU, who may not appreciate the difference!

As for the European Commission, there are two important developments. The first is that from 2014 the size of the Commission will be reduced and consist of members corresponding to two-thirds of the number of Member States. At present there is one nominated Commissioner for each Member State and it will be interesting to see how the system will work for those who by rotation are not allowed to put forward a candidate for this office. There will also be a Union Minister for Foreign Affairs by merging the present role of the Commissioner for External Relations and the High Representative for the Common Foreign and Security Policy. The European Parliament benefits from an extension to more EU policy areas of the co-decision procedure which gives the Parliament a positive role in legislation. The number of MEPs is capped at 750 so any additional Member States will mean a reduction in the number of existing members. More importantly, the European Council must take into account the outcome of the European Parliamentary elections when nominating a candidate for Presidency of the Commission. This should increase the influence of the European Parliament and encourage greater participation in the election of MEPs.

Much discussion took place in the Convention about how to involve national parliaments more in the EU legislative procedure. One suggestion was to create another chamber in the European Parliament so that representatives drawn from national parliaments could be involved on the basis that all the parliaments of the Member States involved two chambers, so why not at EU level? This was rejected but there is a link between the role of national parliaments and the principle of subsidiarity. National parliaments will have to be informed about draft legislation and given six weeks to respond with their views. Under the **Constitutional Treaty** they were to have the power to send any legislative proposals back for review by the EU institutions if one-third of them agree that it infringes the principle of subsidiarity. There are also to be different terminologies for the laws passed by the European institutions, with the term 'laws' being used in place of regulations and 'framework laws' replacing directives, in order to make such terms easier to understand.

The need for the **Treaty Establishing a Constitution for Europe** was unanimous as the Treaty that emerged from the process of the Convention and the IGC seemed to meet the challenges set by the **Laeken Declaration**, including making the **Charter of Fundamental Rights** part of the Treaty and therefore legally binding. However, the Treaty signed in 2005 will not come into force because it was not ratified by all the existing 25 Member States. Under **Article 48** of the **Treaty on European Union (TEU)**, any Treaty amendments must be ratified by all the Member States in accordance with their respective constitutional requirements. Although those countries whose constitutional system required ratification by their national parliaments, such as Germany, successfully passed the domestic legislation, some Member States requiring ratification by referendum did not fare so well. In Spain, the referendum agreeing to the ratification of the **Constitutional Treaty** was passed by a small majority but the polls held in France and the Netherlands in May and June 2005 gave a 'no' majority. The Treaty should have come into law in November 2006 but following these votes the European Council voted for a period of 'reflection, explanation and discussion'. The outcome of this reflection was the **Reform Treaty**, very similar to the **Constitutional Treaty** in many respects although not seen as a stand-alone treaty but a traditional amending treaty like its predecessors. The **Reform Treaty** (or the **Lisbon Treaty**, as that was where it was signed, on 13 December 2007) was rejected in a referendum in Ireland on 12 June 2008. The result is that the failure of the ratification of the **Constitutional Treaty** followed by the same failure for the **Lisbon Treaty** means that the EU of 27 nations is operating on the basis of the **Treaty of Nice**, which was drafted on the basis of meeting the needs of enlargement but without tackling some of the fundamental problems of a greater number of Member States.

Question 50

Critically review the **Maastricht Treaty** in the development of the European Community.

Answer plan

The **Maastricht Treaty** recognised the need for reform in both institution and policy areas of the EU. This discussion question provides the opportunity to raise issues arising from the Inter-Governmental Conferences which were held to discuss developments. It is important with this type of question to know what is happening in the European Union, something which can be gleaned from good newspapers rather than textbooks. Your answer should cover the following points:

- background to the **Maastricht Treaty**;
- the meaning of 'European Economic and Monetary Union' and 'European Political Union';
- the need to deal with the democratic deficit in the Community and the measures implemented to achieve this;
- changes to the institutional balance, especially the co-decision procedure;
- the principle of subsidiarity;
- citizenship of the European Community; and
- developments in the **Treaty of Amsterdam**.

Answer

On 11 December 1991, the leaders of the 12 Member States agreed on the text of a **Treaty on European Union** (**TEU**, or the **Maastricht Treaty**), 17 associated protocols and 33 declarations. The protocols are additional agreements between some, but not all, of the signatories. For example, the **Protocol on Social Policy** included all the Member States except the UK. The declarations do not have legal force, but outline the ways in which the provisions of the Treaty should be interpreted or implemented. The agreement was the culmination of long and arduous negotiations following the reports of two Inter-Governmental Conferences (IGCs) between the 12 Member States. One was on Economic and Monetary Union and the other was on Political Union.

The anticipated completion of the internal market required the Community to review future developments. In addition, there had been revolutionary changes in Eastern Europe, providing new opportunities, problems and the acceptance of enlargement of the EU from its then 15 Member States. Businesses within the EU were pressing for an end to fluctuating and uncertain exchange rates which imposed increasing problems for the movement of goods and services within the Community. The payment of commission and losses on the different buying and selling rates added to the problems encountered by businesses. A possible solution was a move towards European Monetary Union, with a single currency based upon the European Currency Unit (ECU) that could be used freely throughout the Community. These factors provided the catalyst for the establishment of the IGCs.

However, any move towards European Monetary Union would increase the powers of the Community. To offset this, there had to be a strengthening of the democratic accountability of the Community to balance this increased power. The increase in democratic accountability centred on the European Parliament and the concept of subsidiarity. The move towards European Union, a term which is given to the next stage in the process of integration between the 15 Member States, creates two inter-governmental bodies dealing with a common foreign and security policy and home affairs and justice.

The institutional revisions were mostly designed to improve the efficiency and democratic nature of the Community's institutional structures and decision-making processes. The result has been an increase in the powers of the European Parliament and the complexity of the Community's decision-making procedures. Different procedures apply to different areas of legislation. For example, with a proposal for environmental legislation from the Commission, there are four possible decision-making procedures: co-operation procedure; co-decision; consultation with unanimity; and unanimous decision to vote by majority. The **Treaty of Rome**, in 1957, provided for the consultation procedure with a single Parliamentary reading, providing an opinion and unanimous or majority voting in the Council of Ministers. The co-operation procedure was introduced by the **Single European Act 1986 (SEA)** and gave greater involvement for the European Parliament when dealing with legislation on particular policies associated with the completion of the internal market.

The **TEU** introduced a new procedure called co-decision. For the first time, Parliament can prevent legislation being adopted, and in the Council of Ministers majority voting is required, with two exceptions where unanimity applies. Although this procedure is generally called co-decision, to differentiate it from the other procedures, the term does not appear in **Art 251** of the Treaty. Co-decision has some of the elements of the co-operation procedure, but it goes further by giving the Parliament the power to veto a legislative proposal. The veto can only be exercised after the convening of a conciliation committee, comprising members of the Council or their representatives and an equal number of representatives of the European Parliament. This committee must approve a joint text within six weeks, which is followed by a further period of six weeks during which the Council and the Parliament have to adopt the proposal; otherwise it fails. The time period can be extended by common agreement of both the Council and the Parliament for a further two weeks. If the committee fails to agree, the Council may confirm its common opinion within six weeks, which would require the Parliament to reject the text by an absolute majority of its members to stop the proposal being finally adopted. This is what is referred to as Parliament's veto. **Article 49** of the **TEU** also provides the Parliament with the power of veto with regard to the accession of new members. The Council has to obtain the assent of the European Parliament before acting.

A new institution was added to the list of Community institutions. Previously, there were four institutions: the European Parliament, the Council, the Commission and the ECJ. Now there is a fifth one, the Court of Auditors. Although the Court of Auditors has existed since 1977, its place in **Art 7** indicates an upgrading of its status. This increased the influence of the Court of Auditors at a time when the completion of the internal market will bring added pressure on combating fraud and financial accountability for Community funds. A new advisory body was also added to the existing Economic and Social Committee. Under **Arts 264** and **265**, a Committee of the Regions has been established, to give opinions either in cases where they have been consulted by the Council or Commission or in cases where they consider it appropriate. **Article 8** establishes a European System of Central Banks and a European Central Bank to add to the existing European Investment Bank.

The **TEU** added **Art 5** to the **EC Treaty**. This Article deals with the principle of subsidiarity. According to the words of the Article, the Community may take action 'only if and in so far as the objectives of the proposed action cannot be sufficiently achieved by the Member States and can therefore, by reason of the scale or effects of the proposed action, be better achieved by the Community'. The principle is strengthened by the inclusion in the Preamble to the Treaty of the objective of a closer European Union, where decisions are taken as closely as possible to the citizen in accordance with the principle of subsidiarity. It would appear that it is for the

Commission to justify its chosen action when presenting a proposal, that is, why it is not leaving the action to be taken at another level, such as within a Member State. Thus the validity of a proposed Community measure may be successfully challenged on the grounds that it offends against the principle of subsidiarity. As **Art 230** continues to give the European Court the power to hear actions for annulment, it will be necessary to wait until such an argument is brought before the judges.

The last major change introduced by the **TEU** concerns citizenship of the Union under **Arts 17–21**. Citizenship of the Union is mandatory for nationals of the Member States as there is no provision for opting out. Thus, citizenship of the Union has been grafted onto the body of the **EC Treaty**. This means that, as citizens of the Union, nationals of the Member States have, for example, the right to move and reside freely within the Community. They also have the right to vote and stand as a candidate in local and European Parliament elections in whichever Member State they reside. In addition, the European Parliament is required to appoint an Ombudsman to receive complaints from any citizen of the Union concerning maladministration in the activities of the Community institutions, with the exception of the Courts. In July 1994, the first legal attempt was made to identify the rights of a citizen of the Union when Gerry Adams challenged, in the High Court, the ban by the UK Government which prevented him addressing a group of MPs at Westminster. Generally, the rights of a citizen of the Union are stated with regard to movement between Member States, but here, the argument was about movement within the UK.

The **TEU** was finally ratified by all the parliaments of the Member States, although there were some problems in Germany, Denmark and the UK, where there was opposition to its adoption. The Treaty is an attempt to deal with the challenges facing the Community. The 'democratic deficit' has been tackled by increasing the power of the Parliament and the addition of the Council of the Regions as an advisory body. At the same time, the Community has widened its scope of activities. Many of the additions to the original Treaty are not economic, representing the social and citizenship dimension of the Community. It is for this reason that the word 'economic' has been removed from the Treaty, so that it is now referred to as the EC or European Community Treaty. It would seem that the **TEU** was a natural extension to the Community, indicating its maturity and development towards the aims of its founders.

If the Community is to grow, more reforms involving its institutions are required. Unfortunately, the opportunity to deal with these reforms was not taken in the **Treaty of Amsterdam 1997**, although some changes were flagged up in the December 2000 IGC held in Nice. This IGC was held to deal with the issues associated with the growth to 27 Member States (25 in 2004). Some of the reforms did not come into operation until 2005, but at least some reform of the Council and the Commission did take place. The **Treaty of Nice**, implemented in February 2003, is a natural extension of the **Maastricht Treaty**.

INDEX

acte clair 80, 86–9; application 87–8; exceptions 87; misuse issues 88–9; principle 86–7
Advocates General (ECJ) 8, 9
association agreements 183–4

budget procedures (European Parliament) 5–6

Cassis principle 93–5, 97–9, 100–1, 104–5
CFI (Court of First Instance) 11–12
citizenship of the Union 204
co-decision 5, 7, 203
Commission *see* European Commission
Committee of Permanent Representatives (COREPER) 10–11
Committee of the Regions 203
common commercial policy 182–3, 190–1
community institutions 1–20; background 1–2; CFI *see* Court of First Instance; Commission *see* European Commission; COREPER *see* Committee of Permanent Representatives; Council *see* Council of Ministers; ECJ *see* European Court of Justice (ECJ); European Coal and Steal Community (ECSC) 1; European Parliament *see* European Parliament
company law 156–9; European Company 159; freedom of establishment/to provide services 157–8; minimum safeguards 158–9; mobility of companies 157
competition policy 109–32; basis 117–18; concerted practice 126–7; dominance *see* dominant position; European Commission role 19; exclusive contract 125–6; fines 119–20; importance 109, 110; information gathering 118–19; mergers *see* mergers; powers of Commission 118–20; restrictive practices *see* restrictive practices
concerted practice 126–7

Constitutional Treaty 19–20, 196–201; Convention 198–9; European Commission and 200; European Council 199–200; national parliaments and 200; ratification issues 200–1
copyright 101
COREPER (Committee of Permanent Representatives) 10–11
Council of Ministers 6–7, 14–17; business burden 15; COREPER and 13; European Parliament and 16–17; objectives 14; personnel 14–15; Presidency 14–15; qualified majority voting 196; voting procedures 15–16
Court of Auditors 203
Court of First Instance (CFI) 11–12

Dassonville formula 93–4, 97
decisions, direct effect and 40
democratic deficit 204
direct effect 33, 37–41, 45–9; basic requirements 38–9; domestic law and 47–9; parliamentary sovereignty and 47; test 40–1; vertical/horizontal effect 46–7
directives 41–5; benefits to individuals 41–2, 44–5; direct effect 39–40, 42–3, 47–8; indirect effect 44; timescale for implementation 43–4
discrimination *see* freedom from discrimination
dominant position 111–13, 127–8; abuse 112–13, 121–4; elements 111–12, 122–3; principle of dominance 111; remedies 113

ECJ *see* European Court of Justice
Economic and Social committee (ECOSOC) 12–13
employment discrimination 167–8
enlargement issues 194–7
equal pay 170–2

equality 24, *see also* freedom from discrimination

establishment right 139–40

European Coal and Steal Community (ECSC) 1

European Commission 17–20; competition policy role 19; in Constitutional Treaty 200; COREPER and 11; ECOSOC and 13; enlargement issues 195; European Parliament and 3; executive role 18; external relations of community 18–19; functions 17–18, 19–20; personnel 19–20

European Company 159

European Council 199–200, 204

European Court of Justice (ECJ) 7–10; Advocates General 8, 9; CFI and 11–12; enforcement 9–10; French influence 9; function 7; interpretation process 29–31; personnel 8; preliminary references 9; rapporteur 9; supremacy of EC law 34–7; workload 8–9

European Parliament 3–7; budget procedures 5–6; co-decision procedure 5, 7; co-operation procedure 4–5; Commission and 3; Council of Ministers and 6–7, 16–17; enlargement issues 195–6; proposed legislation 3–4

exclusive contract 125–6

exhaustion of rights 102

expansion issues 194–7

external relations 181–91; association agreements 183–4; background 181; common commercial policy 182–3, 190–1; internal rules and 186–7; parallelism doctrine 185–7; treaty-making powers 182, 188–90

free movement of goods 91–106; importance 91, 96, 100; intellectual property rights 100–3, 106–7; quantitative restrictions *see* quantitative restrictions, equivalent effect; restrictive practices 105–6

free movement of workers 133–47; background 133; basic rights 134–5, 137–8, 141; definition of worker 141–2, 144–5; dependants 135–6, 138–9; professional qualifications 139, 154–6; public policy and 145–7; public service and 142–3; right of establishment 139–40

freedom of establishment/to provide services 149–64; background 149; basic rights 150–1; company law and *see* company law; discrimination/non-discrimination 162–3; lawyers' rights 154–6; professional qualifications 139, 154–6, 160–2; professional sportsmen 163–4; public policy/security and

151–2; right of establishment 139–40; students' rights 152–3

freedom from discrimination 165–80; background 24, 165; employment discrimination 167–8; equal pay 170–2, 176–7; equality principle 24, 166–7; extension of law 169, 175–6; indirect discrimination 174, 177; national law and 178; occupational pensions 178–80; retirement ages 178; sex discrimination 167, 172–6; transexuality 168–9

fundamental rights 25–6

goods *see* free movement of goods

indirect effect 44

intellectual property rights 100–3

internal market developmentbackground 193; enlargement issues 194–7, *see also* Constitutional Treaty; Treaty on European Union

judicial remedies/review 51–69; actions against member states 52–5; background 51; community measure, individual's challenge 59–62; direct and individual concerns 66–7; faulty regulation 67–8; individual's challenge to regulation 56–9; legislative economic policy actions 68–9; member states *see* member states, actions against

judicial remedies/review, indirect action 71–89; *acte clair see acte clair*; background 71; *locus standi* issues 83–5; national courts/ECJ dialogue 79–82; preliminary references 72–5; preliminary references *see* preliminary references; validity issues 85–6

law *see* sources of law

lawyers' rights 154–6

legislative economic policy actions 68–9

Maastricht Treaty *see* Treaty on European Union

member states, actions against 52–5; administrative stage 53; Commission duties 52, 54–5; effective compliance 54; individual complainants 54–5; judicial stage 53–4; liability in damages 62–5; types 52

Merger Task Force (MTF) 130

mergers 129–32; categorisation 130; collective dominance 131; notification requirement 129; one stop procedure 132; role of Commission 130

national and EC law 33–49; background 33; conflict guidance 36–7; direct effect *see* direct effect; directives *see* directives; supremacy of EC law 34–7; uniformity of application 35, 36
non-discrimination *see* freedom from discrimination
non-pecuniary barriers *see* quantitative restriction, equivalent effect

parallelism doctrine 185–7
parliamentary sovereignty 47
patents 101
preliminary references 72–5; guidelines 75–8; judicial discretion 77–8
procedural rights 26
professional qualifications 139, 154–6, 160–2
professional sportsmen 163–4
proportionality 24
protection of legitimate expectations 25

qualified majority voting 196
quantitative restriction, equivalent effect 92–5; *Cassis* principle 93–5, 97–9, 100–1, 104–5; *Dassonville* formula 93–4, 97; definition/identification 93, 96; national law and 93–4; rule of reason 94–5

regulations 27–8; definition 27; effect 28, 40; faulty 67–8; individual's challenge to 56–9; requirements 27–8
restrictive practices 105–6, 114–16; agreements 115–16; definition 114–15; powers of Commission 118; remedies 116
right of establishment 139–40

sources of law 21–31; background 21–2; ECJ *see* European Court of Justice, interpretation process; equality 24; fundamental rights 25–6; general principles 23; non-discrimination 24; primary/secondary 21; procedural rights 26; proportionality 24; protection of legitimate expectations 25; regulations *see* regulations
sportsmen 163–4
students' rights 152–3
subsidiarity 203–4
supremacy of EC law 34–7

three-pillar structure 199
trade marks 101–2
transexuality 168–9
Treaty on European Union (Maastricht Treaty) 202–4; background 202; citizenship of the Union 204; co-decision 203; Committee of the Regions 203; Court of Auditors 203; democratic deficit 204; institutional revisions 202–3; subsidiarity 203–4

workers *see* free movement of workers